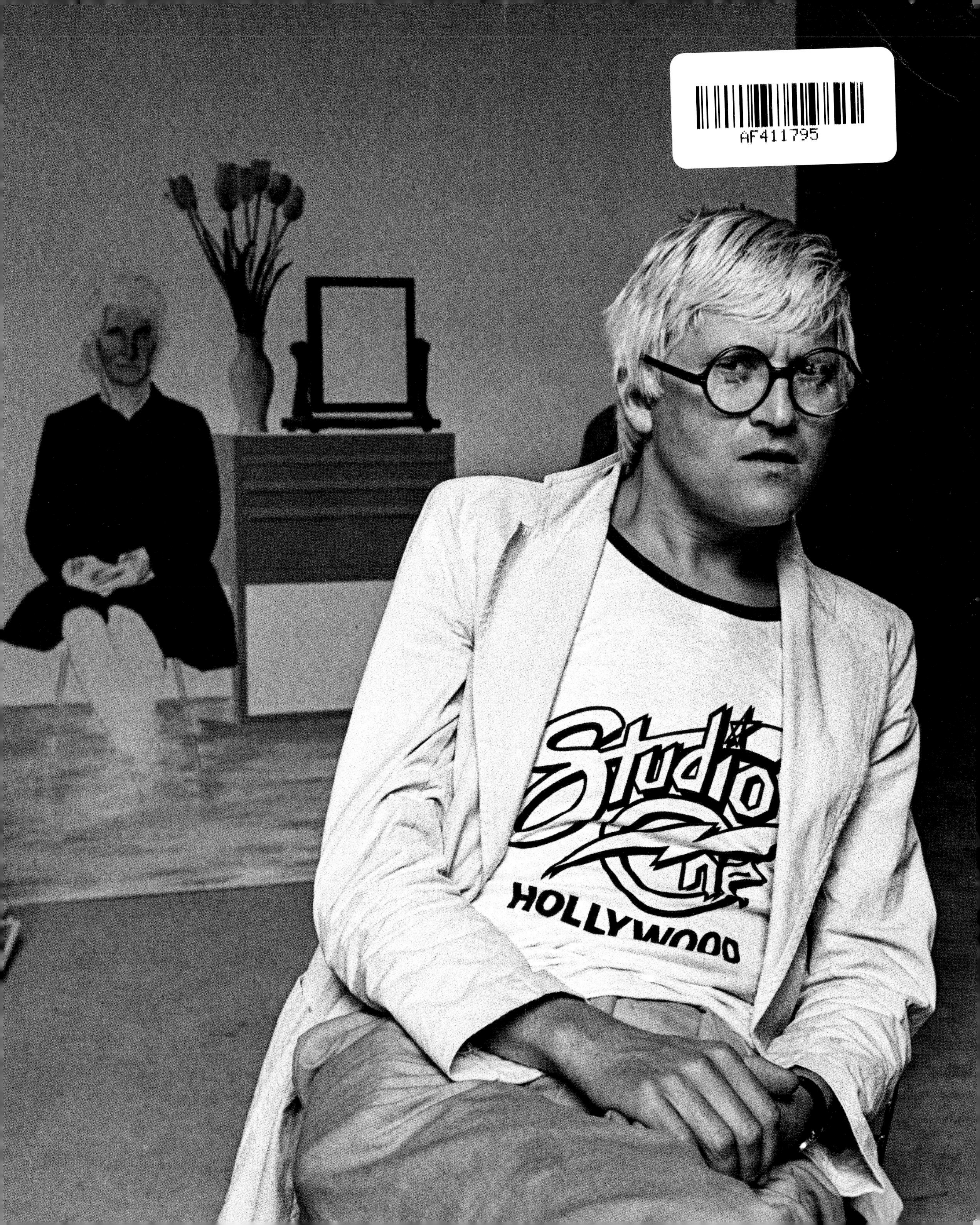

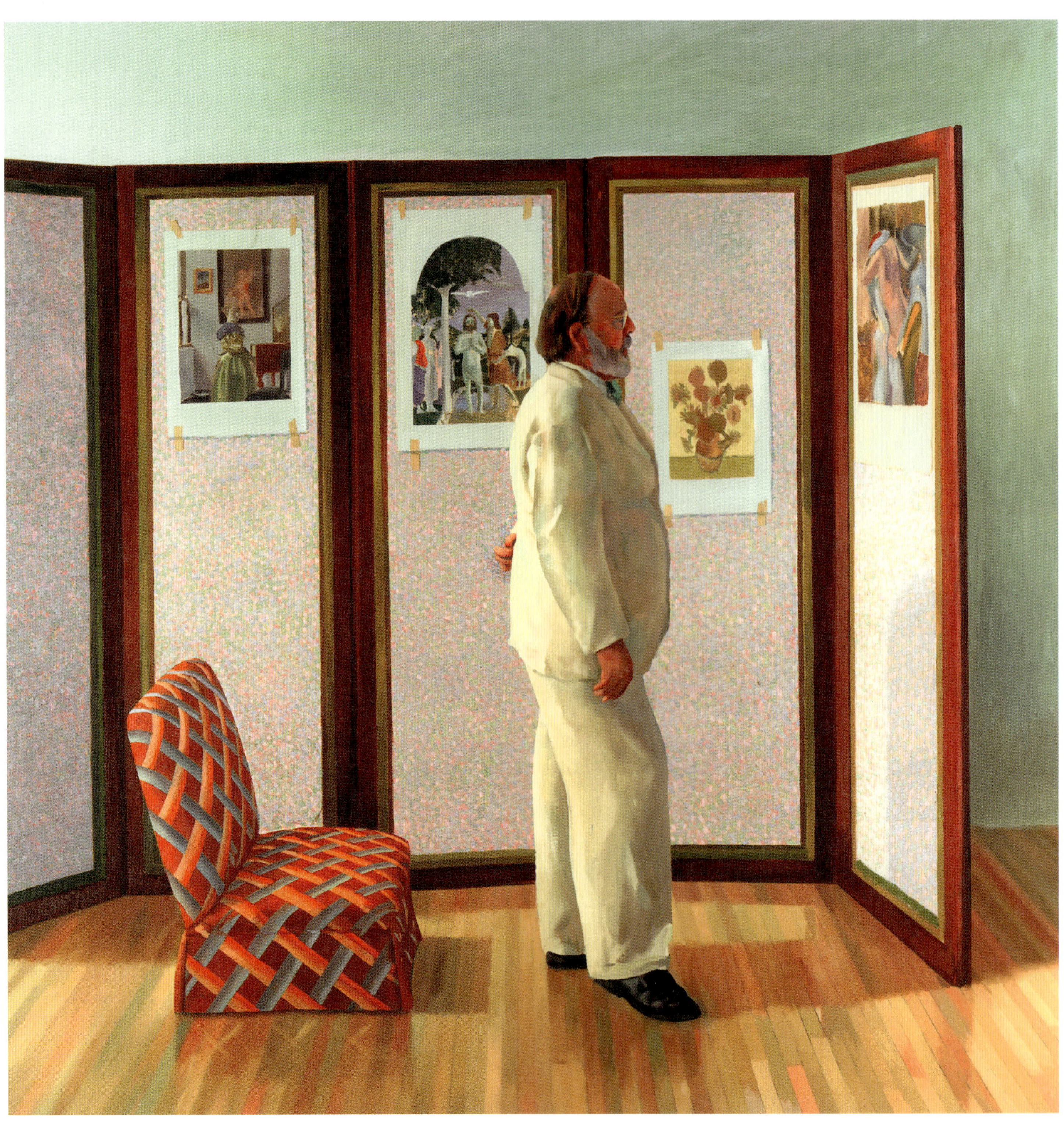

Fig. 1
David Hockney (born 1937)
Looking at Pictures on a Screen,
1977
Oil on canvas, 188 × 188 cm
Private collection

Fig. 2
Piero della Francesca
(about 1415/20–1492)
The Baptism of Christ,
probably about 1437–45
Egg tempera on wood,
167 × 116 cm
The National Gallery, London

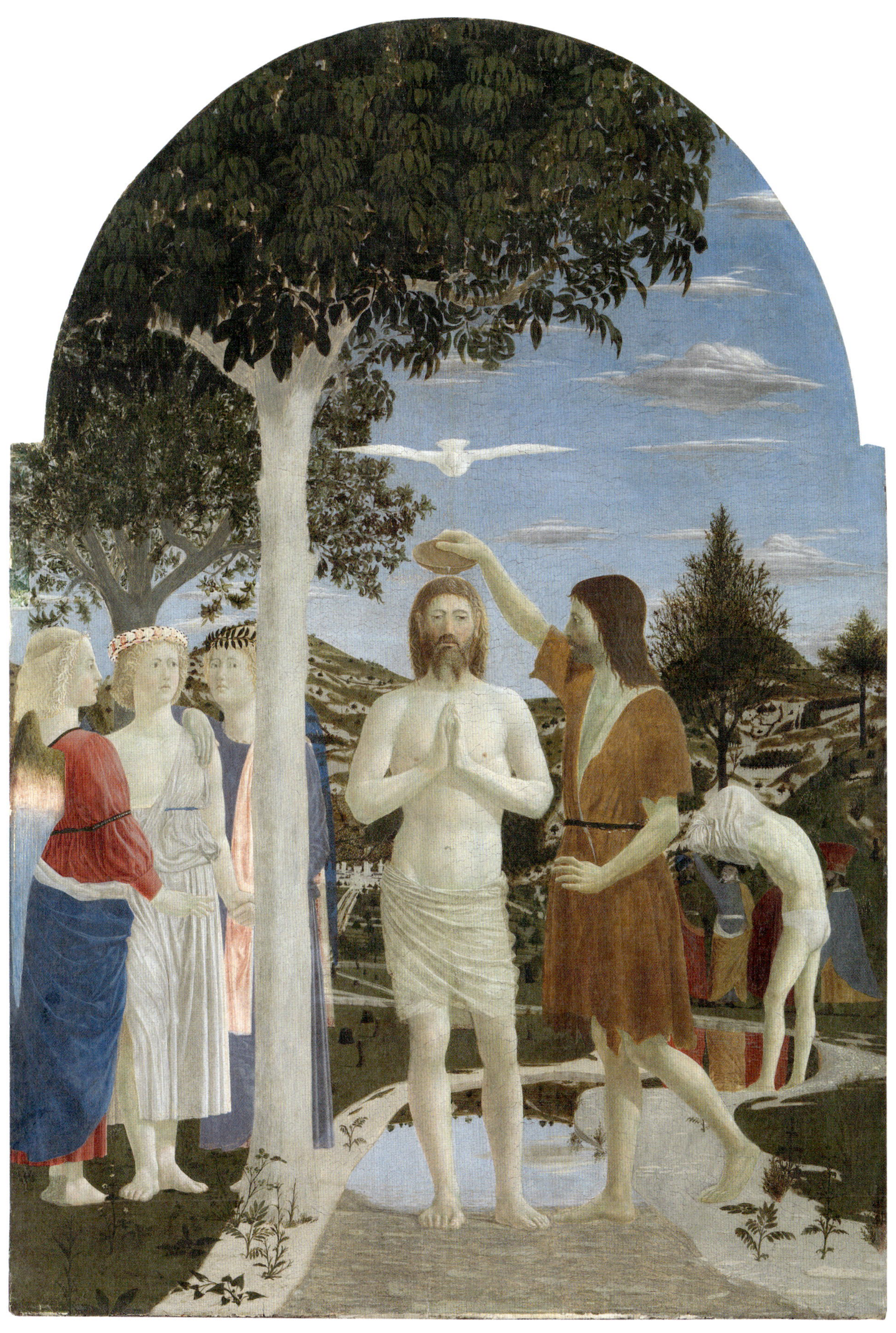

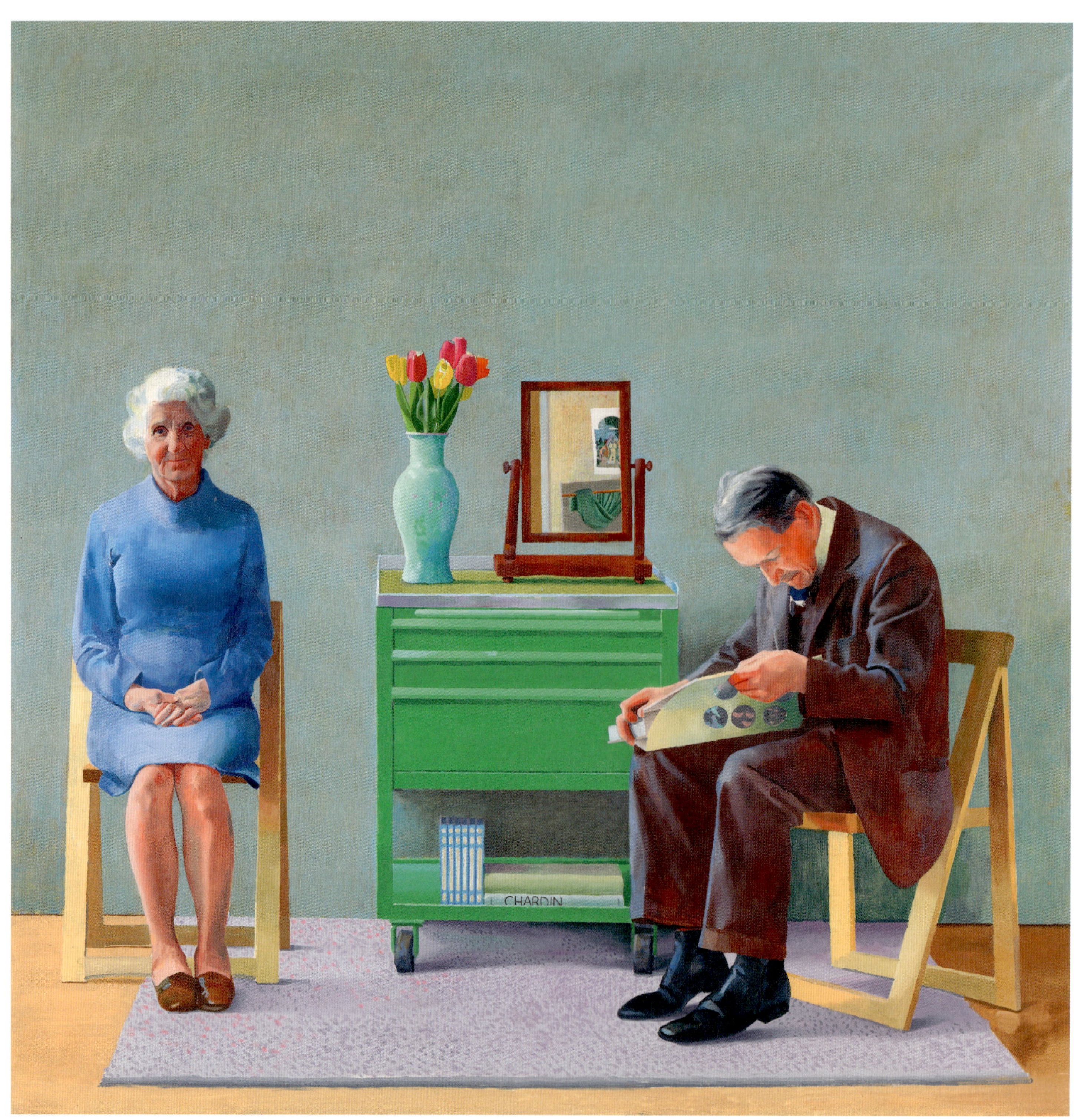

Fig. 3
David Hockney (born 1937)
My Parents, 1977
Oil on canvas,
182.9 × 182.9 cm
Tate, London

HOCKNEY AND PIERO

A LONGER LOOK

SUSANNA AVERY-QUASH

WITH CONTRIBUTIONS BY
MARTIN GAYFORD
DAVID HOCKNEY
SACHA LLEWELLYN

NATIONAL GALLERY GLOBAL, LONDON
DISTRIBUTED BY YALE UNIVERSITY PRESS

Published to accompany the exhibition
Hockney and Piero: A Longer Look
The National Gallery, London
8 August–27 October 2024

The H J Hyams Exhibition Programme
Supported by The Capricorn Foundation

Exhibition supported by

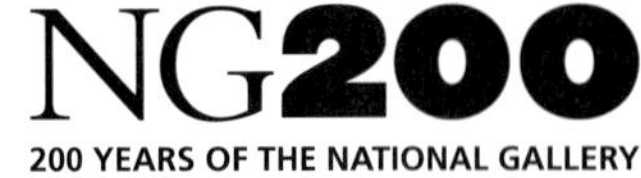

The life you want to live
riverstoneliving.com

This exhibition has been made possible by the provision of insurance through the Government Indemnity Scheme. The National Gallery would like to thank HM Government for providing Government Indemnity and the Department for Culture, Media and Sport and Arts Council England for arranging the indemnity.

First published in 2024 by
National Gallery Global Limited
Trafalgar Square
London WC2N 5DN
www.shop.nationalgallery.org.uk

ISBN: 978 1 85709 722 1
1053826

British Library Cataloguing-in-Publication Data
A catalogue record is available from the British Library
Library of Congress Control Number: 2024930697

Publisher: Laura Lappin
Project Editor: Catherine Hooper
Copy-editor: Jenny Wilson
Proofreader: Phoebe Colley
Picture Researcher: Rebecca Thornton
Production: Davina Cheung

Designed by Hoop Design, www.hoopdesign.co.uk
Origination by DL Imaging, London
Printed in Italy by Printer Trento

All measurements give height before width.

Front cover
David Hockney (born 1937), *My Parents*, 1977 (detail from fig. 3)
Back cover
Piero della Francesca (about 1415/20–1492), *The Baptism of Christ*, probably about 1437–45 (detail from fig. 2)
Frontispiece
David Hockney, Saint Germain, Paris, 1979
Derek Hudson
Page 8
David Hockney (born 1937), assisted by Jonathan Wilkinson, *In the Studio, December 2017* (detail), 2017
Photographic drawing

Page 10
Bern Schwartz (1914–1978), *David Hockney*, 5 July 1977
Dye transfer print, 47 × 37.8 cm
National Portrait Gallery, London
Page 28
Photograph in *Gay News*, July 1981
The Robert Workman Archive
Bishopsgate Institute, London
Page 46
David Hockney working in his London studio, 1977
Martyn Goddard
Page 68
Detail from Hockney's poster for *The Artist's Eye* exhibition (fig. 55)
Pages 98–9
David Hockney (born 1937), assisted by Jonathan Wilkinson, *25th June 2022, Looking at the Flowers*, 2022
Photographic drawing

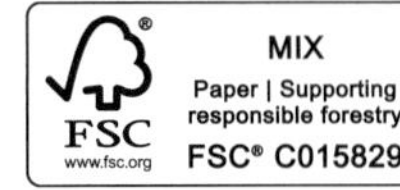

CONTENTS

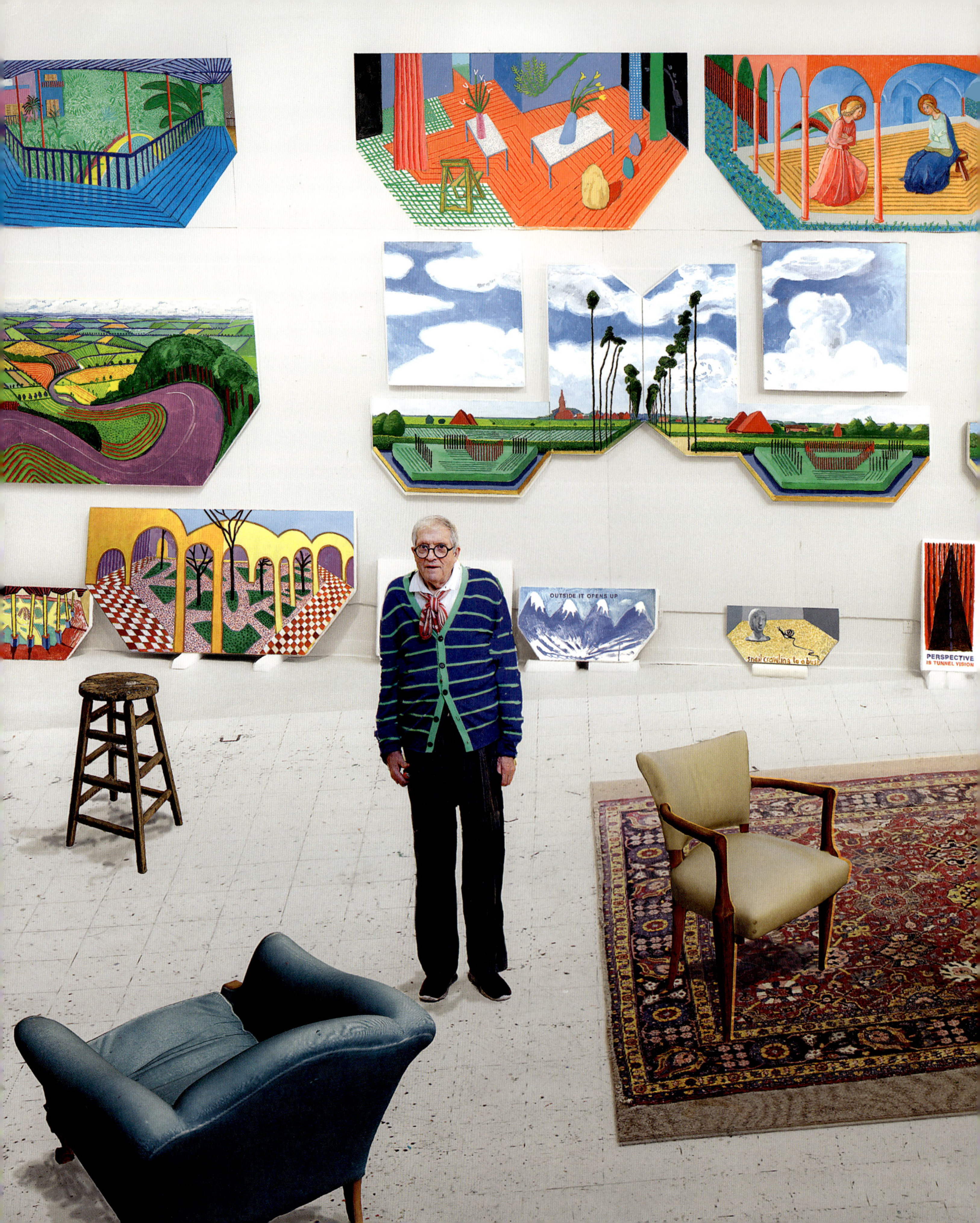
OUTSIDE IT OPENS UP
PERSPECTIVE IS TUNNEL VISION

DIRECTOR'S FOREWORD

One of the ways in which the National Gallery is celebrating its Bicentenary year is through a collaboration with David Hockney. This small-focus exhibition brings together a 'triptych' of works comprising Piero della Francesca's *The Baptism of Christ* and two paintings by Hockney, both of which depict the Piero as an integral part of their making and meaning. In *My Parents*, Piero's *Baptism* is featured as a reproduction reflected in a mirror set between Hockney's father and mother. It is a painting that speaks to his genealogy, both familial and artistic. In *Looking at Pictures on a Screen*, a poster reproduction of Piero's *Baptism* is pinned to a screen alongside three more posters of Gallery paintings by Vermeer, Van Gogh and Degas.

The exhibition sheds light on the National Gallery's origins as a place that promotes dialogues between artists and between artists and audiences. It also represents an interaction between the Gallery and a living artist. This is a narrative in which the National Gallery has played an indisputably significant and often pioneering role over its 200-year history.

Hockney has a long association with the National Gallery; indeed, he is, perhaps of all living painters today, the one whose links with Trafalgar Square are the most deeply rooted. His interactions started when he came to London from Bradford in the mid-1950s and was astonished by the paintings he encountered on the walls. Over almost 70 years, he has produced numerous works and designs, including stage sets for opera, which are related to paintings in the collection.

Furthermore, Hockney has been invited to engage with the collection for particular events. In 1981, he was asked to curate the fifth of the Gallery's pioneering *Artist's Eye* exhibitions, while in the year 2000, he was one of 25 leading artists commissioned to create a new work in response to one in the permanent collection. In both exhibitions, Hockney conveyed his appreciation for the role of the National Gallery in making great art available for all. He also promoted the value of close observation. The work he produced in 2000 was an assemblage of 12 closely observed portraits of National Gallery room stewards, whose job is to look at people looking at pictures.

Hockney told Director Michael Levey in March 1979 that 'I love the collection of the National Gallery', and to Susanna Avery-Quash, curator of this exhibition and author of this book, he noted in February 2024 that he had 'never fallen out of love with Piero'. In Hockney's writings about the Gallery, he has always stressed the life-enhancing benefits of looking at a painting for a long time and going back to look at it again and again for further inspiration and insight.

This is an encouraging birthday message for the National Gallery as it enters its third century: here, people can look at art for free and then they can return and take 'a longer look'. A favourite Chinese proverb of Hockney's states that three things are needed to look profitably at art: the hand, the eye and the heart. Hockney promotes this vision in the knowledge that an ever deeper, more committed engagement of people with pictures will induce curiosity, openness and connection.

Our thanks go to David Hockney for a lifetime of image-making, to curator Susanna Avery-Quash and to the authors of this publication, to the Capricorn Foundation, who support the H J Hyams Exhibition Programme at the National Gallery, and to Riverstone, who have also generously supported this exhibition.

Gabriele Finaldi
Director, The National Gallery

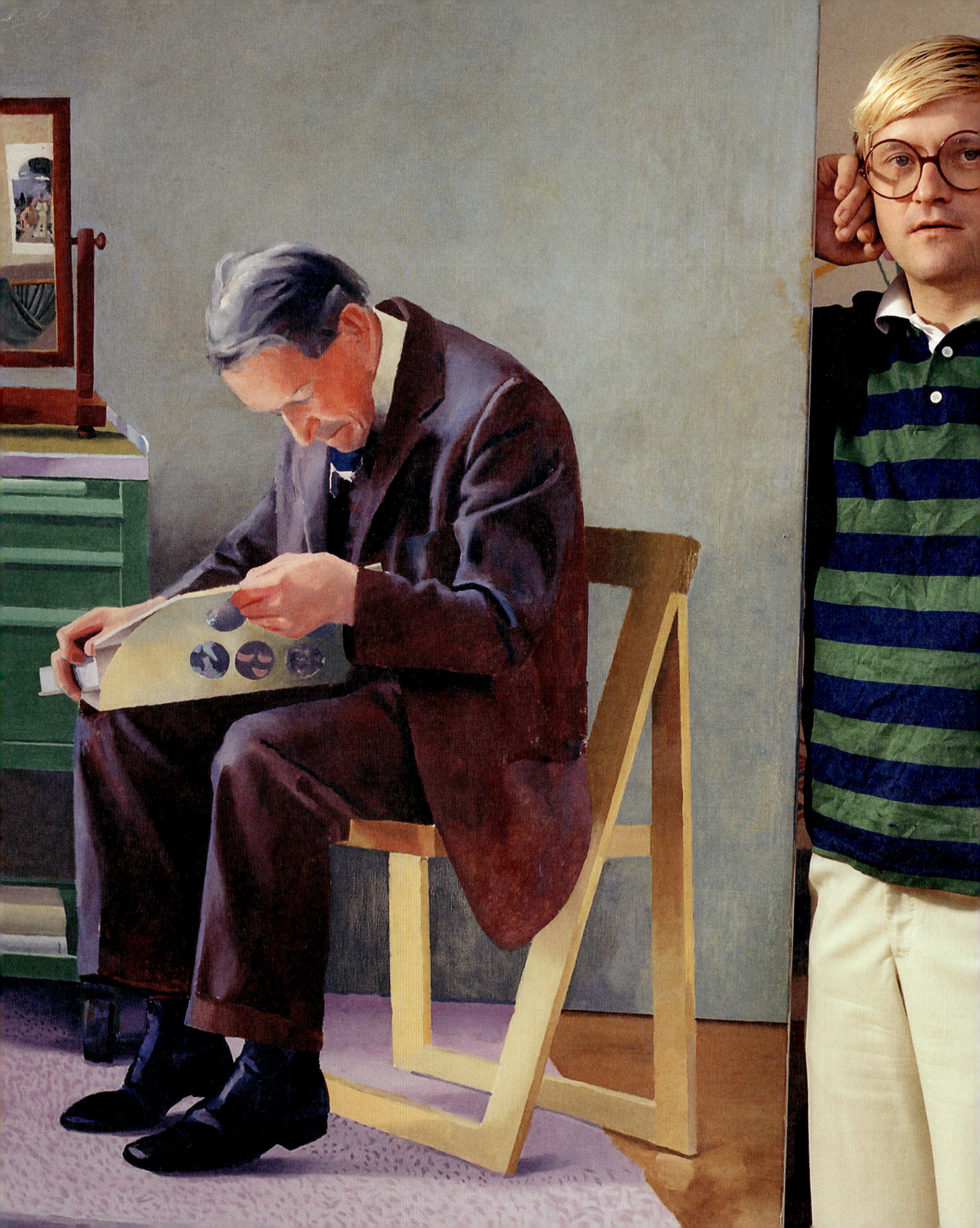

CHAPTER 1

LOOKING AT PICTURES FOR A LONG, LONG TIME

David Hockney in conversation with Martin Gayford

Happy birthday! The National Gallery is doing a great job, isn't it? It's keeping all those pictures there, safe and on view. DAVID HOCKNEY [1]

MARTIN GAYFORD When did you first see Piero della Francesca's *The Baptism of Christ*?

DAVID HOCKNEY **I'm not sure. I remember as a student I was given a little book on Piero – it cost 3s. 6d., I think – which had perhaps one colour picture, all the rest were in black and white. I won this as a prize at Bradford School of Art. It was a Sketch Club prize and I really *valued* that book. In fact, I've probably still got it somewhere, I wouldn't have given it away.**

MG And *The Baptism* would have been included in that book and made an impression on you?

DH **Yes.**

MG So was that the moment you set eyes on *The Baptism*?

DH **I don't think so, because when I got it I thought, 'How marvellous! A book about Piero della Francesca!' At home we had some books that** must have been from just before the war, about people and places. There were paintings in these books too, some of them great paintings. And I think it was probably in one of those that I first saw the Piero. These were all black and white, but some pictures stood out. This was when there wasn't much colour in printing.

MG Yes. Colour reproductions were rare and expensive for a long time. The more deluxe art books might have them but they were printed separately on glossy paper and hand-glued onto the ordinary pages.

DH **Yes. Piero was obviously an important artist for Seurat, for example. But Seurat never went to London or Italy, and there are no paintings by Piero in Paris. So he must have seen them in black-and-white engravings or maybe black-and-white photographs in art books and magazines.**

MG But you can see the connections in his pictures, such as the National Gallery's *Bathers at Asnières*. He was fond of juxtaposing figures in absolutely straight-on full faces with others in sharp profile. You get that in his *Three Models*, for example, and Piero did the same thing in *The Baptism* and several other paintings. You made just the same profile/full-face comparison in quite a few pictures too, by the way. The double portrait of *Henry Geldzahler and Christopher Scott* is an example (fig. 5).

DH **Yes, I did. But just as Seurat would have found out about Piero mainly from monochrome images – engravings and photographs – I often did too, at least to begin with (fig. 4).**

Over the years I watched a printing revolution really. Everything today is in colour. But even in 1976 when my first book [*David Hockney by David Hockney*] was done they said, 'You can have more colour but the price will be £20, but if you have fewer pictures in colour it can be £10.' I thought, well, better to have more people read it and do it for £10.

Although of course not all paintings can be reproduced in black and white. Rothkos are just a greyish smudge. Even in colour they don't really work. There is a superb work, *Earth and Green*, at the Museum Ludwig in Cologne. It's fabulous when you see it there, but impossible to photograph.

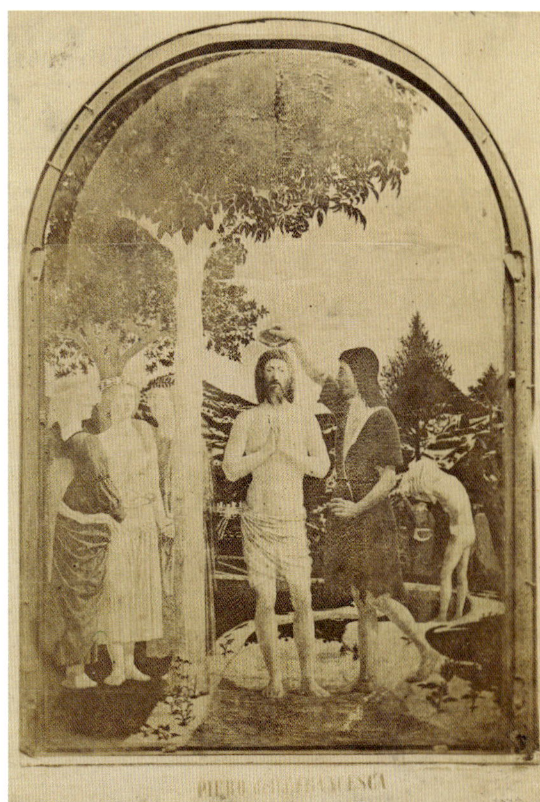

Fig. 4
Monochrome reproduction of
Piero della Francesca's
The Baptism of Christ,
nineteenth century
12.7 × 17.8 cm
The National Gallery, London

Fig. 5
David Hockney (born 1937)
*Henry Geldzahler and
Christopher Scott*, 1969
Acrylic on canvas, 214 × 305 cm
Private collection

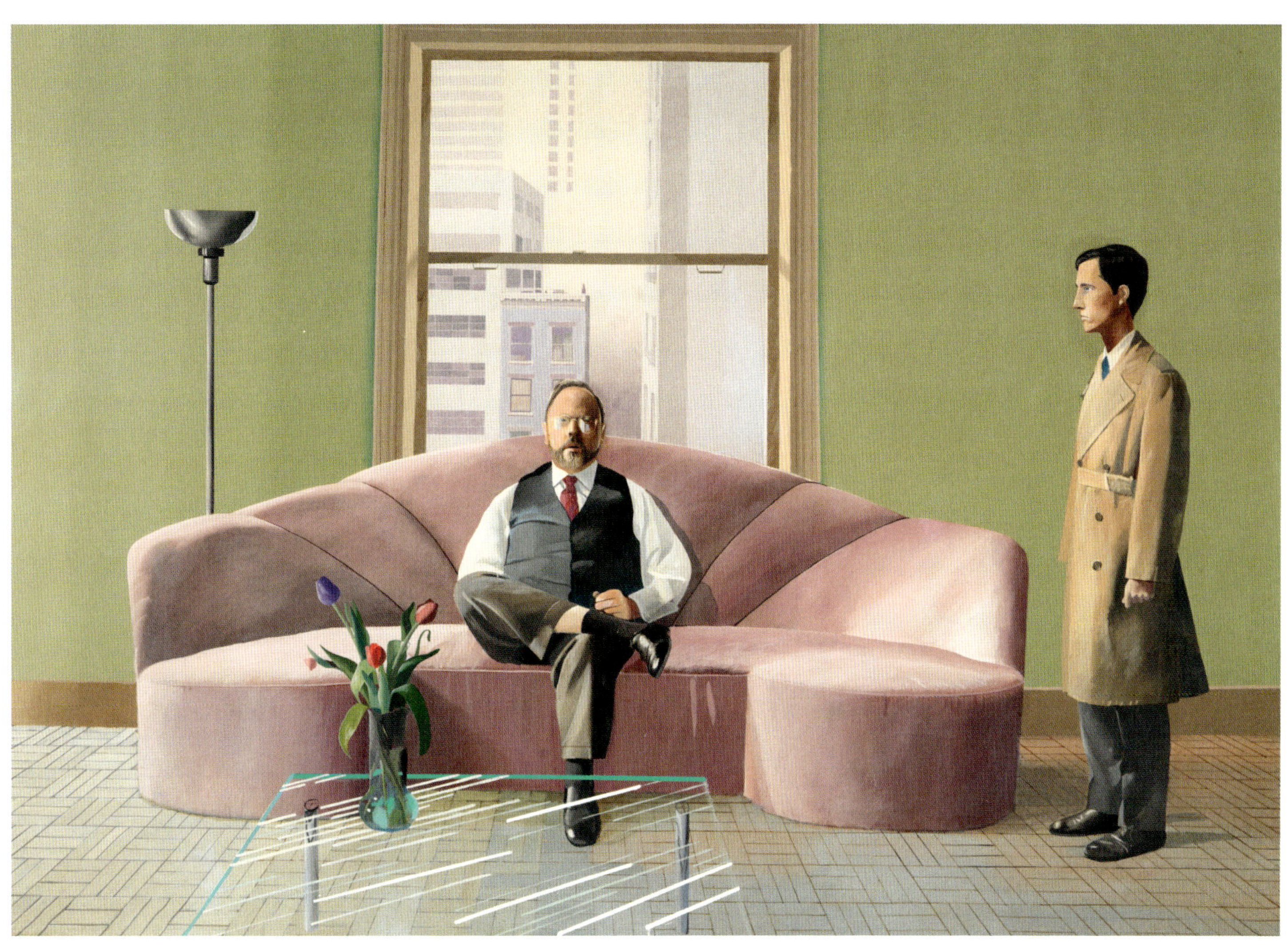

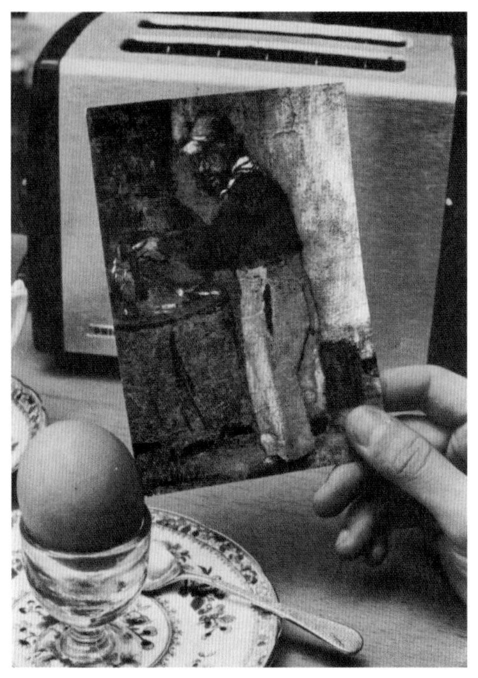

MG When you did your *Artist's Eye* exhibition at the National Gallery in the summer of 1981, you made a distinction between three ways of encountering a painting. Included there was your work entitled *Looking at Pictures on a Screen*. The exhibition itself was called *Looking at Pictures in a Room*. And the little accompanying catalogue was *Looking at Pictures in a Book*. So, to borrow a phrase from John Berger, here were 'three ways of seeing'. These days I suppose you would have to add a fourth: *Looking at Pictures on a Phone*, because that is how many people make a record of what they see in art galleries.

DH **That's true. You can get very good colour just with your phone. I've always been interested in reproductions, as I said, because I followed developments in printing. I realised that's how most people would see pictures. In *The Artist's Eye* we had the reproductions on show as well as the real paintings (and the actual screen and chair in my painting too) (see fig. 42).**

MG Looking at a photograph of a painting is a different experience to standing in front of the original, but that doesn't mean it isn't a valuable one. You wrote in your catalogue for *The Artist's Eye* exhibition that even when a painting is in 'a cheap reproduced form, it can still give off a lot of its magic'.

DH **Yes. And I pointed out that a little postcard, which I bought at the Toulouse-Lautrec Museum in Albi, was still giving off 'vibrations'. It was of Toulouse-Lautrec cooking, painted by Vuillard. He has on a red shirt and yellow trousers and looks a bit like a monkey at work. It was a small painting. I've still got it on the wall above my bed. It's in an elaborate frame but it's actually just the postcard. I bought a lot of copies of this postcard and sent it out to people I knew because I thought it was so good. Then I photographed it as if the recipients were seeing it at their breakfast tables, so there was a boiled egg and a toaster behind the postcard (fig. 6). The morning they received**

this postcard must have been a delight for lots of people. Certainly, I would have been delighted to receive it. It's just a reproduction, but it can give you a lot of pleasure. Bigger reproductions of course are better. They're more accurate. But this postcard still gave off magic.

MG What magic is missing from a reproduction?

DH **Well, scale for one thing, and texture. Once, in the Kröller-Müller Museum at Otterlo in the Netherlands, I was looking at Van Gogh's *Cypresses*, and I could see that it was not quite reproducible, when you look at the paint on it, how thick it is in the trees and the clouds. I said to a friend, 'I've seen this reproduced but it's just not the same at all. You get the *image* but you don't get the *painting*.'**

MG Or the texture is actually wrong. Most fifteenth-century Italian paintings were painted in fresco and tempera, so their surfaces are matt. But reproductions are often on shiny paper.

DH **Yes, Piero's paintings aren't glossy, but a lot of reproductions *were* glossy – and still are – nonetheless. But there were books on Piero and Fra Angelico printed on a paper that is almost transparent, which gives the impression of being a fresco. They are very beautiful books.**

MG You wrote that you'd chosen four National Gallery pictures for *Looking at Pictures on a Screen* because you liked them, but that if other pictures from the collection had been available in the same large format you might have chosen them.

DH **Yes, I bought quite a few reproductions in the 1970s. My mother had one of Piero's *Baptism* on her bedroom wall for 30 years. She had it there until the day she died. I'd bought it together with some reproductions of paintings for myself and given it to her. She always liked it – but probably because it was a religious picture.**
    When I was young, I mainly knew old master paintings from reproductions. There was one of Fra Angelico's *Annunciation* from San Marco on the top corridor at Bradford Grammar School. I think it was in colour. I remember being very attracted to it. I thought it was the best picture there. So,

when I was 11 years old, I was already looking at it. Maybe it was a collotype [a photo-based printing process invented in the nineteenth century]. The artist Russell Flint used to do a lot of them, bare-breasted dancing girls in Spanish settings; businessmen bought them. I used to see them in a shop in Bradford, and they weren't cheap. They cost maybe £20 when you could have got anything else for £2. Collotypes had a matt look that would have been great for Fra Angelico, or Piero's *Baptism* for that matter.

MG Colour reproductions were still a bit of a rarity, a treat, until perhaps the 1960s.

DH **Yes, they were. Even the ones from the National Gallery that I bought were printed about 1970, I think.**

MG Photographs of your London studio at Powis Terrace in the mid-1970s document how you were surrounded by images of great pictures. Piero's *Baptism* is visible in several, and others include Pissarro's *Fox Hill, Upper Norwood*.

DH **They were in different places (fig. 7), finally on a screen [as in *Looking at Pictures on a Screen*, fig. 1].**

MG The whole conception of *The Artist's Eye* was built around reproductions, wasn't it? Because the paintings your friend Henry Geldzahler is gazing at on the screen are reproductions you'd bought from the National Gallery. And those were the ones included in the exhibition.

DH **When they asked me to make a choice for *The Artist's Eye*, I thought it would be great to include this picture of Henry just looking at the pictures I'd chosen.**

MG There's a paradox in that painting, isn't there? In the exhibition the viewer was looking at a real painting in oil on canvas of someone meditating on reproductions.

DH **Yes. That's what you are doing when you look at that picture: looking at a picture on a canvas of someone looking at photographs of paintings on paper. But in *The Artist's Eye*, I thought, the real pictures would be in the gallery. That would**

give people a special thrill that postcards and reproductions can't provide, however good they are. So that's what I did.

I understand what reproductions do. They've enriched my life a great deal, and I've learnt a lot of things from looking at them. I'm very glad there are lots of them. Otherwise, you'd have to be living in Florence to see Fra Angelico and Piero, or travelling all over the place. On the other hand, when you see the real paintings, it is a different experience.

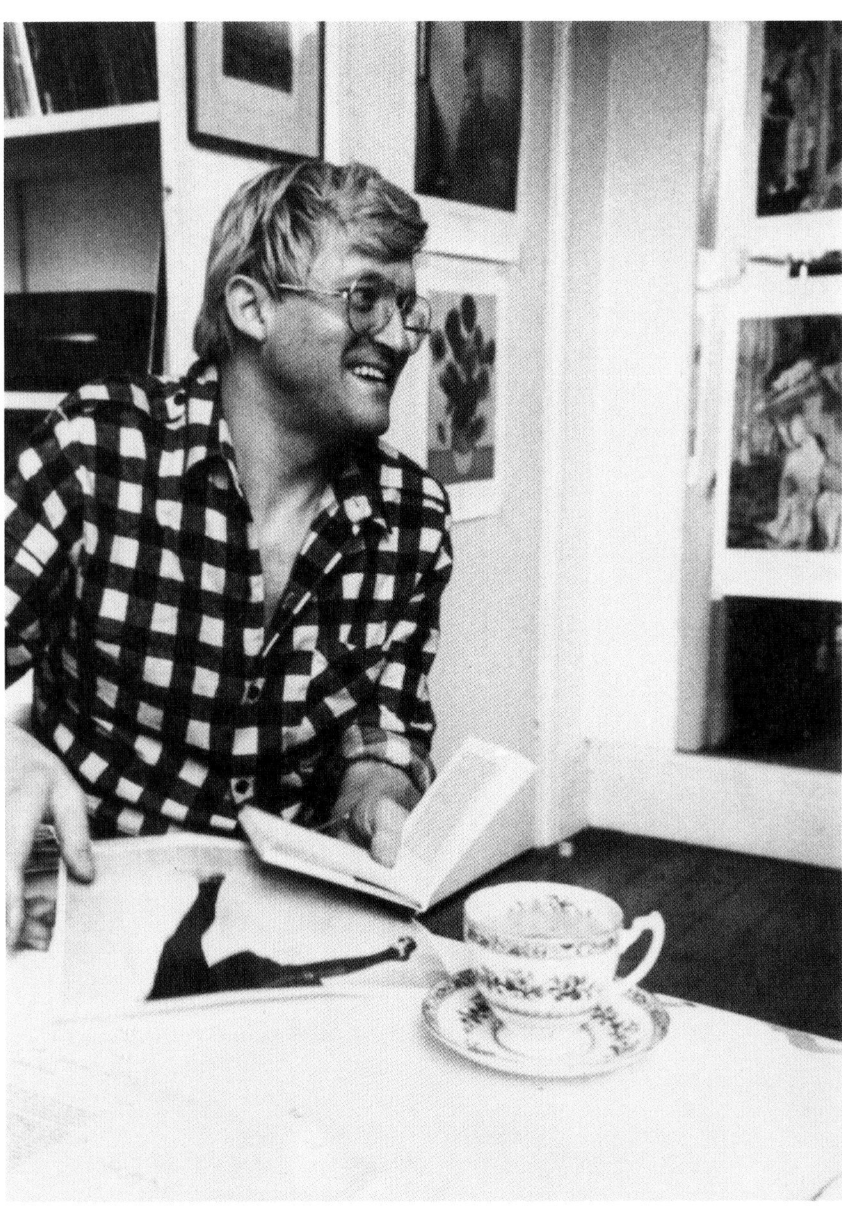

MG So in *The Artist's Eye* there was quite a complex thesis about various ways of absorbing paintings? When did you first have that thrill of seeing the actual Piero of *The Baptism of Christ*?

DH **I saw the real picture when I first came to London, which was when I was about 18 years old. It must have been in 1955; I came down with my friend Norman Stevens and we stayed at his uncle's on the kitchen floor. We went to the National Gallery, the Tate Gallery and a few other galleries. That was all we did.**

I thought it was *fantastic* because in Bradford there was nothing much in the art gallery. Leeds had a few more things, a Bonnard and a Derain of the Thames from the time that the dealer Vollard had sent Derain to London to paint the Thames like Monet.

On those early visits I remember being affected by Piero's *Baptism* and the Rembrandt portrait of Margaretha Trip with her hands on the arms of the chair (fig. 8). I thought that was a fantastic painting. I remember both very well, and also van Eyck's Mr and Mrs Arnolfini [*The Arnolfini Portrait*]. That's a very, very moving picture. But the Piero is just marvellous.

MG It's not hard to see connections between your own work and all three of those. Your double portraits are, like van Eyck's, masterpieces depicting just two people in a room (with, in the case of *My Parents*, a mirror in the background [see fig. 3]). And your pictures of your mother often put me in mind of Margaretha Trip (fig. 9).

I suppose that, once you were settled in London, going to galleries and museums was an important activity for you.

DH **Well, yes. You see, I'm a provincial person. As I said, I didn't visit London until I was 18 years old. My family and I thought London was miles and miles away; we didn't even know people who had been there. Or they might have been *once*. So, when I started coming down it was always to see exhibitions and museums. I remember seeing the Jackson Pollock show at the Whitechapel in 1958 (I hitchhiked to see it), and shows in the Tate. The Picasso exhibition at the Tate in 1960 is another I remember.**

The National Gallery was just *there*. They didn't do exhibitions in those days. But I often went there

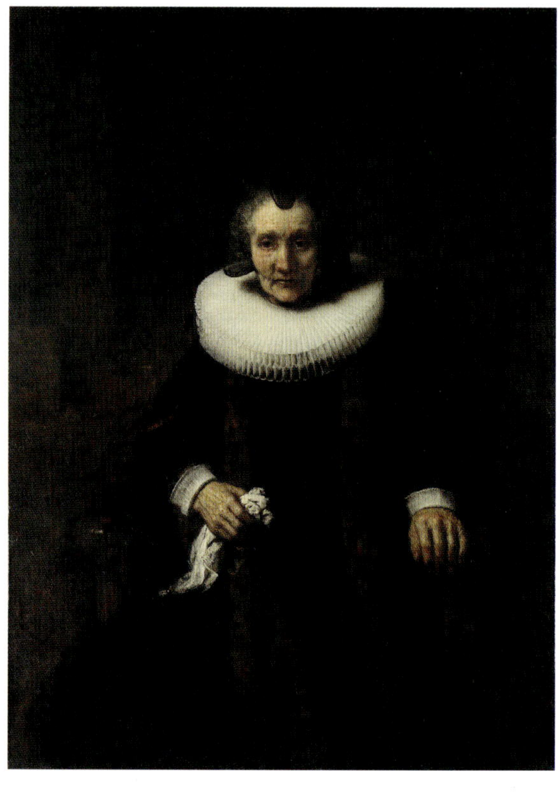

as a student. Most of the other students did too, but not everyone. I remember being told off by someone who used to carry around magazines about contemporary art. 'What do you want to go *there* for?' But you would think that if you are a painter, you'd want to understand the history of your own activity. I wouldn't always go through everything. Sometimes I'd just go in to see two or three rooms – the Rembrandts or the Van Goghs.

MG All of the artists in *The Artist's Eye* show were important to you, weren't they? Van Gogh, Vermeer and Piero especially?

DH **I was always looking at Fra Angelico, Piero, Vermeer and Van Gogh.**

MG I've often thought that the range of colours you use is a bit quattrocento: light, clear and bright. And you've admitted to borrowing a few motifs from Piero and Fra Angelico in your picture *California Art Collector* (fig. 10).

DH **That was because the climate and the houses reminded me a bit of Italy. That's part of the charm**

Fig. 8
Rembrandt (1606–1669)
Portrait of Margaretha de Geer, Wife of Jacob Trip, about 1661
Oil on canvas, 130.5 × 97.5 cm
The National Gallery, London

Fig. 9
David Hockney (born 1937)
Mother, Bradford, 19 Feb 1979, 1979
Sepia ink on paper,
35.6 × 27.9 cm
The David Hockney Foundation

1 Looking at Pictures for a Long, Long Time

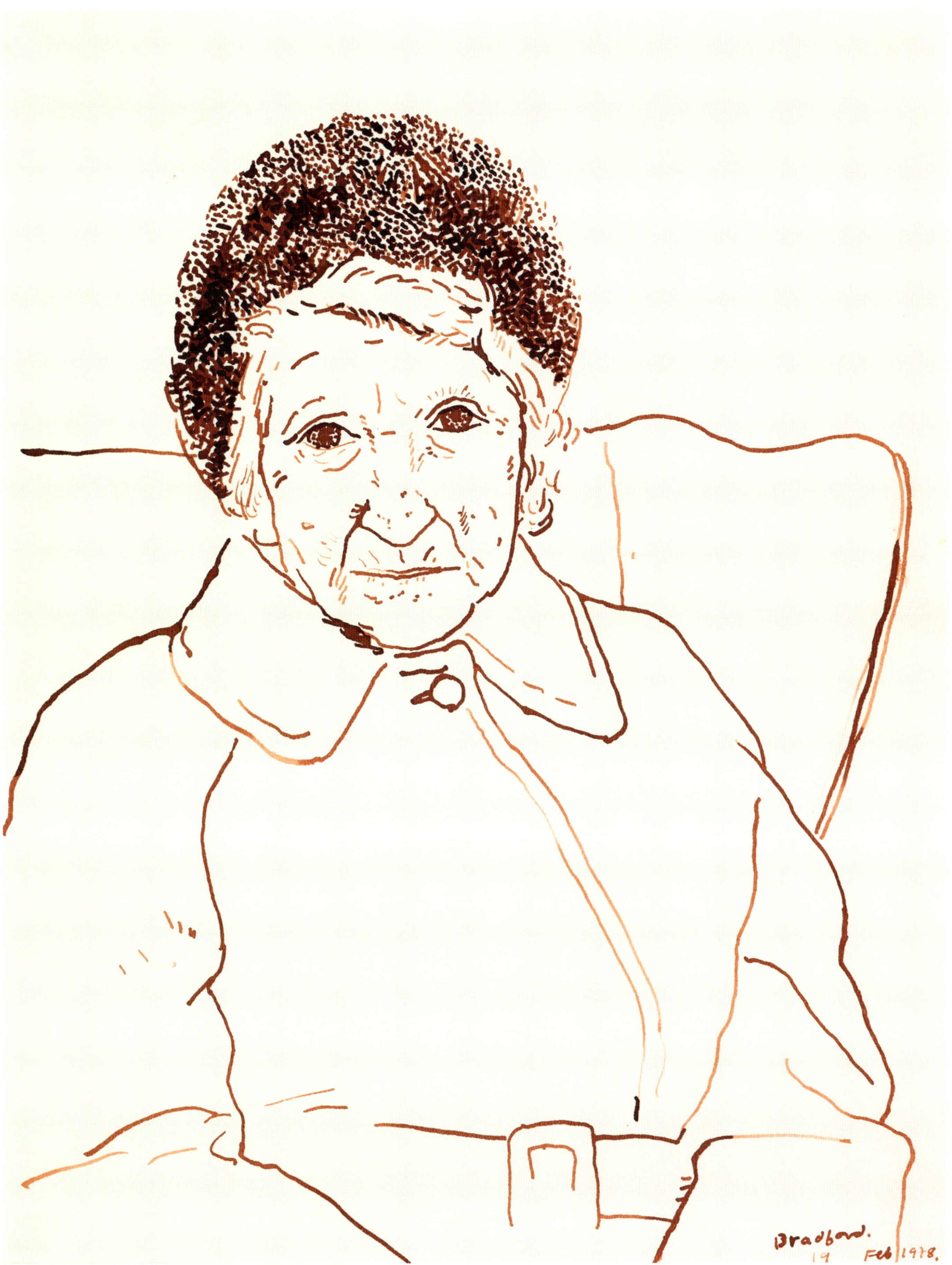
Bradford.
19   Feb 1978.

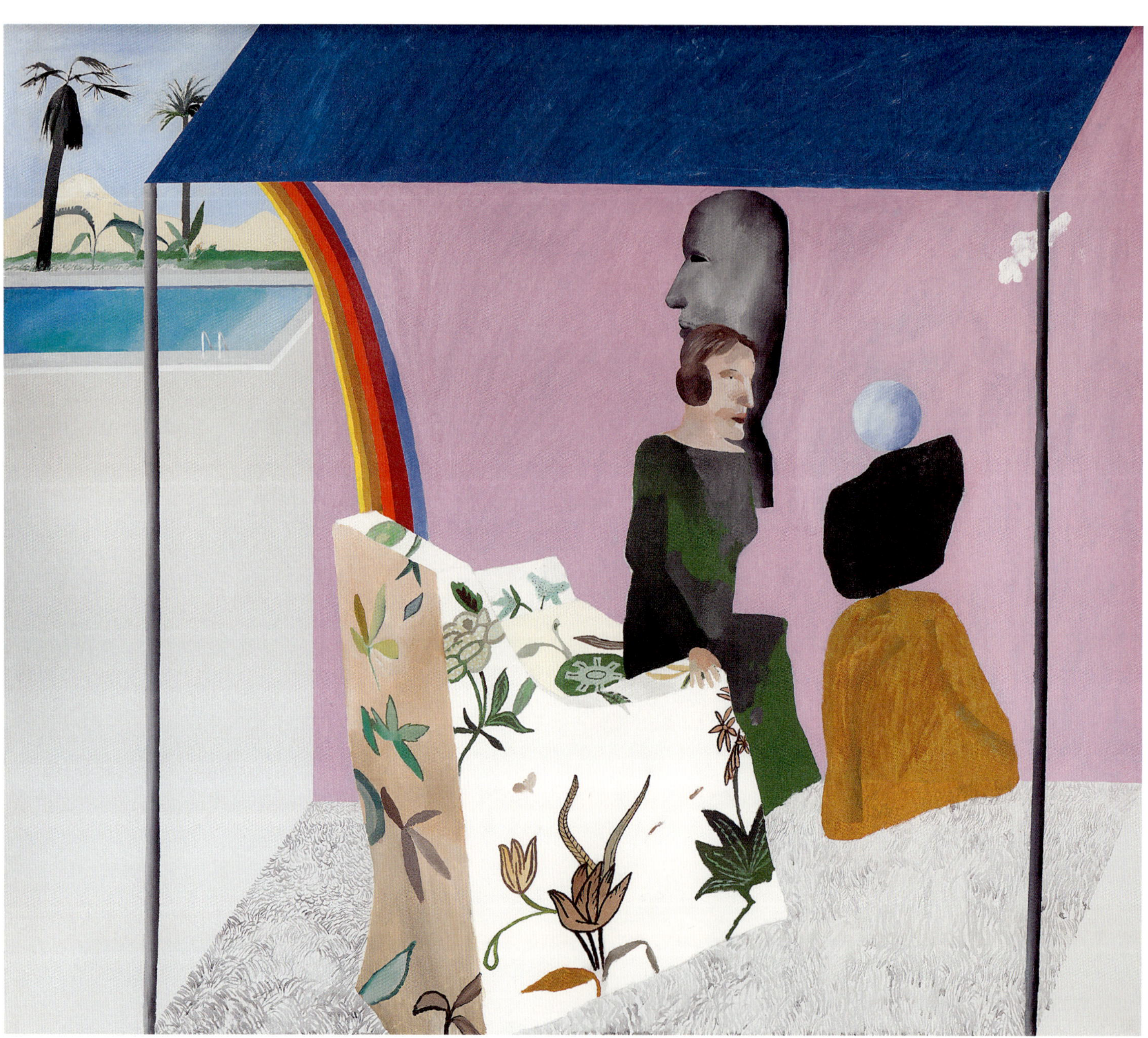

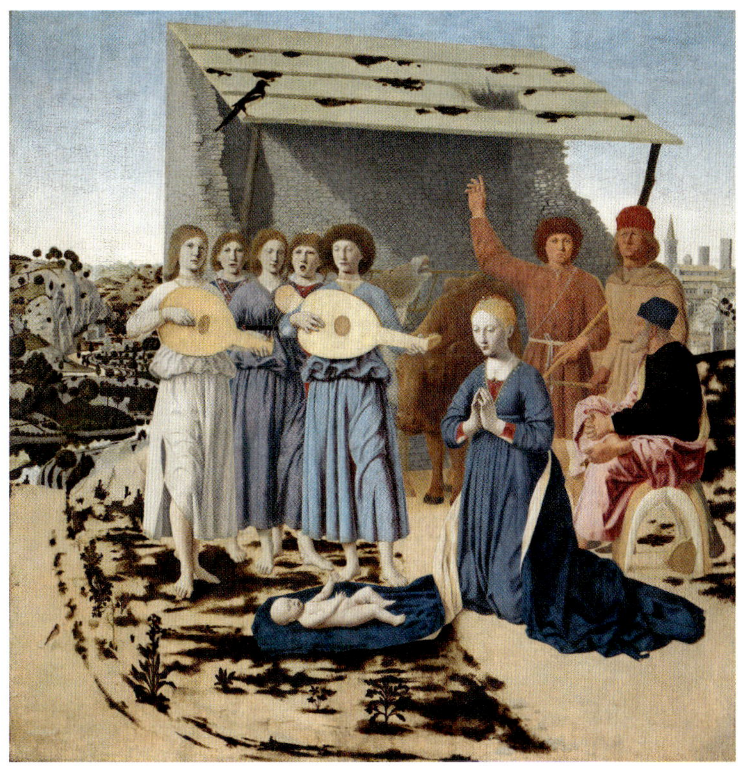

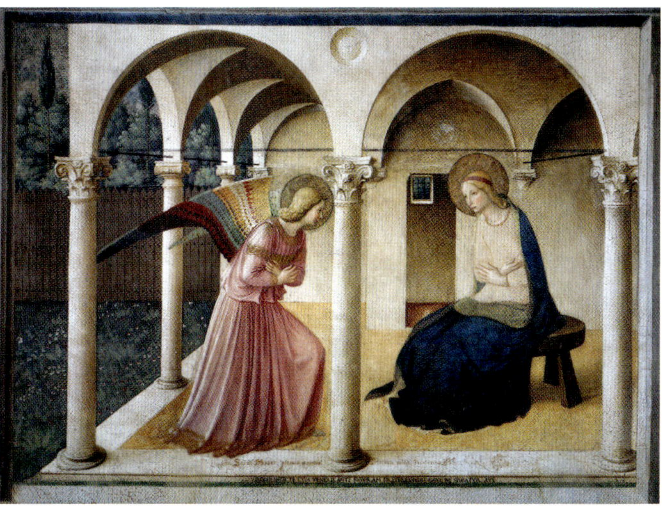

the mountains in Scene 1 of *The Magic Flute* [Hockney designed a production of Mozart's opera for Glyndebourne in 1978].

MG I noticed you also recycled Uccello's dragon from *Saint George and the Dragon* in the National Gallery. It turns up as the serpent that chases Tamino at the very start of the opera (figs 14 and 15). Uccello and Gozzoli fit well with the fairy-tale mood of *The Magic Flute*. But Piero's *Baptism* has more to it than that, hasn't it?

DH **It is a very, *very* beautiful painting, isn't it? The clarity of it is *stunning*.**

MG In your first book, published in 1976, you cite Piero's pictures as an example of paintings that are 'marvellous and exciting to look at, that delight you'. Obviously, you still feel that.

DH **Yes. Anybody must be delighted. You couldn't not be!**

MG And of course you are far from being the only artist to admire Piero. He was a stated favourite of many twentieth-century British artists – Euan Uglow, for example, and Craigie Aitchison.

DH **Well, I can't imagine any good painter would ever knock Piero della Francesca. And *The Baptism* is a truly magnificent picture.**

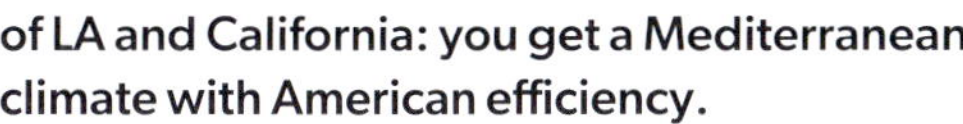

of LA and California: you get a Mediterranean climate with American efficiency.

MG The figure in the picture is looking at some contemporary sculpture by William Turnbull, but she's underneath a canopy taken from Piero's *Nativity* in the National Gallery (fig. 11), while the rainbow behind her seems to derive from the brilliant plumage of Fra Angelico's angel in *The Annunciation* (fig. 12), a work that, in turn, inspired you to create a version of your own (fig. 13). Could you put into words the attraction of quattrocento Italian paintings for you?

DH **They saw things in a wonderfully *clear* way. I saw the Fra Angelico frescoes in San Marco the first time I went to Italy, and I've seen them since, when I've been back to Florence. It closes at one o'clock, so last time I went every morning with JP [Hockney's partner]. We were more or less the only people there. There are huge queues at the Uffizi. But at San Marco you just pay and go in.**
    By the way, the other works that really affected me in Florence were the frescoes by Benozzo Gozzoli in the Palazzo Medici, just down the road from San Marco. That's where I borrowed

Fig. 10
David Hockney (born 1937)
California Art Collector, 1964
Acrylic on canvas,
152.4 × 182.9 cm
Private collection

Fig. 11
Piero della Francesca (about 1415/20–1492)
The Nativity, early 1480s
Oil on wood, 124.4 × 122.6 cm
The National Gallery, London

Fig. 12
Fra Angelico (active 1417; died 1455)
The Annunciation, 1440–5
Fresco
Convent of San Marco, Florence

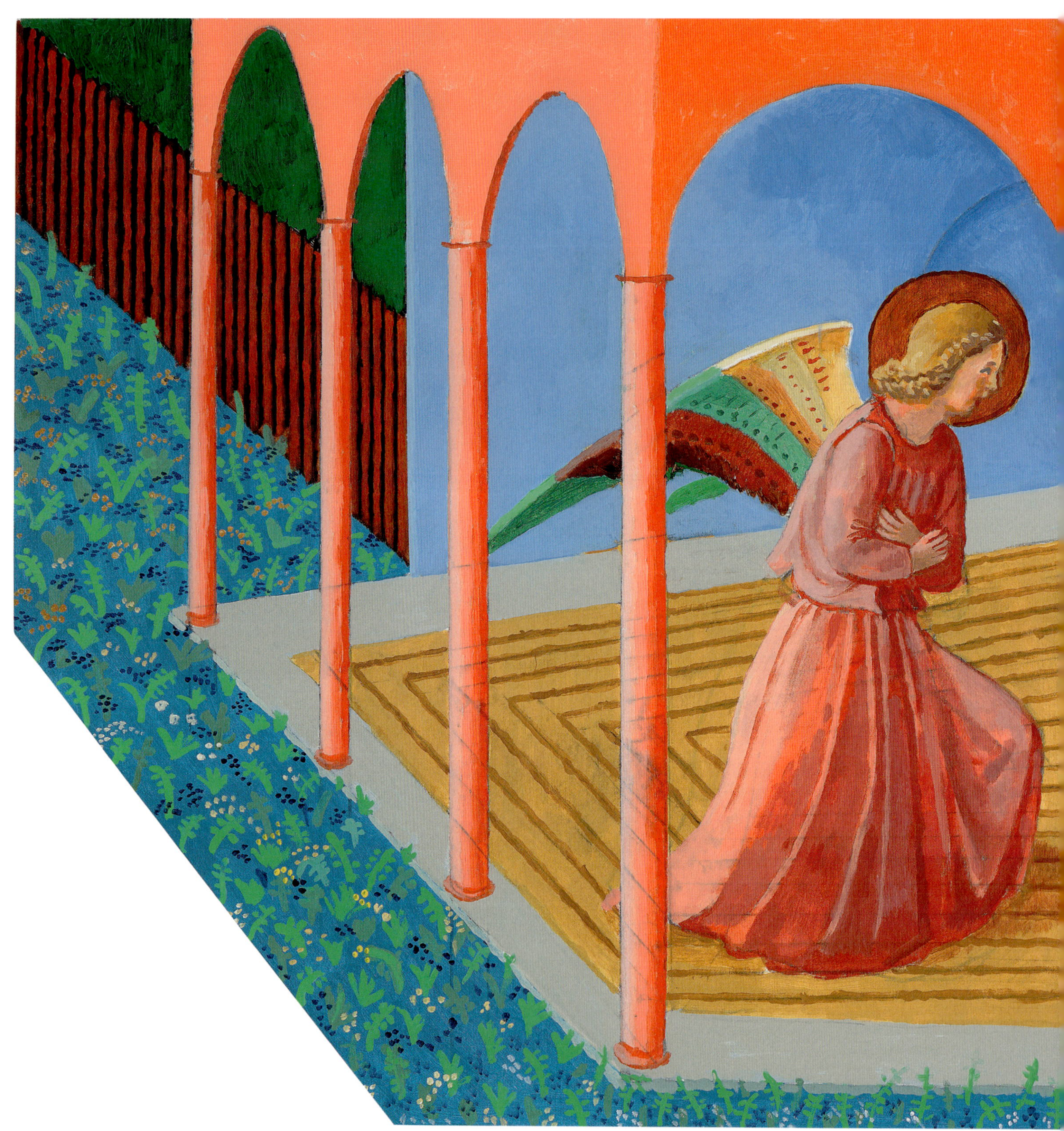

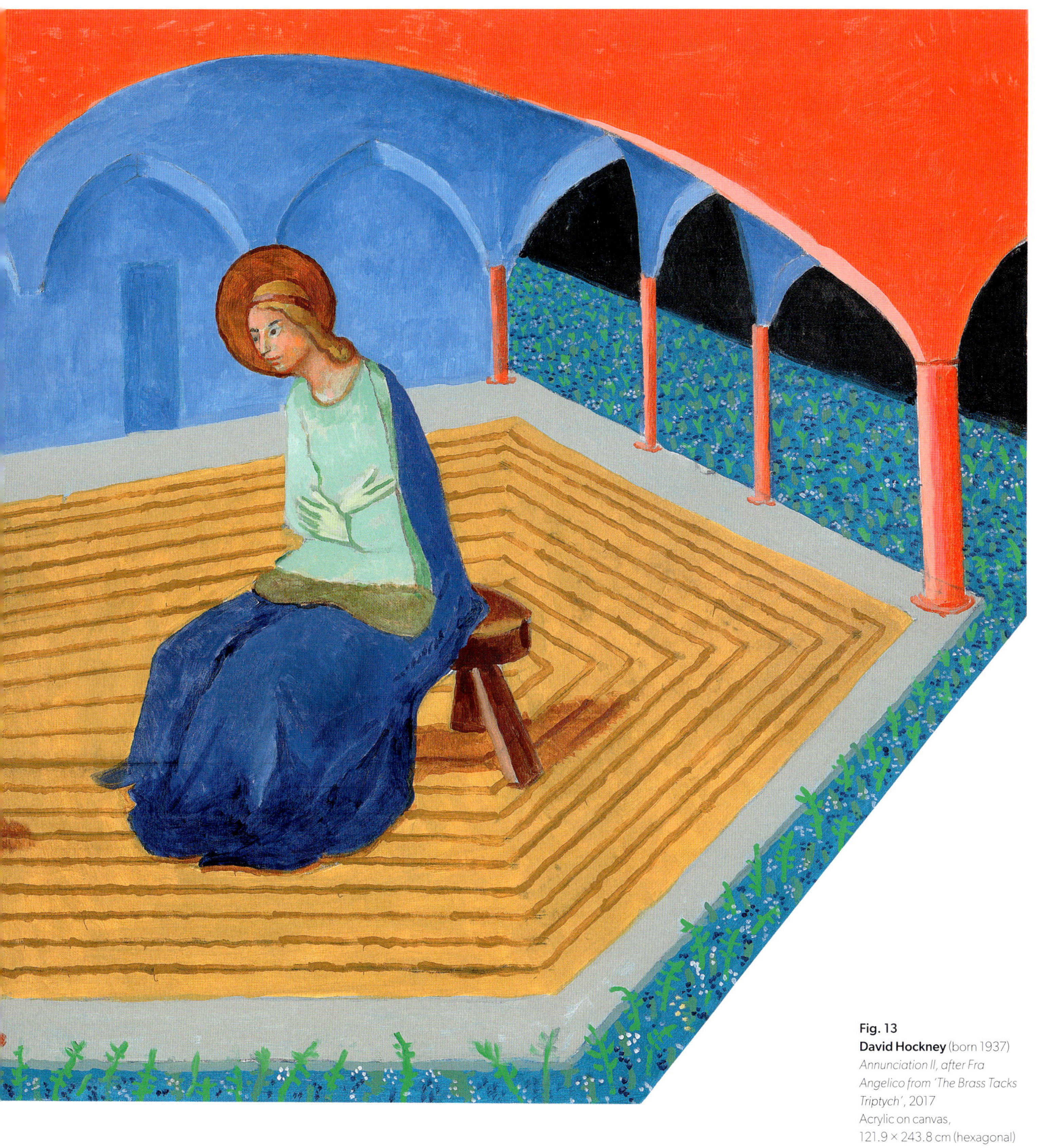

Fig. 13
David Hockney (born 1937)
Annunciation II, after Fra Angelico from 'The Brass Tacks Triptych', 2017
Acrylic on canvas,
121.9 × 243.8 cm (hexagonal)
Collection of the artist

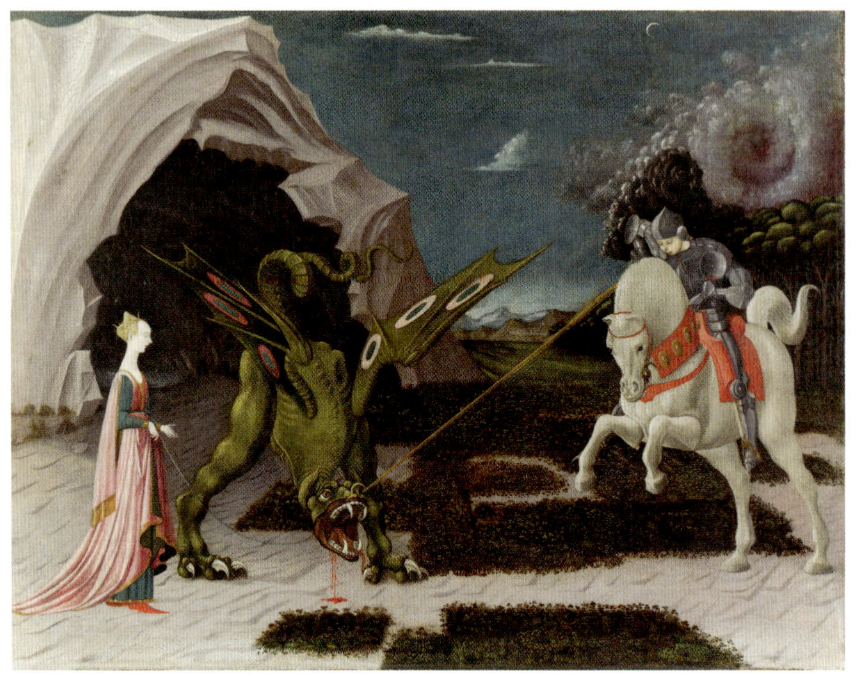

MG It's interesting that it was the quattrocento Renaissance – the fifteenth-century artists – who had an impact on many modern artists, not the generations that followed, the so-called High Renaissance.

DH **Raphael's painting was about roundness and finish. I don't like his work in the way I do Piero's or Fra Angelico's. I *love* them.**

MG In 1976, when an interviewer asked you whether you bought works of art, you answered, 'No, but I'd love to have that Piero della Francesca [*The Baptism*, pinned to the studio wall], just so I could look at it every day for an hour.' Would you still like to own *The Baptism*?

DH **Well, yes. It would be fantastic!**

MG An hour is quite a long time to look at a picture, but perhaps not too long.

DH **I don't think so. You would look at the landscape with those little mountains in the background (see fig. 43), the figures, everything. It's beautiful! I enjoy looking at pictures for a long, long time.**

MG I agree. They take you over and you stop thinking. You sink into them.

DH **Yes. It's wonderful to sit and just look for a long time.**

MG In a way, that's the subject of *Looking at Pictures on a Screen*. It was intended as an 'imaginative portrait' of your friend Henry Geldzahler, but obviously it's also about the calm contemplation and enjoyment of painting.

DH **I often went round museums and galleries with Henry. His eye really was fantastic. Some people, a few, have fantastic eyes. Henry always had it.**

MG Occasionally people pooh-pooh the notion of 'a good eye'. But certain individuals really have astonishing powers of discernment when it comes to art. A few dealers maybe, but not so many historians and critics.

DH **[laughs]**

MG Henry Geldzahler was the first Curator for Twentieth-Century Art at the Met [Metropolitan Museum of Art, New York] and Commissioner of Cultural Affairs for New York. But he was also an amazing spotter of artistic talent. He's said to have visited Jean-Michel Basquiat's studio the very day that Basquiat made his first proper painting, as opposed to graffiti. It still wasn't dry. Geldzahler bought it on the spot.

DH **I remember that painting when it was in Henry's apartment.**

MG But what's the 'marvellous and exciting' thing that delighted him – or you – when you look at those pictures?

DH **With pictures you can never quite know exactly how or why they affect you: what it is. Though you do know that this is fantastic – a really great, great painting. But I think for me in Piero's *Baptism* it is a *spatial* thrill – seeing fantastic figures in space.**

MG You once made that point taking another great Piero, the fresco of the pregnant *Madonna del Parto* in Monterchi, not far from Arezzo, as an example. You argued that 'it is an amazing spatial, visual experience', and while we may think it's her pregnancy or her face that's moving us, it is actually the way that the figure

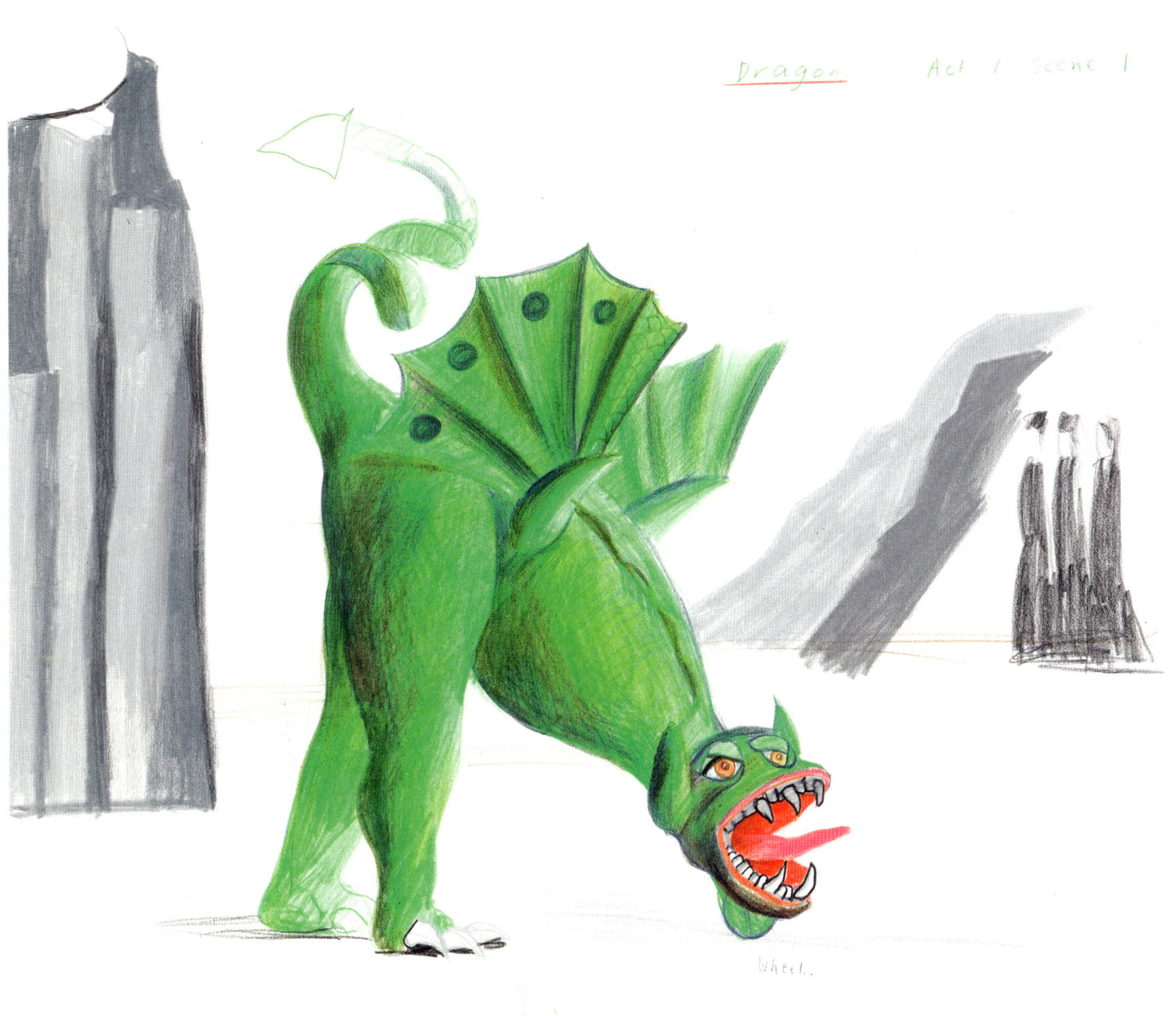

Dragon.   Act 1 Scene 1
Wheel..

is placed in space: 'The magic is in the space, not the objects.'

DH **Yes. As I've often said, I think being able to draw means being able to put things in believable space. That's what drawing is. And photography can't do it very well. Photographs see surfaces, not space. That's why landscape photography is not so good. A long time ago, walking on a beach at Bridlington, my sister Margaret said to me, 'Sometimes I think space is God.' I thought that was a very nice, poetic idea.**

MG There is certainly an enormous amount of space in *The Baptism*. It shoots back behind Christ's legs and hips perhaps half a mile to the little town in the distance and the hills beyond. You write somewhere that in a Piero you could measure where all the figures are; you could make a model of it.

DH **Well, yes, I suppose you could.**

MG But there is also time in *The Baptism*. In the catalogue you describe how while you were looking at a reproduction of it one day it struck you that 'the bird that is hovering over the head of Christ seems not to be moving' (see fig. 63). But, you go on, although it is a still picture, 'there are marvellous suggestions of movement elsewhere in the picture. Just below, the water being poured doesn't seem still; it's an action that's going on, you *feel* it going on.'

DH **There is a quantity of time in every picture, but there's much less in a photograph than in a painting. The time makes the space somehow.**

MG We don't really have the vocabulary for talking about space. Bernard Berenson wrote about 'space composition'. He thought it was the particular strength of Central Italian painters such as Perugino and Piero.

DH **It's a good phrase, but it doesn't really tell you any more than those two words: that it's a composition involving space. Painting is like music in that you can't talk about it that well. You've just to *listen* to music. That's all. And you've just to *look* at paintings.**

MG You've written about the paradoxes and problems for many modern viewers when looking at pictures such as Piero's. You pointed out that almost every one depicts a Christian story or scene, 'Yet our delight in the pictures is in the way they are constructed; that's what makes them stand out, not the story.' Do you still feel that?

DH **Yes, because the subject, which is something that happened in the life of Jesus, doesn't really mean much to me. I'm not a devout Christian, though I was brought up as one. My mother was a believer. But for me the picture doesn't lose anything as a result of that. So it can't be just about the subject.**

Why does *The Baptism of Christ* by Piero work for me when I'm not really a Christian? There are many paintings that you get great pleasure from, without really needing to know much about them. Lots of people who go to galleries don't know the Bible stories. It demonstrates that pictures are really just abstractions. And of course, in a sense, every picture in two dimensions is an abstraction. Nothing in the world is truly two-dimensional.

Mind you, it's possible to get meaning from a picture without understanding the theology. I was told about a group of visitors from East Asia who were being shown round a gallery and were entranced by a painting of the Madonna and Child because it was such a beautiful picture of a baby.

MG Did you follow the Piero trail to see more of his works in Tuscany?

DH **Yes. I went to Arezzo to see his frescoes in the church of San Francesco, I think the first time I went to Italy, in 1962. Some of them are very high up so that they must have been seen only by God. I thought that was fantastic, that Piero works up there, probably for months, then comes down and nobody ever sees the entire frescoes other than the Almighty!**

MG But the lower scenes, which are easily visible, would have had a tremendous impact on someone seeing them in the fifteenth century.

DH **Enormous.**

MG In a way, all the artists whose work appeared on the screen and in *The Artist's Eye* exhibition were tutelary spirits in your work and studio, not just Piero but Vermeer, Degas and Van Gogh too.

DH Van Gogh must have liked Piero, mustn't he? He would have loved the clarity.

MG I suppose he would have seen *The Baptism* if he went to the National Gallery.

DH He must have made a visit there while he was in London in the 1870s because he'd seen Hobbema's *Avenue at Middelharnis*, which I've always loved myself, recently making a picture inspired by it (see p. 8). He commented on that. When his brother Theo was going to London, he advised him to look out for the Hobbema when he was in the National Gallery.

MG Like Piero's, Vincent van Gogh's works have had quite an effect on your own. You exhibited side by side with him at the Van Gogh Museum in 2018. And some years after *The Artist's Eye* exhibition, you made a number of your own versions of *Van Gogh's Chair* in reverse perspective (figs 16 and 17).

DH That was a commission for the centenary of Van Gogh's arrival in Arles in 1888. I've always loved the painting; it was a favourite of my father's, too.

MG You must have seen the *Sunflowers* and *Van Gogh's Chair* when you first visited the Tate in 1955.

DH Yes, and I saw a Van Gogh exhibition in Manchester in 1956 while I was still at Bradford College of Art. I remember thinking that if he could use two whole tubes of blue to paint a sky, he must have been quite rich.

MG That's funny! Tracey Emin expressed just the same idea. Van Gogh felt he was poor, but in a way it was voluntary. His family was rich, and his brother was always telling him just to ask for more money if he needed it. So the lesson you drew from looking at Van Gogh was partly economic, partly technical.

DH Technique affects so many things. If you use paint the way Vincent did, you've got to paint fast. The method isn't good if you paint slowly, simply because of the thickness of the paint and the fact that it all has to dry at once. Obviously, Vincent knew all this, which is why he worked fast. I don't think he spent more than three or four days, even on some of the rather complicated pictures he did in Arles. All painting is a sort of performance art, but you particularly feel that with Van Gogh, and it's stunning.

MG You can see the speed when you look at the pictures. It's interesting that the lessons you learned from galleries and museums were partly practical: how to paint a picture.

DH There are rules of painting. You can break them if you want to, but if you do, the painting won't last very long. Monets and Cezannes are still a pleasure to look at, because those artists put the paint on right and there's not too much white in it. If you look at paintings that are old and in quite good condition, you will see they are mainly painted very thinly. Vermeer used very thin paint; so did Caravaggio. Most Picassos are thinly painted too, actually.

Even Van Goghs, if you look at them, are not that thick – he put a lot of paint in the brushstroke, but they are not made up of many layers. They are 130 years old and they haven't gone dark, though some pigments have faded. The colours still vibrate.

MG It was the same with Vermeer. Some of the lessons you took from him were concerned more with *how* he painted than *what* he painted. I remember sitting in front of his *Art of Painting* with you when it was in an exhibition at the National Gallery in 2001. It was another example of long, slow looking; we were there for quite a while. And you began by saying that, although its title was *The Art of Painting*, it was also very much about the *craft* of painting.

DH Well, yes. In Vermeer, what is so amazing is the way the figures fit in space, and it's also to do with tonalities and edges. For instance, the difference in tonality between the dark in the blacks and the dark in the blues is stunning. Your eye sees it.

MG In *The Artist's Eye* you had a selection spread through time from the fifteenth century onwards.

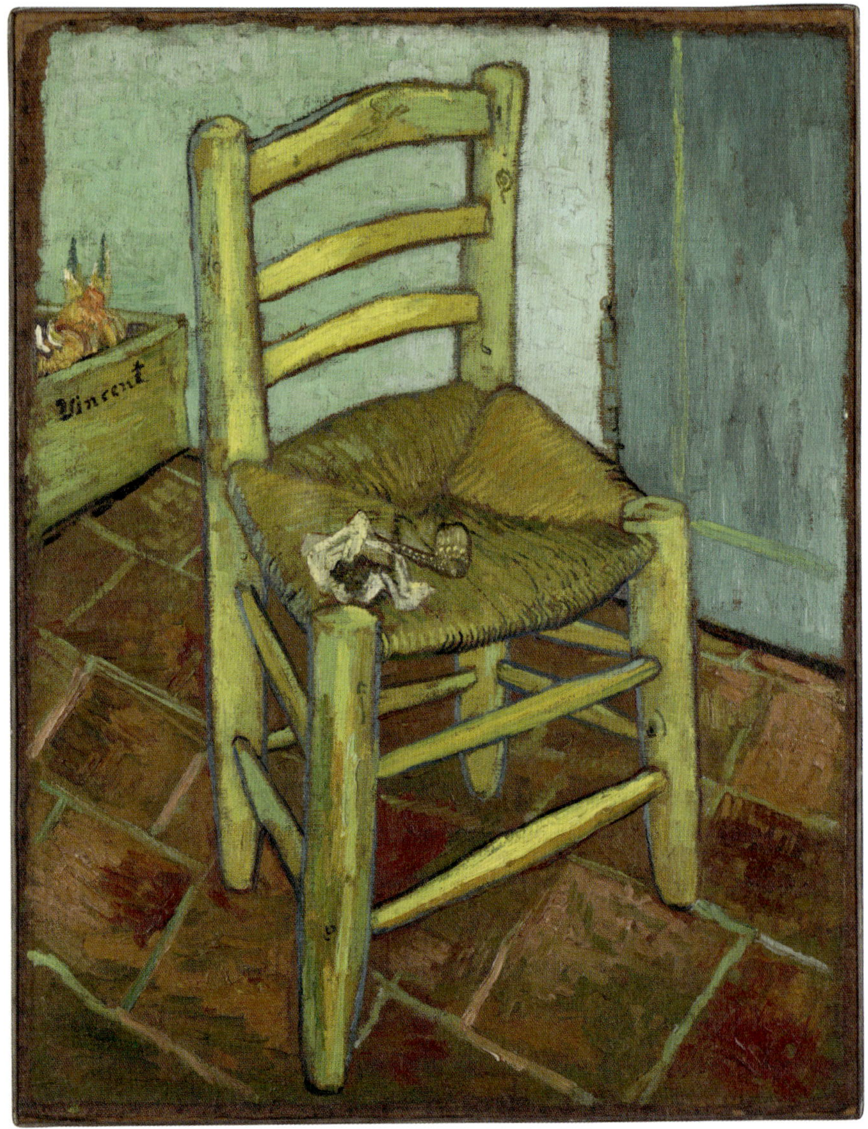

Fig. 16
Vincent van Gogh
(1853–1890)
Van Gogh's Chair, 1888
Oil on canvas, 91.8 × 73 cm
The National Gallery, London

Fig. 17
David Hockney (born 1937)
Vincent's Chair and Pipe, 1988
Acrylic on canvas,
91.4 × 91.4 cm
Fondation Vincent Van Gogh

DH Yes, they were from a period of over 450 years, but they were all fantastic pictures.

MG That's a thing about painting. It communicates over time. A picture on the wall of a cave from 30,000 years ago speaks to you directly. When you look at it, you know that the person who made it had sensations and feelings just like yours.

DH It's obvious. I was once talking to a friend who was going on about his eighteenth-century ancestors, and I said, well, one of my ancestors was a cave painter.

MG Well, if you go back that far, we are probably all related to just about every human being who was alive then. In a deeper sense, every painter and maker of pictures is related to the artists of Lascaux and Altamira because fundamentally they are doing the same thing. As we've been discussing, your own work has been deeply affected by works from long ago.

DH One of my early paintings was entitled *A Grand Procession of Dignitaries in the Semi-Egyptian Style* [1961]. I called it 'semi-Egyptian' because I made a few additions to the Ancient Egyptian stylistic repertoire. Even then I was fascinated by Egypt. I had a book: *Egyptian Sculpture*. It was all in black and white, but it was beautifully printed. The photographs were obviously taken with care, the sculptures were all very well lit, so they looked really good. I *loved* that book. And I did a few paintings from it. *Egyptian Head Disappearing into Descending Clouds* [1961] was another one.

MG I remember that when you were going to see the great Pieter Bruegel the Elder exhibition in Vienna in 2018 you told people you were off to see some contemporary art.

DH Well, if paintings speak to you, it's happening now. So they *are* contemporary. They're living. The artist might have died but the pictures are still alive. They just get better and better.

MG Do you have any wishes for the National Gallery on the Bicentenary of its foundation?

DH Happy birthday! The National Gallery is doing a great job, isn't it? It's keeping all those pictures there, safe and on view. They have to protect them, look after them, and they are doing that. Everything in the collection is good, every single picture is good. It's a classic collection of paintings – one that might grow a bit but remains quite fixed. If you took a few pictures off the walls in the National Gallery a lot of people would miss them, wouldn't they? They are images from the past that really live today, and I think they'll be there for a long, long time in the future.

1 Looking at Pictures for a Long, Long Time

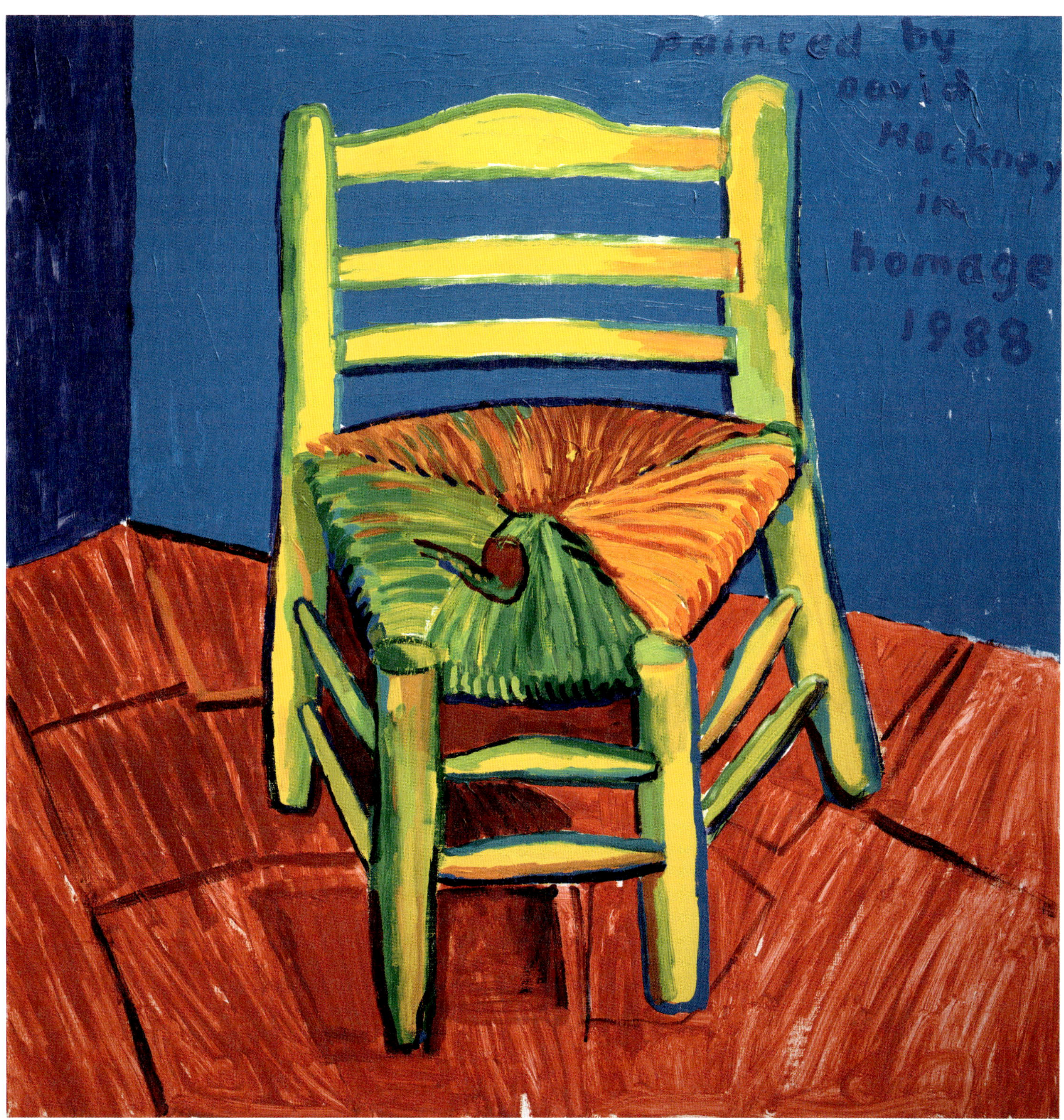
painted by
David
Hockney
in
homage
1988

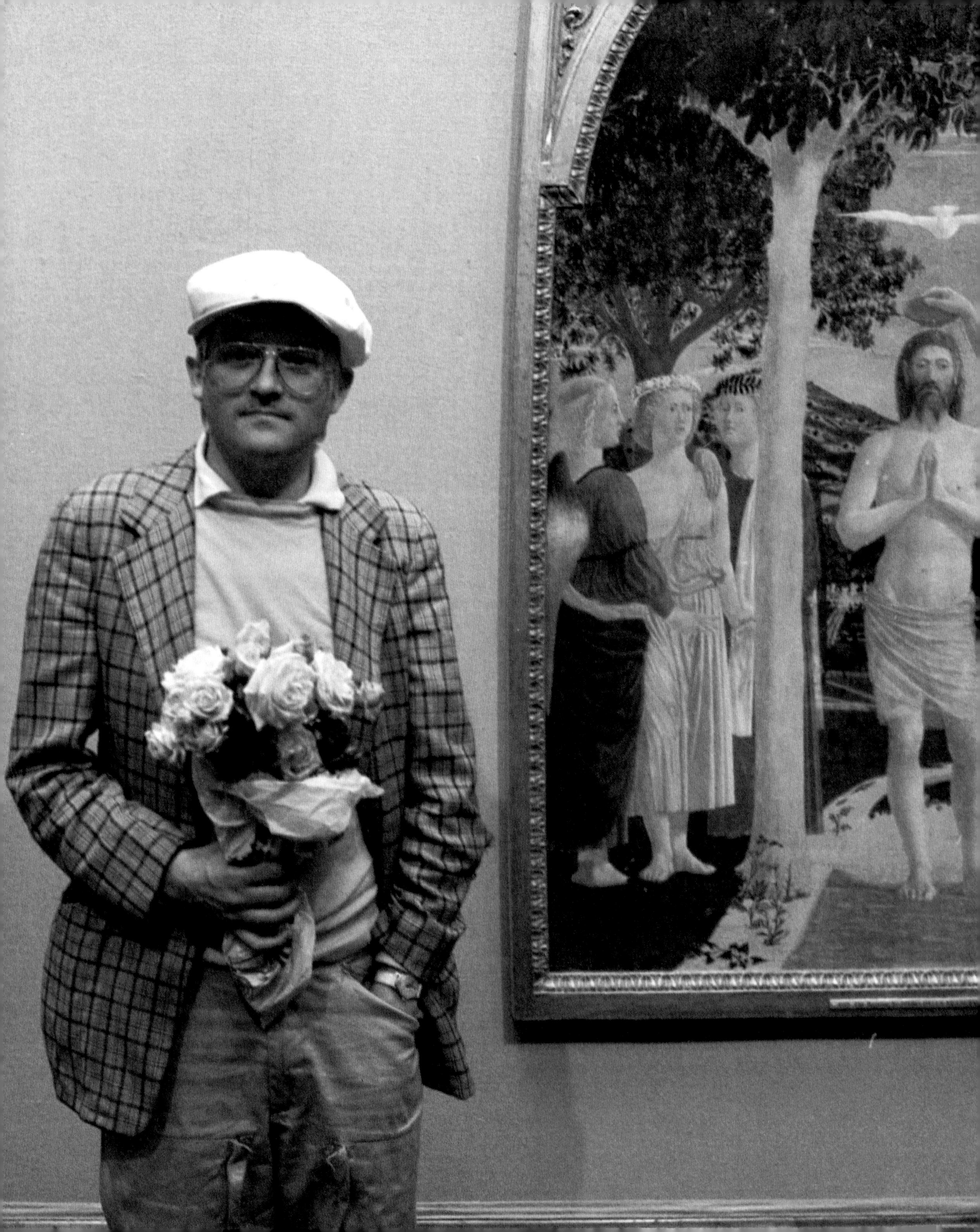

TRANSCENDING THE CENTURIES: ARTISTIC CONVERSATIONS WITH PIERO

Susanna Avery-Quash and Sacha Llewellyn

Look at Piero della Francesca's wonderful pictures that are marvellous and exciting to look at, that delight you. I would think anybody who likes painting at all would like a Piero della Francesca. DAVID HOCKNEY [1]

I t has recently been claimed that 'Piero's work ... has
captivated audiences more thoroughly than any
15th-century artist other than Leonardo'.[2] This chapter
explores how one of the best loved pictures by Piero
della Francesca, *The Baptism of Christ*, painted probably
about 1437–45 (fig. 2), has inspired artists, and in
particular British painters, since it entered the National
Gallery's collection in 1861, leading to the creation of
a rich variety of exciting visual responses.[3]

'EXQUISITE ARCHITECTURE': PIERO'S *BAPTISM* ENTERS THE NATIONAL GALLERY

Although now regarded as one of the supreme
artists of the Renaissance, after his death in 1492
Piero was neglected for almost four centuries, and,
when remembered, was given more credence as a
mathematician than as a painter. The famous sixteenth-
century artist-biographer Giorgio Vasari was lukewarm
in his praise, and the fact that Piero's frescoes lay off
the beaten track and were in an increasingly poor state
of repair did not help matters. By the late nineteenth
century, however, Piero's star was beginning to rise.
In Britain, a small group of pioneering connoisseurs,
museum officials and collectors was responsible for
putting his name back onto the artistic map, and the
purchase and display of *The Baptism* by the National
Gallery in 1861 was a pivotal moment in establishing
his reputation in Britain.

Sir Charles Lock Eastlake (1793–1865), appointed
Director of the National Gallery in 1855, acquired the
first examples of Piero's work. Eastlake's acquisition
strategy, following a governmental directive, aimed
to fill gaps in the nascent collection (in existence since
1824), not least in relation to early Italian art, so that a
more comprehensive survey of the history of European
painting might be displayed at Trafalgar Square. As far
as Eastlake's contemporaries were concerned, art had
reached its apogee in 'the period of Raphael and his
contemporaries',[4] and the work of Piero came to be
seen as an important milestone on that journey towards
perfection. Piero was introduced into the Gallery's
Foreign Schools catalogue of 1858 as 'one of the
most distinguished of the early Umbrian painters' and
'according to Vasari, the master of Perugino [and] Luca
Signorelli' – the former being particularly important in
Italy's artistic lineage as the master of Raphael (1483–
1520).[5] Eastlake was fulsome about the artist's 'exquisite
architecture' and 'most careful' perspective. In his
estimate Piero was not, however, the best model for
aspiring painters, given that his female figures had 'large

features', 'thick lips', 'descending corners of mouths',
'wide noses', 'dropsical ancles [*sic*]', and lacked
requisite Raphaelesque charm.[6]

Although Eastlake saw *The Baptism* in its original
location during a visit to Borgo San Sepolcro in
September 1856, he dismissed it on account of its poor
state of repair. Instead, the following year, he purchased
what he thought would be the Gallery's first 'Piero',
Portrait of a Lady in Red, although the attribution was
soon questioned and it is now catalogued as 'Florentine
School'.[7] A similar scenario occurred in 1861, when
Eastlake bought a second profile portrait of a woman (in
yellow), although in this case the misattribution to Piero
was retained as late as 1915.[8] Indeed, 1861 was a crucial
year Piero-wise. Not only did Eastlake also purchase
The Baptism at the Matthew Uzielli Sale, London, on
13 April 1861,[9] but the ground was laid for two further
Piero acquisitions. Eastlake started negotiations over
Piero's *Saint Michael* for his own collection (see fig. 64),
which he bought the following year, albeit it as by Fra
Carnevale (born by 1416; died 1484). That work came
to the Gallery in 1867, when the recently widowed
Lady Eastlake offered it to the Trustees, along with all
the other works that her husband had acquired during
his directorship, at the prices he had paid for them. It
was also in 1861 that Eastlake first encountered Piero's
Nativity (see fig. 11) in Florence, when it still belonged
to 'descendants of P. della Francesca', and which he
attributed to 'either Pietro [*sic*] della Francesca or Fra
Carnevale', noting that 'the execution [is] generally
thinner than Pietro [*sic*] the hair of one of the angels like
corkscrews – like an early or young artist other parts
finely drawn ... The face of the M.[adonna] longer than
Pietro [*sic*] & his peculiar mouth only to be traced in
the shepherds'.[10] It seems that he might have acquired
this work for himself had he not been beaten to it by his
compatriot Alexander Barker. In the end, the Gallery
secured it at a sale of Barker's collection in 1874.

That same year, following the National Gallery's
purchase of Piero's *Nativity*, John Charles Robinson,
formerly an art referee of the South Kensington Museum
(now Victoria and Albert Museum), published three
letters in *The Times*, in which he claimed that he was
the person who had singlehandedly negotiated *The
Baptism*'s export from Florence, and 'mainly, too' the
one who had 'caus[ed] it to be placed in the National
Gallery'.[11] Certainly, Robinson was responsible for its
first public UK debut, through organising its loan to
the South Kensington Museum in 1860–1.[12] By 1874,
Eastlake was no longer alive to defend his record.

What is clear is that as soon as it entered the Gallery, *The Baptism* was regarded as a prime 'specimen' of early Italian art. According to diary entries by the Gallery's Keeper, Ralph Nicholson Wornum, on 10 May 1861 it was hung in a new frame '<u>with glass</u>', prominently in the 'Small Vestibule' with works by Filippo Lippi. The following day, thanks to publicity in *The Times* nearly 5000 visitors came and the 'new room … caused a sensation'.[13] It has never been loaned away from Trafalgar Square and, during discussions of the new Sainsbury Wing extension, it was one of a handful of 'key exhibits' chosen to 'occupy conspicuous positions, chiefly at the end of vistas, enabling them to be seen and recognised at a distance'. When the Sainsbury Wing opened in 1991, *The Baptism* was displayed, alongside Piero's *Nativity* and *Saint Michael*, in Room 66, a 'chapel-like room',[14] in a specially created shallow niche that terminated a vista.

'ENERGETIC BUT UNREFINED': FIRST RESPONSES TO *THE BAPTISM*

Eastlake purchased *The Baptism* for £241 10s., a modest sum compared to the £2,500 he paid that same year for three early Italian works by Fra Filippo Lippi, Carlo Crivelli and Ortolano, and the £800 he spent on a self-portrait by Rembrandt (1606–1669).[15] While the modest sum disbursed for *The Baptism* is partly explained by its poor condition and its being an incomplete work, Piero was also not yet part of nineteenth-century consciousness of Renaissance art. What Eastlake described perceptively as the sculpturesque qualities of Piero's style were generally negatively recast as stolid inelegance. For instance, the report of the purchase by the *Illustrated London News* in June 1861 dismissed *The Baptism* as 'a curious example of the Umbrian School in the fifteenth century, a school in which the old traditions and dry manner of painting survived', exemplified by a 'great stiffness about the figures'.[16] The *Encyclopaedia Britannica*'s first entry on the artist, which appeared in 1885, was equally uncomprehending. While noting that *The Baptism* was 'an important example' of the painter's earlier style, this phase was described as 'energetic but unrefined', while Piero's entire oeuvre was dismissed as 'lack[ing] selectness of form and feature. The types of his visages are peculiar, and the costumes … singular.'[17] Again, the first English monograph on Piero, published in 1901, noted of *The Baptism* that 'Piero has here undoubtedly failed in the drawing of the extremities of his figures, the legs of Christ being thick and clumsy, and those of the Baptist loosely and incorrectly drawn – a

curious lapse in a picture where minor accessories such as the dove and the shell from which St. John pours the water over Christ's head are most carefully rendered.'[18] Even the art critic John Ruskin (1819–1900), who almost more than anyone else appreciated the maturity of the so-called Italian 'primitives', remarked only that Piero had a pretty name.[19]

'THE GREATEST ARTIST IN ITALY AFTER GIOTTO': THE ASCENDANCY OF *THE BAPTISM*

However challenging Piero's work appeared to a nineteenth-century audience, by the early twentieth century, scholars, critics and artists alike began to look on *The Baptism* with fresh eyes. In 1906, Edward Verrall Lucas, the author of *A Wanderer in London*, considered it to be the most remarkable painting in the National Gallery: 'surely never did dove so brood before: nor … has any man ever so divested himself of his shirt as the figure in the background'.[20] In 1923, the art critic Charles Lewis Hind described how Piero won 'the hearts of all who pause before his *Baptism*', while at the same time Sir Charles Holmes, the Director of the National Gallery, declared the painting to be among the 'greatest treasures in the collection'.[21] The following year, when, as part of the Gallery's centenary celebrations, *The Guardian* asked 19 leading artists 'which of the pictures in the National Gallery gave them the most delight', five – Muirhead Bone, Charles Ricketts, William Rothenstein, Charles Haslewood Shannon and Ethel Walker – chose *The Baptism*.[22]

How might this change of perception in Britain be accounted for? The ground had been laid by several important developments, including a growing admiration for the French painter Pierre-Cécile Puvis de Chavannes, whose *Beheading of Saint John the Baptist* (fig. 18), strongly indebted to Piero, had entered the National Gallery's collection in 1917.[23] In 1924, *Young Spartans Exercising* (about 1860) by Hilaire-Germain-Edgar Degas (1834–1917) and *Bathers at Asnières* (1884) by Georges Seurat (1859–1891) also entered the collection, providing two more striking examples of the influence of Piero – and, in particular, *The Baptism* – on two great modern French painters.[24]

Arguably, however, the most significant development was the interest shown in Piero by Roger Fry (1866–1934), an expert in Renaissance art and one of the most distinguished art critics of his age, who declared Piero to be 'the greatest artist in Italy after Giotto, incomparable beyond the men of the high Renaissance … an almost pure artist'.[25] Not only did

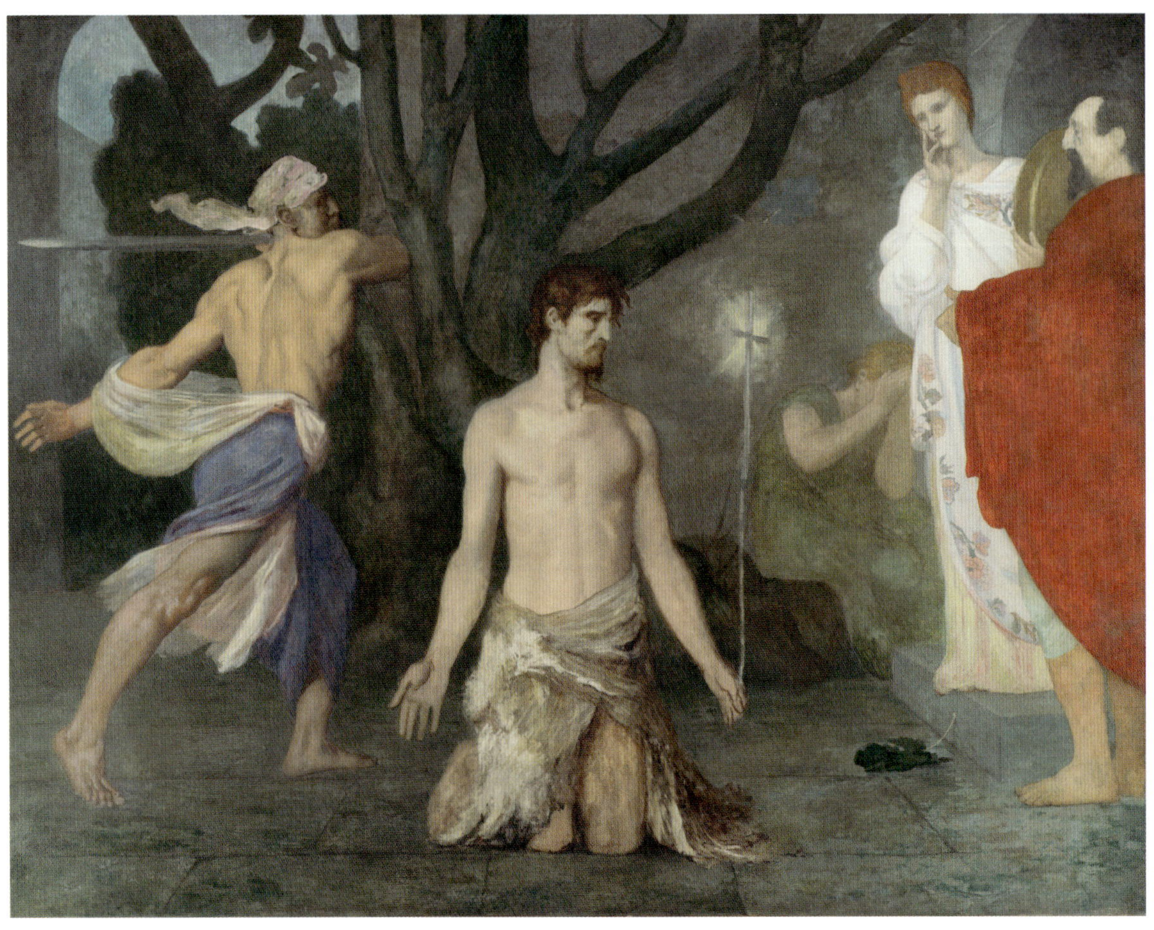

Fry dedicate an entire talk to *The Baptism* as part of his Cambridge University Extension lecture course but he also cited 'the modernism of Piero's attitude' as a major inspiration for the artists he promoted in his two celebrated exhibitions of Post-impressionism held at London's Burlington Galleries in 1910 and 1912.[26] According to Fry, the sensibility of Seurat's paintings echoed Piero's motionless groups, and the monumental quality of the art of Paul Cezanne (1839–1906) had similar roots, ideas that were repeated and expanded by other influential writers, including a later Director of the National Gallery, Philip Hendy (1900–1980), in his 1968 book on Piero.[27] When the French painter-critic André Lhote (1885–1962), who was included in Fry's Post-impressionist exhibition of 1912, hailed Piero in 1930 as the 'first Cubist',[28] the die was cast.

Piero's impact on British art was especially evident among the Bloomsbury group, of which Fry was in many ways the visionary leader. Piero's visual and cultural inheritance would also inform the work of Duncan Grant, another central figure of the group. Not only did Grant study at first hand Piero's stand-alone altarpieces in the National Gallery and his large-scale fresco cycles in Arezzo, but he even made copies of Piero's work, including of the angel musicians in the National Gallery's *Nativity* and of the portrait of the Duke of Urbino in the Uffizi (his copy of the latter hangs today at Charleston, East Sussex). Grant submitted both of these copies with two others to an exhibition organised in 1917 in Fry's Omega Workshops titled *Copies and Translations (by English painters – Fry, Grant, Bell – of paintings by the masters)*. In the preface to the accompanying catalogue, Fry stated: 'Each generation … has to remake its old Masters. If we did not go on continually revaluing and remaking them they would be not merely old but dead.'[29] In particular homage to Piero's *Baptism*, Grant went on to produce his own version of the biblical episode (fig. 19), playfully overwriting the silence, stasis and restraint of Piero's version with a sensual and fluid eroticism. By contrast, it was the gravity and stillness

2 Transcending the Centuries

of Piero's art that found expression in the paintings of
Vanessa Bell (1879–1961), another Bloomsbury group
member. In paintings such as *Studland Beach* (about
1912), the simplified bodies and geometric shapes are
borrowed directly from Piero's reductive aesthetic, while
her palette references the tawny gold and oxblood hues
of Piero's *Baptism*.[30]

At the Slade School of Fine Art (the art school of
University College London), where Fry taught art history
between 1909 and 1914, Piero's preeminence was
naturally promoted, and students were encouraged
to study his work face to face in the nearby National
Gallery, a vital supplement to the mostly monochrome
lantern slides and reproductions in books. Some Slade
students, perhaps in need of post-war fantasy and
escape, even went so far as to impersonate characters
from Piero's paintings. '[D]ressing like figures from the
world of Piero della Francesca', recalled the engraver
Clare Leighton, writing of her Slade years (1921–3),
'we did not need to search for other stimulation'.[31]
At the New English Art Club, the main exhibiting venue
for Slade pupils and alumni, the connections with Piero's
work ran so deep that in a 1920 review of an exhibition
there, *The Athenæum* quipped, 'When a Slade student
applies the term "good" to Piero della Francesca's
Baptism he means that it reminds him of things he has
seen at the New English Art Club.'[32]

Augustus John (1878–1961) provided a particular
connection to Piero for Slade students. A Slade
alumnus, his superstar personality continued to
radiate in Britain right up until his death. Referring to
his Umbrian predecessor as 'my darling Piero', from
around 1909 John started to saturate his works with
references to Piero.[33] According to a reviewer of John's
Grafton Galleries exhibition of 1909, the results were
akin to salvation: 'It would appear that the *mauvais
pas* of his career has been traversed and surmounted
… The directness, the monumental calm, the joyous
yet dignified colour scheme, even the treatment of
the landscape, as regards the foreground … all these
are Piero's.'[34] During the early 1910s, such a vision and
aesthetic particularly shaped a group of Slade School
students, self-styled as the 'Neo-primitives', who looked
initially to John's output and then increasingly to the
early Italian art that he promoted. A characteristic work
is a multi-figure portrait by Neo-primitive member John
Currie (1883–1914), painted in tempera, depicting an
Italianate landscape, and evocatively titled *Some Later
Primitives and Madame Tisceron* (1912, The Potteries
Museum & Art Gallery, Stoke-on-Trent) – all references

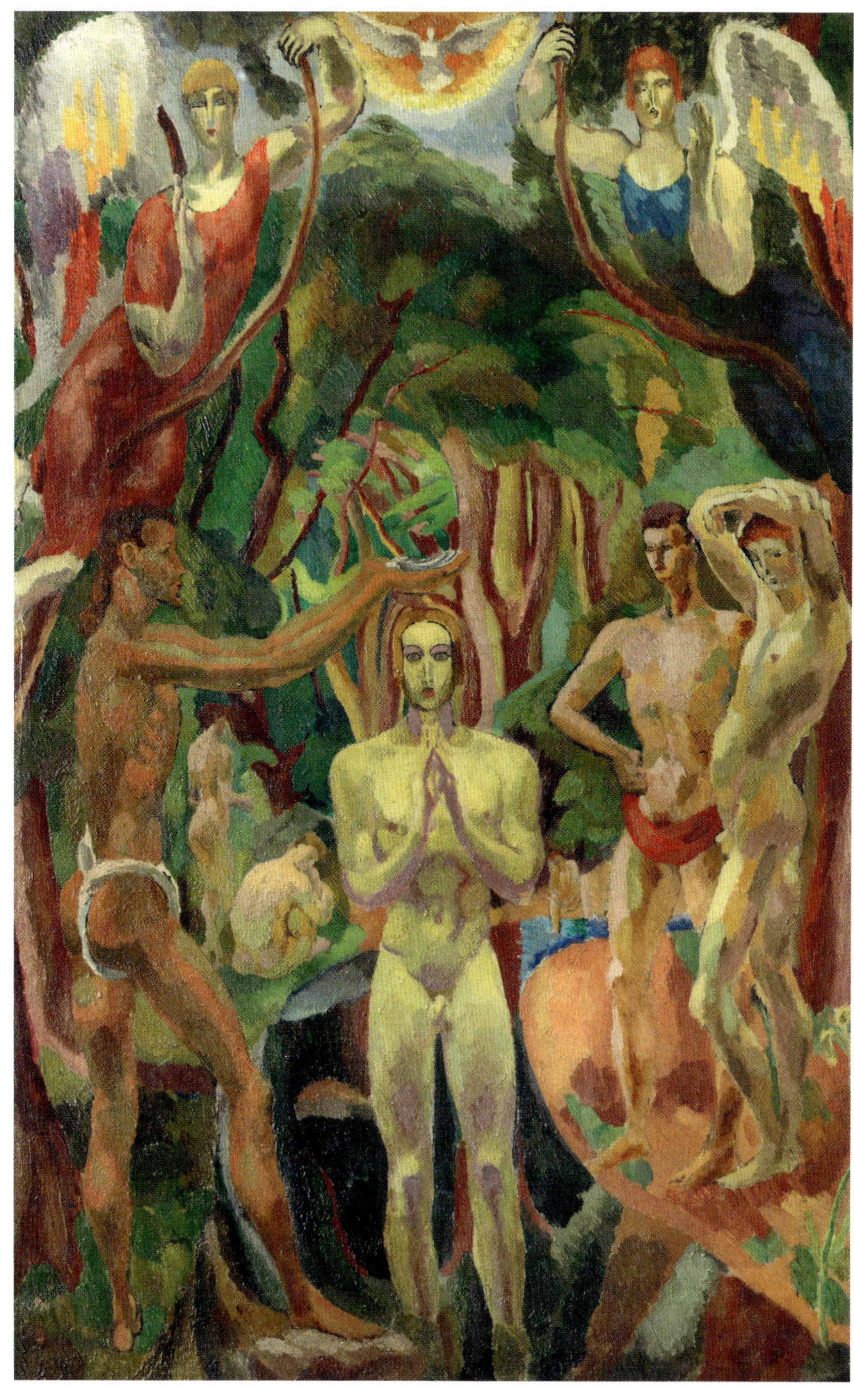

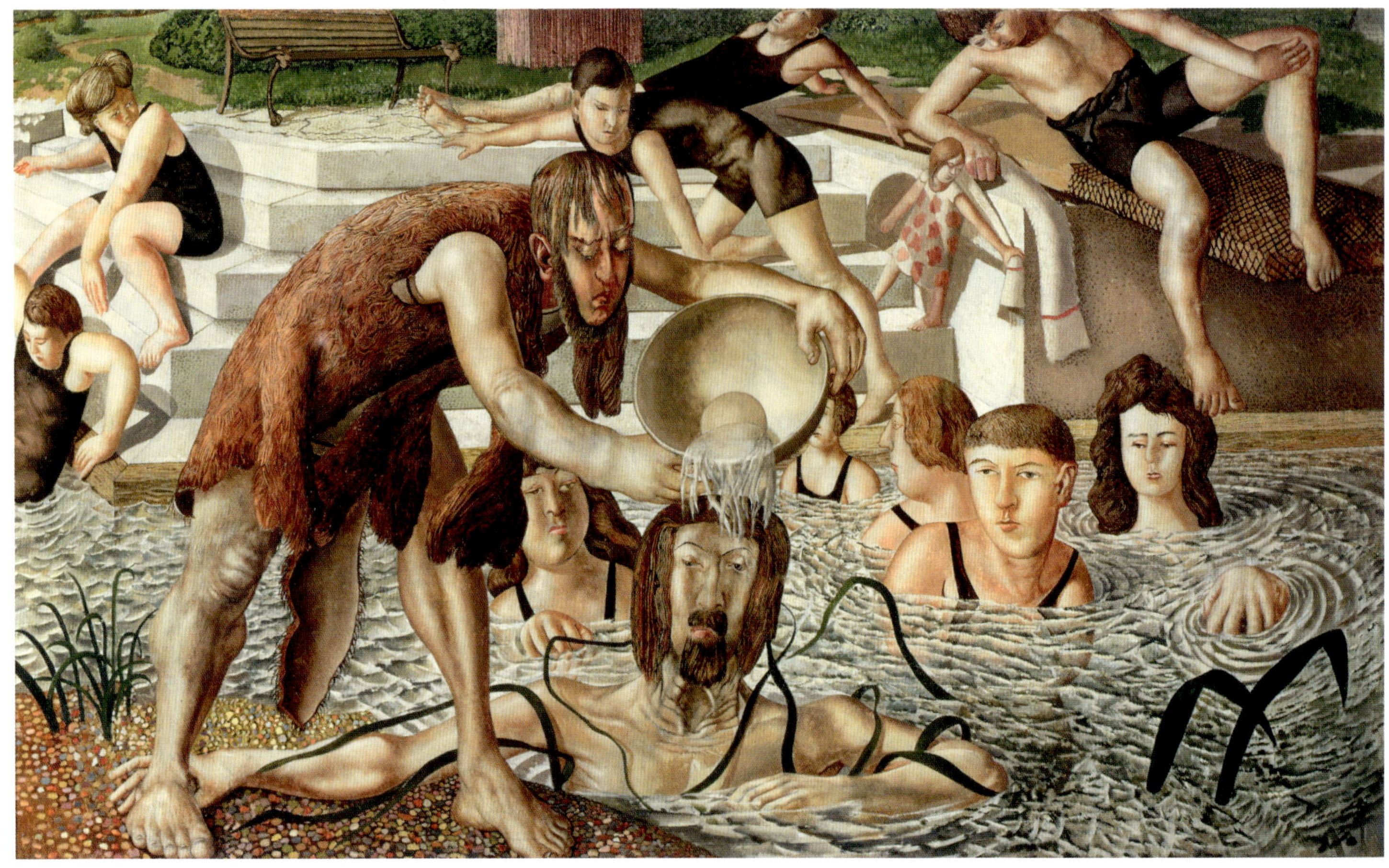

to what he perceived to be an artistic lineage stretching back to painters like Piero.

Of these 'later primitives', Stanley Spencer remained the most committed to early Italian art, with his use of statuesque, pared-down figures, anachronistic settings taken from his own locality and time, and a technique and palette that resembled tempera painting (even though he worked in oil). Famously, when asked about his allegiance to the then most celebrated avant-garde artist Pablo Picasso (1881–1973), Spencer replied that he had not 'got past Piero della Francesca yet'.[35] Spencer's passion was fostered through studying paintings *in situ* at the National Gallery – he always lamented the fact that the Gallery was not located in Cookham, his beloved birthplace in Berkshire. And given that he never travelled to Italy, Spencer was reliant otherwise on reproductions in books and postcards.[36] In one such postcard, addressed to his brother Gilbert (1892–1979) and written from Italy about 1913, Spencer's Slade School friend Gwen Raverat

(1885–1957) compared the colours of the Tuscan landscape to a Piero at Trafalgar Square so that the reader could visualise the enchantment of what she saw: 'Nearly every day we go off for great walks in the hills round Florence: it's incredibly beautiful: the colours are all so light & dry & fine: it's like the background of The Nativity by Piero della Francesca in the Nat. Gal.'[37] As late as 1952, Spencer painted his own version of *The Baptism* (fig. 20). Like Piero, Spencer set his scene in familiar territory – in his case, the bathing pool on the Thames at the Odney Club, Cookham, and, as a nod to Piero's *Baptism*, the features of Spencer's front-facing Christ, with his shoulder-length brown hair, moustache and beard, are almost a direct replica of Piero's.

'THE SENSE OF FORM': HOW *THE BAPTISM* INSPIRED THE VORTICISTS

Piero's appeal was not limited to the proponents of descriptive painting and Bloomsbury-inflected Post-impressionism; he also played a central role in the

2 Transcending the Centuries

short-lived modernist group of Vorticists, formed in 1914 and named by American poet Ezra Pound (1885–1972). Vorticism embraced the stark realities of modern urban and industrial life and was, according to Pound, 'an attempt to revive the sense of form – the form you had in Piero della Francesca's *De Prospettive Pingendi* [*sic*], his treatise on the proportions and composition'.[38] Readers of *Mr Eliot's Sunday Morning Service* (1918) by the poet T.S. Eliot (1888–1965), who became associated with Vorticism through his friendship with Pound, would most likely have recognised Piero's *Baptism* when they read about the artist of 'the Umbrian school' who painted 'upon a gesso ground / The nimbus of the Baptized God'.[39] *The Baptism* also informed *The Mud Bath* of 1914 (fig. 21) by fellow Vorticist David Bomberg, inspired by Schewzik's Vapour Baths in Whitechapel's Brick Lane, which the local Jewish community frequented for ritual purification. Based on the same evenly spaced, horizontal and vertical linear grid, both compositions are divided in half by a tree. In addition, the figures enlivening the right half of Bomberg's picture are reminiscent of the lithe, semi-naked man in Piero's painting. Bomberg claimed he

had, in similar vein to Piero, simplified his artistic vision and 'stripped it of all irrelevant matter'.[40]

'PEARLY AND COOL': PIERO AND THE REVIVAL OF TEMPERA AND MURAL PAINTING

Another factor that played into Piero's ascendancy in Britain was the revival of interest in the ancient egg-based medium of tempera. The Society of Painters in Tempera was founded by, among others, Christiana Herringham (1852–1929) in 1901 to improve 'the art of Tempera painting by the interchange of the knowledge and experience of the members'.[41] Herringham not only produced faithful copies of early Italian art that had used the technique, including Piero's *Baptism* (see fig. 38), but also brought out important publications concerning the history of the technique. In this connection, she produced a new scholarly English translation in 1899 of *Il libro dell'arte, o trattato della pittura*, Cennino Cennini's celebrated fifteenth-century treatise on artistic techniques, as well as an essay, based on a lecture she had given on 21 October 1902, titled 'Methods of Tempera as Exemplified in a Few Pictures in the National Gallery'. Here, she compared the technique that Piero

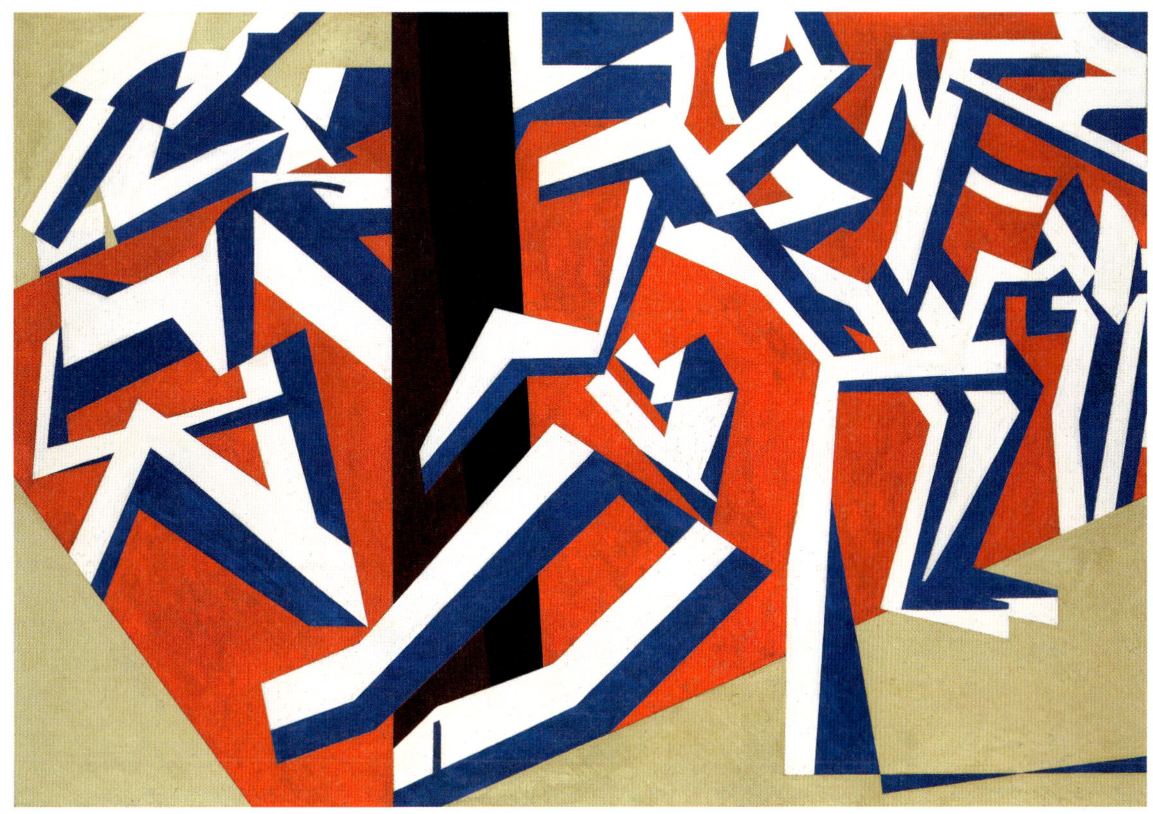

had used in *The Baptism* and *The Nativity*, suggesting that '[t]he first is undoubtedly pure tempera', while the second had a 'viscous, tenacious quality' suggestive of 'a varnish or mixed mediums'.[42] Fry, another founding member of the Society of Painters in Tempera, likewise thought Piero's handling of the medium in *The Baptism* was superlative, enabling the 'pearly and cool' quality of the picture as well as the 'intense luminosity in [the] rendering of flesh'.[43]

One of the leading exponents of tempera in the first two decades of the twentieth century was Frederick Cayley Robinson (1862–1927), for whom Piero's *Baptism* was also a key inspiration. In his First World War memorial for Heanor Grammar School, Derbyshire, painted in about 1919, for example, figures circle round a tall, pale-barked tree in a way that recalls the compositional arrangement of Piero's painting.

The revival in mural painting in the first half of the twentieth century was a direct outcome of the tempera comeback. The creation in 1913 of a scholarship at the British School at Rome in decorative (or mural) painting created a generation of artists, including Colin Gill, Winifred Knights, Alan Sorrell, Reginald Brill and Thomas Monnington, who were trained in the craft of fresco and mural art, and for whom Piero's monumental vision was a key reference. Having already encountered Piero in the National Gallery and during lectures at their respective art schools, the Rome scholars set off on personal

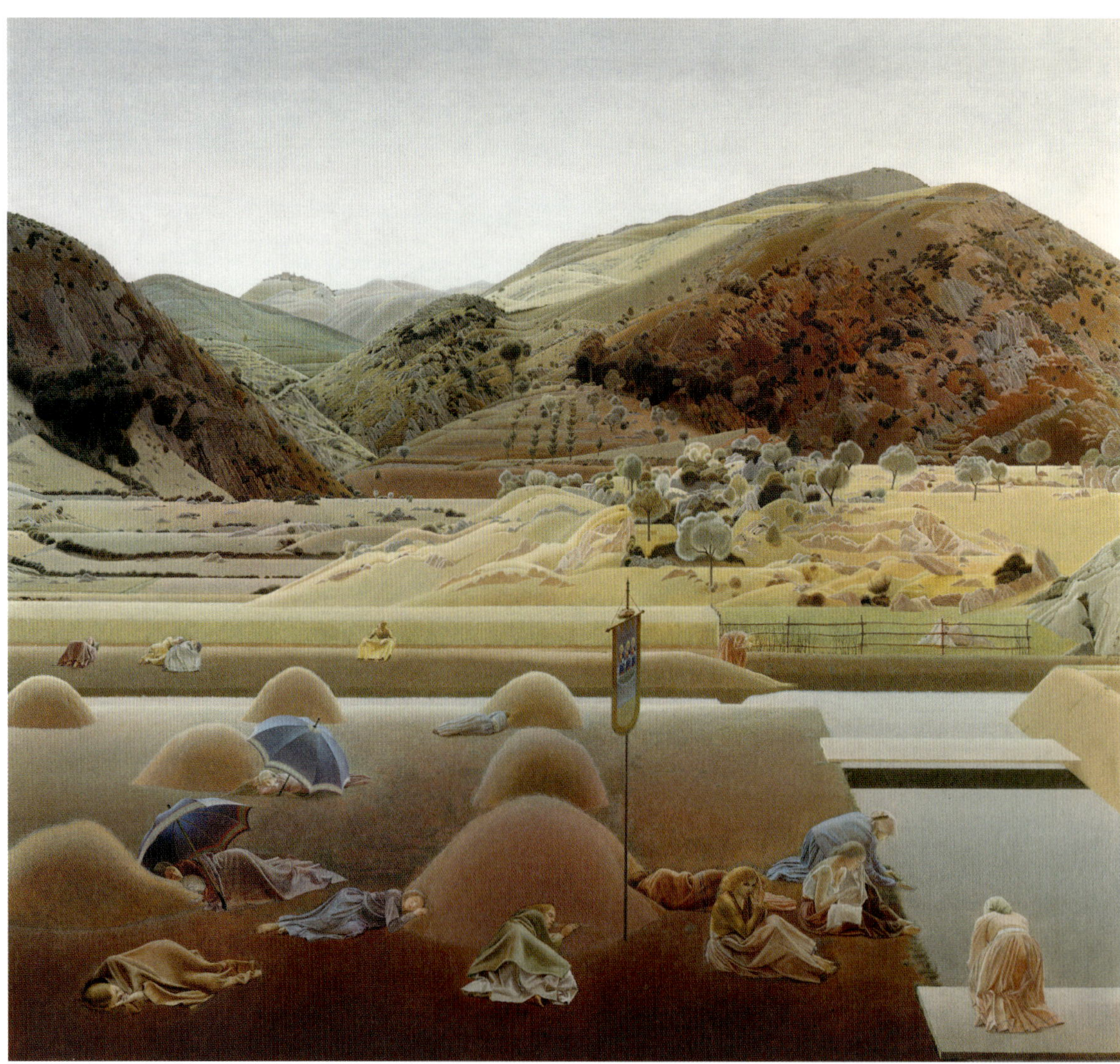

Fig. 22
Winifred Knights (1899–1947)
The Santissima Trinita, 1924–30
Oil on canvas, 102 × 112 cm
Private collection

pilgrimages to discover Piero's larger-scale oeuvre *in situ*, especially in Arezzo, San Sepolcro and Urbino.

When Knights, who became the first woman to win the scholarship in 1920, exhibited *The Santissima Trinita* (fig. 22) – her Rome School magnum opus – at the Imperial Galleries, London, in 1927, *The Manchester Guardian* noted that 'many are comparing it in its sweetness and ecstasy to Piero della Francesca'.[44] Not only does the act of washing depicted in the image suggest the Christian sacrament of baptism, but the highly naturalistic Italianate landscape also has much in common with the background in Piero's *Baptism*. In her notebook, alongside a description of 'the exquisite, indescribable delicacy' of the river with 'shadows gold-grey-green (milky)', Knights wrote 'Francesca!!!', an indication that she additionally sought to reproduce the reflective qualities and mood of stillness that characterised Piero's rendering of water.

Monnington, the 1922 Rome scholar, went so far as to claim that it was seeing Piero's work in the National Gallery when he was a teenager that compelled him to become an artist. The principal picture that Monnington produced in Italy was *Allegory* (about 1924, Tate Britain), an intensely personal project closely bound up with his marriage in 1924 to Knights, his love for Italy and his evident admiration for Piero.

'A STEADY LIGHT': PIERO IN THE SHADOW OF THE SECOND WORLD WAR

As the rumblings of war began to stir (again) over Britain in the late 1930s, Piero's vision – his qualities of calm dispassion and stability – seemed more than ever to provide a timeless and all-embracing sanctuary. The British painter John Armstrong conveyed his sense of dread in his oil painting *Pro Patria* (fig. 23), in which fragments of classical statuary, posters of shouting faces, bomb-damaged buildings and twisted trees are metaphors for the destruction of European civilisation and human values. The sole figure, disrobing, provides the only sign of life, and perhaps hope; it is a direct quotation from Piero's painting (see fig. 62).

When the National Gallery reopened after the end of hostilities in 1945, Vanessa Bell marvelled at seeing Piero's work again: 'how lovely [it] looked, simply dazzling in its airiness and light'.[45] And writing a few years later, in 1951, art historian Anthony Bertram (1897–1978) described Piero as a Christian, mathematician and artist: 'A steady light above our dark turbulence, a certain star, knowing his own way with such assurance.'[46]

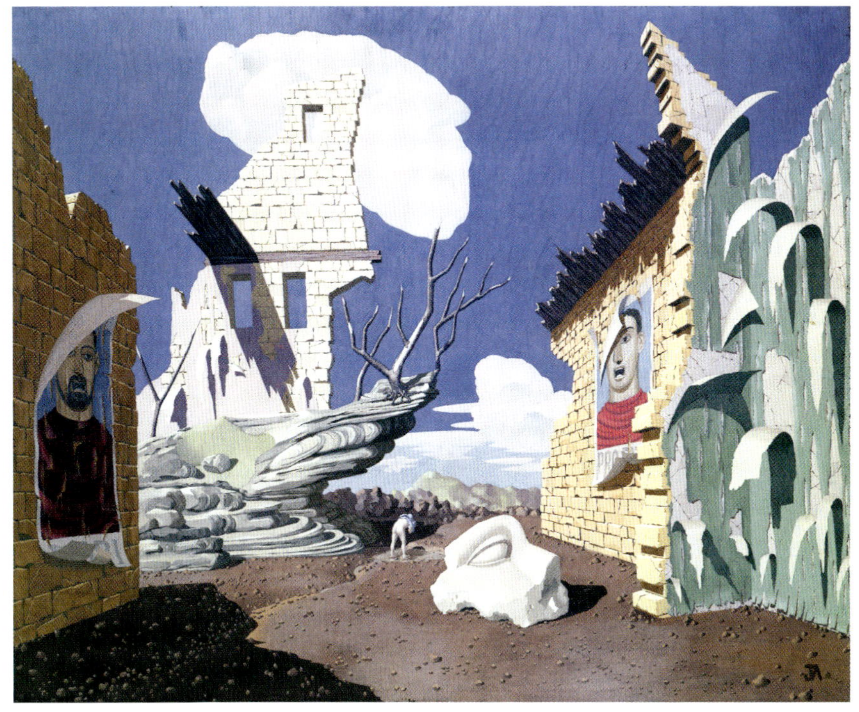

'THE FRINGE OF MODERNITY': PIERO AND THE MODERNISTS

During the twentieth century, the development of painting was shaped by a continuous search for a new formal language – what is loosely grouped under the modernism umbrella and charted in *The Shock of the New* (1980), the eight-part documentary television series by the art critic Robert Hughes (1938–2012). One of the greatest products, or by-products, of this evolution was the 'invention' of abstract art. For many, Abstraction represented a rupture or an end to the narrative that started with artists like Piero and the advent of linear perspective. In Britain, Abstraction came late, some two decades after its waves had broken on the Continent in the work of artists such as Wassily Kandinsky, Kazimir Malevich and Piet Mondrian and their less-famed female predecessor Hilma af Klint. Ben Nicholson, Barbara Hepworth, Paule Vézelay and John Piper were among its first practitioners in Britain. After the Second World War, Abstraction's influence became even more far-reaching with the advent of a second wave, Abstract Expressionism, led by American artists Janet Sobel, Lee Krasner and Jackson Pollock, whose work influenced a new generation of artists and led to the creation of an increasingly divergent discourse as to whether art, to remain relevant, should be figurative or

Fig. 23
John Armstrong (1893–1973)
Pro Patria, 1938
Tempera on board,
75.8 × 93.6 cm
Imperial War Museum, London

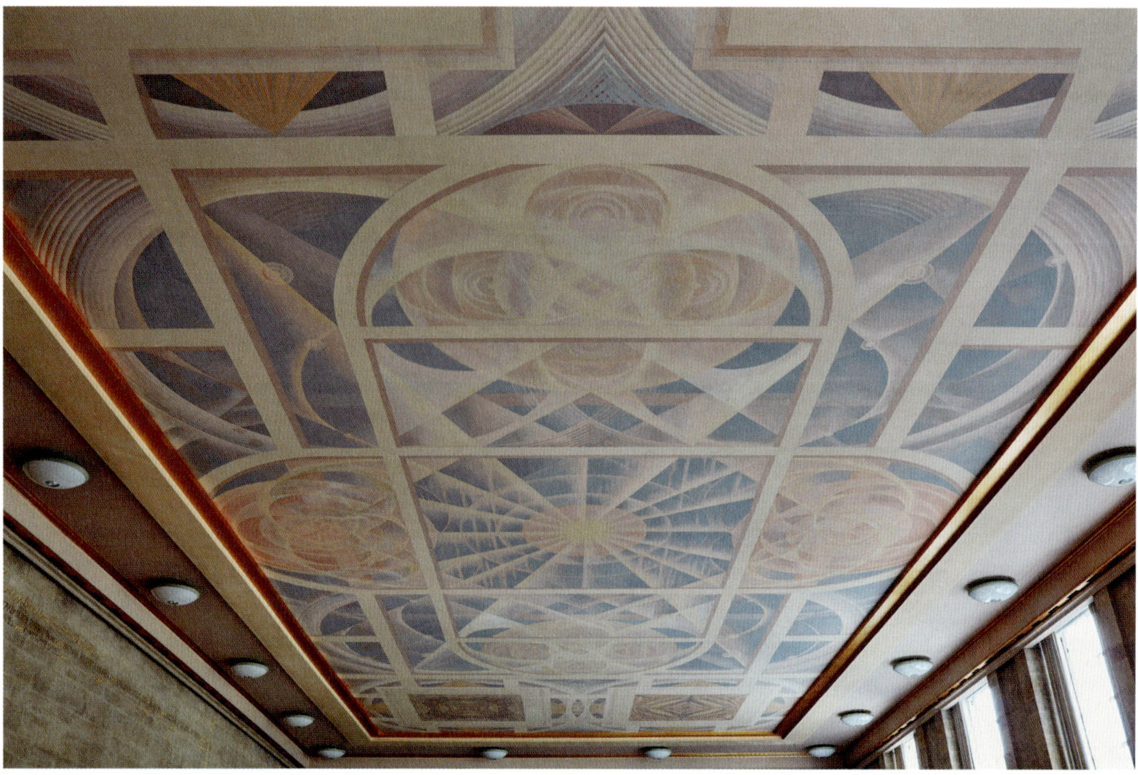

abstract. In this context, surprisingly, many artists hailed Piero as perfectly in tune with modern divergence and, rather than being seen as a fading star in the increasingly distant constellation called the Renaissance, his extraordinary talent continued to shimmer and to attract a new audience.

Monnington, when elected President of the Royal Academy in 1966, advocated his self-declared hero Piero, in particular his sense of perspective governed by geometry, as pertinent to both camps: artists who favoured figuration and artists who favoured abstraction. As an influential teacher, first at the Camberwell School of Arts and Crafts and then at the Slade, he encouraged a new generation of students to share his vision. David Harry Hume, a student of Monnington's from 1949 to 1951, recalled how he was shown 'that serious painting need be neither abstract nor academic. It meant looking at Piero rather than Michelangelo.'[47] Monnington took the helm of the Royal Academy at a low point in its history, when modernists and traditionalists were at loggerheads. His own post-war journey as an artist had led him from Renaissance-inspired figuration to pure abstraction, and he used his odyssey to soothe

a bewildered public. For his gargantuan ceiling at the new Council House in Bristol, produced with help from Scott Medd (1911–1984), Monnington resolved the problem as Piero might have done, with a design whose geometric forms are irradiated by subtle effects of light (fig. 24). With deliberation, Monnington chose to paint his ultra-modern-looking work in the old-fashioned fresco technique, insisting on the daily delivery of hundreds of fresh eggs.[48] His friend, the painter Gordon House (1932–2004), concluded, 'For Monnington the Golden Mean of Piero reconsidered with the experience of the twentieth century had brought him to the fringe of modernity.'[49]

'LOATHING PIERO' OR 'A REVELATION': PIERO AND SOME MORE RECENT ARTISTS

To imply that Piero inspired all aspects of modern British and contemporary art would be misleading. He certainly had his detractors. Lucian Freud (1922–2011), in a deliberately provocative statement that in fact demonstrated just how ubiquitous the adoration of Piero still was, famously declared, 'I always prided myself on loathing Piero.'[50] But the number of artists who openly

   2 Transcending the Centuries

acknowledge their debt to Piero, and to *The Baptism*, is striking, not only for the passion of their affirmations but also for the diversity of their working methods.

David Hockney has always been inspired by Piero's work (see Chapter 1). He has commented on the fact that other painters have likewise engaged with Piero's work, pointing to Seurat's *Bathers at Asnières* as a prime example: 'What I don't understand is this: why is it that Seurat could study a painter of 300 years before – Piero della Francesca – and produce in 1880 a version of Piero's ideas, updated or progressed or whatever word you want to say, and if that was valid in 1880 why is it not valid in 1977? Nothing has happened between then and now to stop somebody carefully analyzing and studying the pictures of Piero della Francesca and making something from the ideas in them.'[51] During one interview, Hockney was able to gesture towards a print of *The Baptism* on the wall behind him, which at that time was placed between a photograph of Hockney (revealing his backside) and another of Francis Bacon.

The Baptism is clearly visible in other photographs that record Hockney in his studio at various times (see p. 10, fig. 7 and p. 46), and his mother also kept a print of it in her bedroom for decades, so clearly the work remained a family favourite.[52]

That Hockney felt a real sense of closeness to *The Baptism* and Piero's work more generally – indeed, even identified himself with it – is revealed by the fact that in two earlier portraits of his parents, Kenneth and Laura Hockney, both titled *My Parents and Myself* (fig. 25), it is not *The Baptism* depicted as the reflection in the mirror but rather a self-portrait of Hockney himself. The substitution in the finished version of *My Parents* of Hockney's self-portrait for a reproduction of *The Baptism* has been discussed by one recent critic in terms of a 'spectral image of the artist based on the artist's professed fondness for Piero's painting', and as 'a substitutive assertion of the self'.[53] We might go further and propose that, given the reflection of the drapery hanging from a rail in the final version (fig. 26),

Fig. 25
'My Parents Posing for *My Parents and Myself*', 1976
Photograph by David Hockney
The David Hockney Foundation

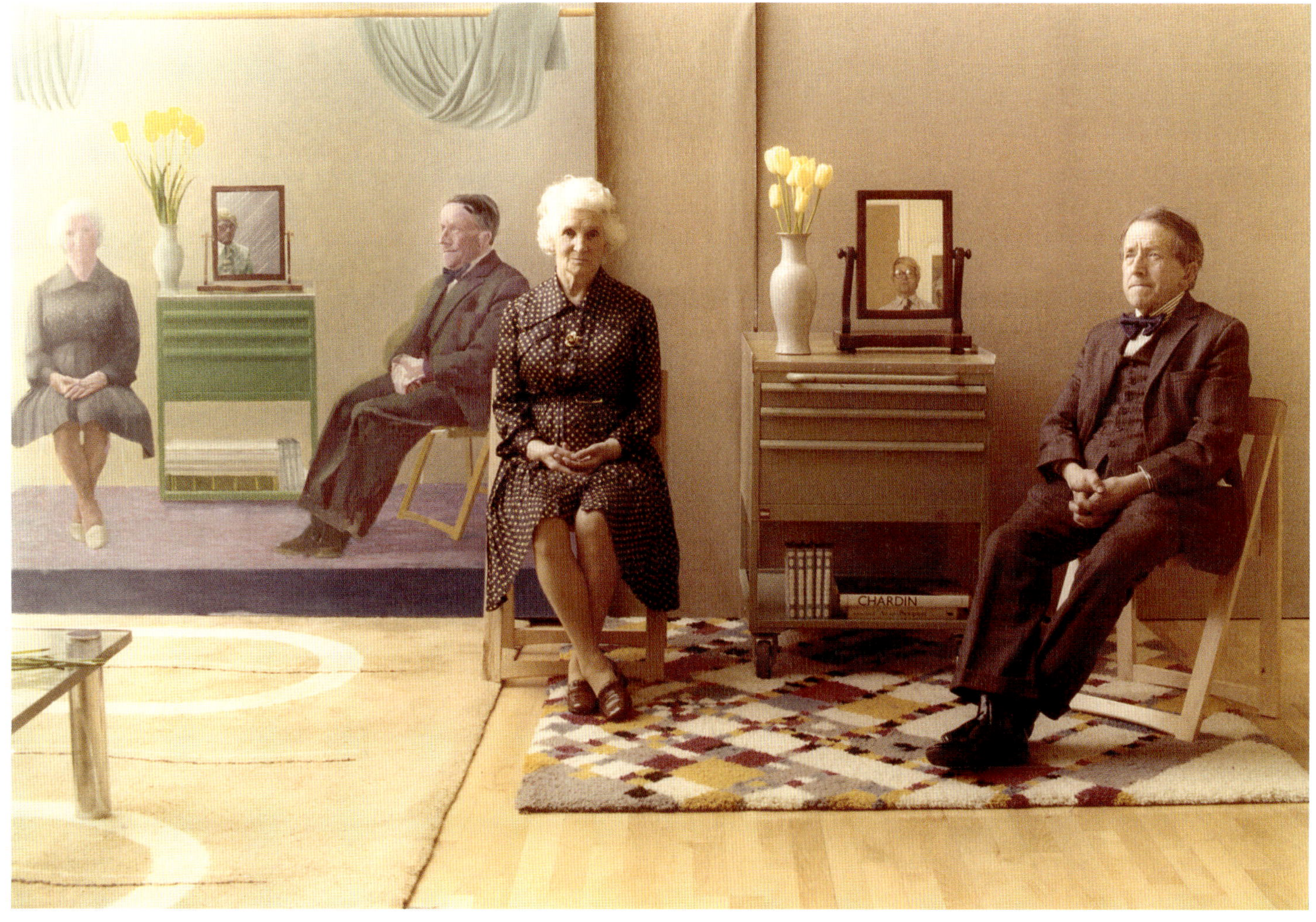

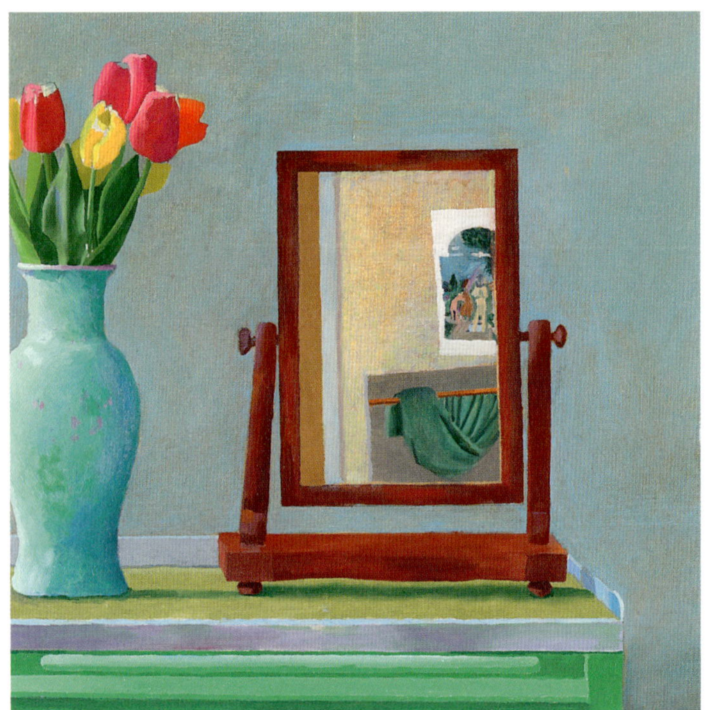

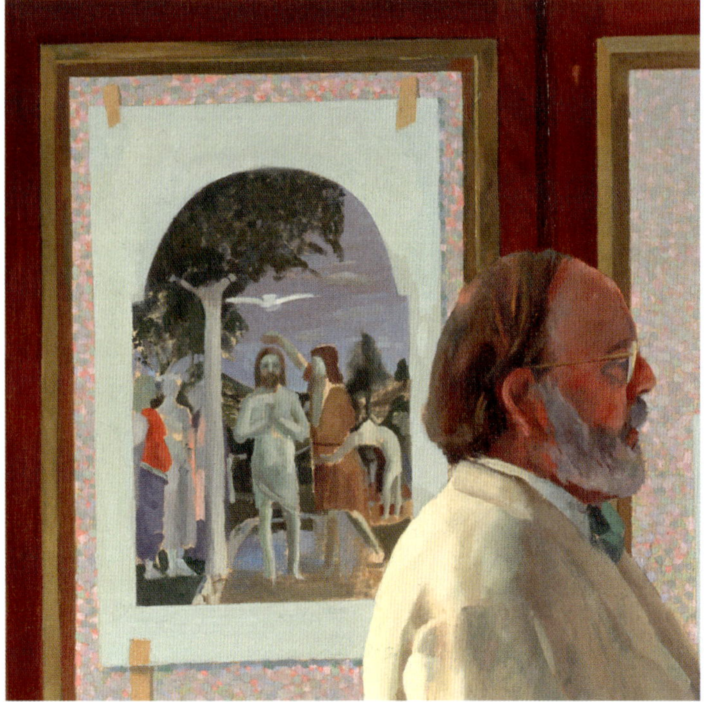

Piero's painting alludes to a 'spiritual rebirth' that in some way Hockney associates with a queerer experience of home and family, having already explored the themes of water, domesticity and gay identity in his pool pictures from the 1960s and early 1970s. In the same way that in *Looking at Pictures on a Screen* Hockney identified himself with the sitter Henry Geldzahler (fig. 27), not least when he substituted his own image for Geldzahler's in the poster he created for *The Artist's Eye* exhibition of 1981 (see fig. 55), through tracing the evolution of *My Parents* it is also possible to point to Hockney's self-identification with the main protagonist of *The Baptism* – the figure of Christ – and with the creator of the work itself – his hero, Piero.[54]

Hockney has found Piero's work constantly intriguing for its dual figurative and abstracted character, from which he has come to believe that representation and abstraction are 'not … two separate things'.[55] Motifs borrowed from or inspired by *The Baptism* informed certain of Hockney's paintings produced in the decades around the time of *My Parents* and *Looking at Pictures on a Screen* (both 1977), especially the combination of two male figures in various stages of undress and associated with water, such as *Domestic Scene, Los Angeles* (1963) (fig. 28), and pairings of figures where one is shown facing the viewer (see fig. 5).

Furthermore, Hockney has been deeply interested by the way that Piero structured his paintings to concentrate on spatial clarity. 'That is why I love Piero', Hockney once explained. 'The magic seems to me to be in the space, not in the objects.'[56] Time is a second factor that Hockney, emboldened by Piero, has attempted to embed in his pictures. In relation to Piero's *Baptism*, Hockney praised the way that stillness and movement are suggested in different areas. While appreciating that naturally 'nothing is moving in the still picture', he drew attention to the sense of water being actively poured, in contrast to the apparently motionless hovering bird (see fig. 63).[57] Hockney has continually promoted the art of painting over photography largely for the reason that a good amount of time has gone into producing a picture, rather than the split second it takes to click a camera lens, a fact that makes the lived experience of the hand-crafted scene portrayed more relatable – and welcoming – to the viewer.

Turning to consider Hockney's contemporaries, another artist, who likewise had a primary interest in the human body, is Neo-romantic painter Keith Vaughan. However, in his case, his studies of male nudes became increasingly abstract, a perennial question being how to reconcile the polarities of realism and abstraction when depicting figures in a landscape. Many of his double

2 Transcending the Centuries

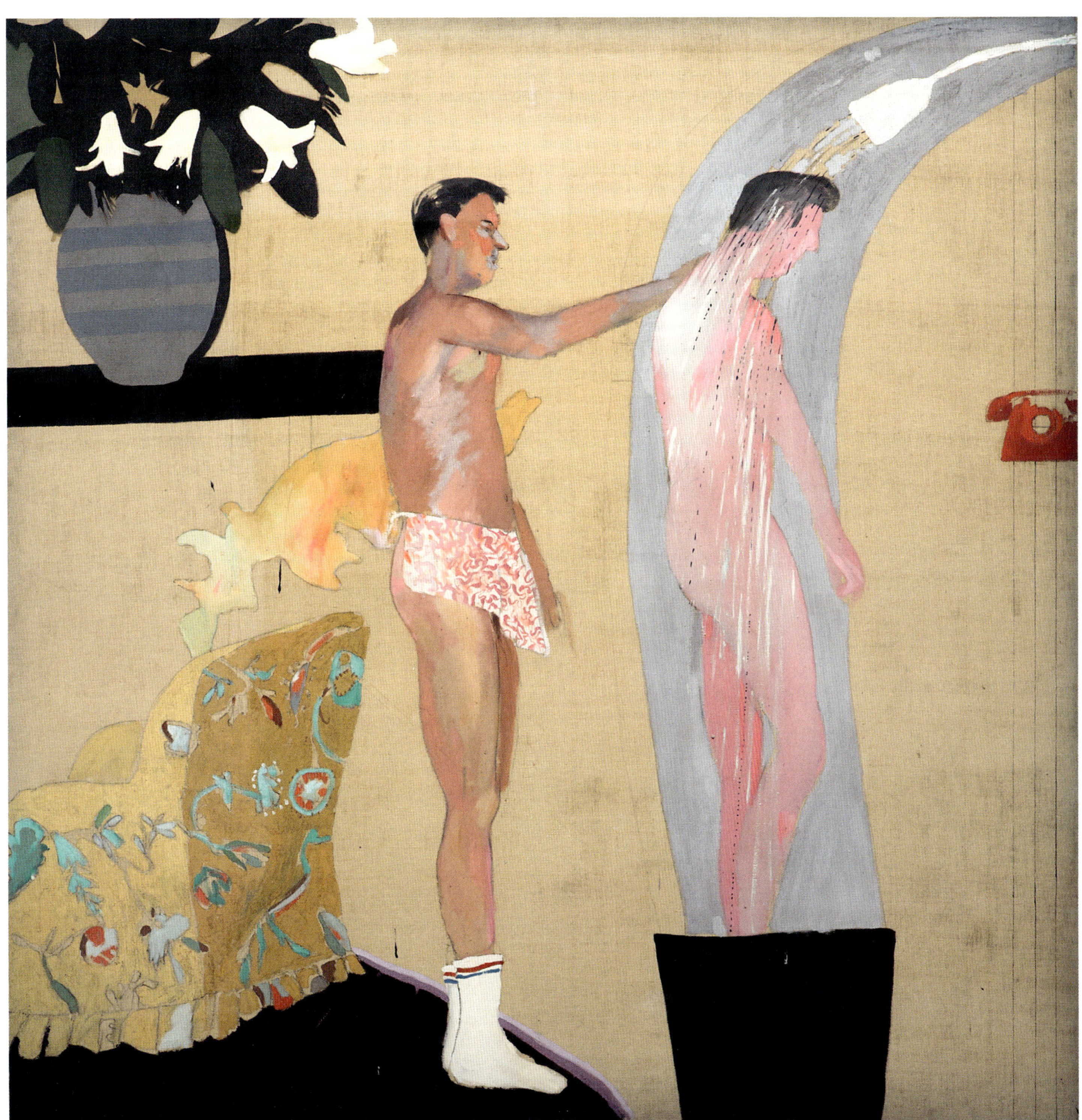

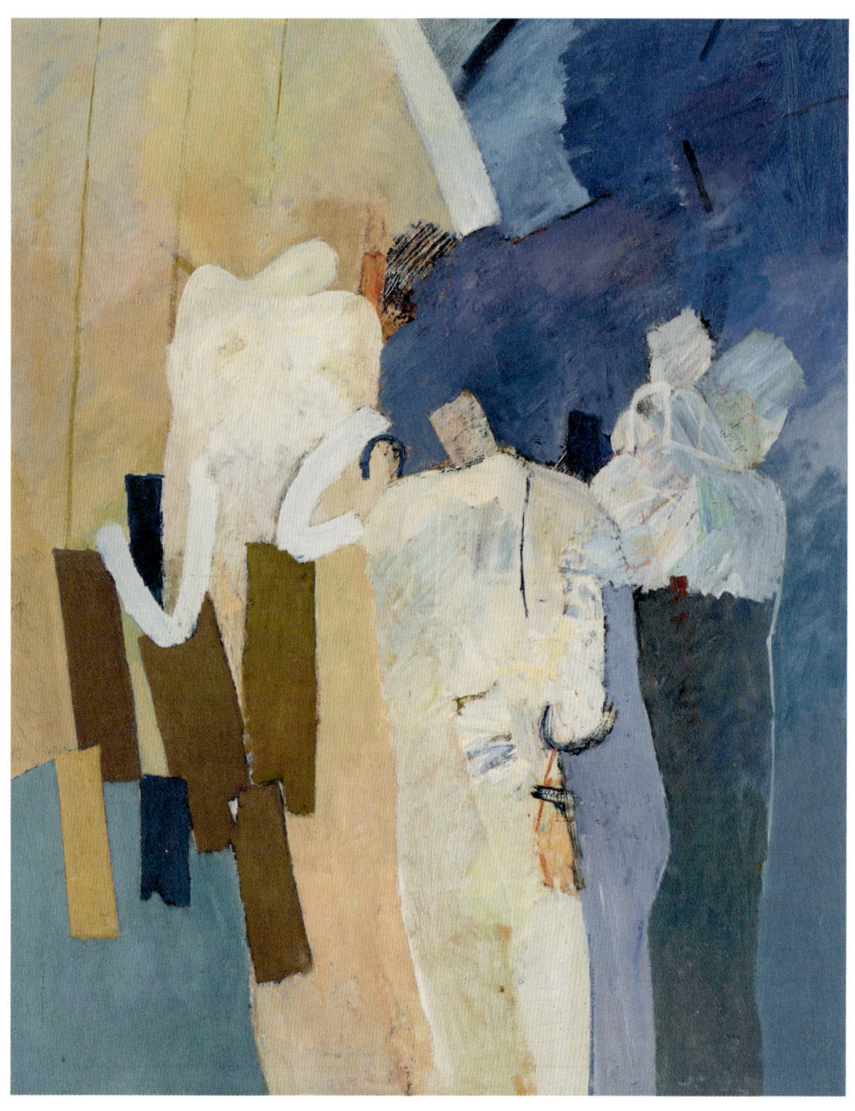

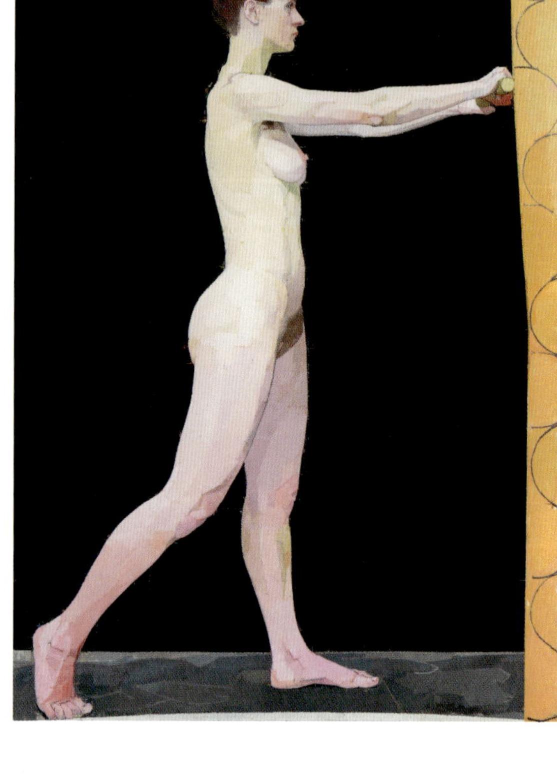

and multi-figure nude portraits, such as *Bathers by Green Bank* (1954), *Neapolitan Bathers* (1951) and especially *Baptism* (fig. 29), evoke Piero not only in their subject matter but also in the poses of individual figures and the palette that employs the same tawny brown, rose, olive green and royal blue. In Piero's *Baptism*, Vaughan was particularly taken, as so many others have been, by the figure removing his shirt, by its 'frozen moment, the revelation of the male form, the awkwardness of the pose' (see fig. 62).[58]

Another painter best known for his nude figures is Euan Uglow, a great admirer of Monnington and Piero. Uglow studied Piero's work in London as well as Italy, where he spent six months on a Prix de Rome

Fig. 29
Keith Vaughan (1912–1977)
Baptism, 1963
Oil on canvas, 127 × 101.5 cm
Private collection

Fig. 30
Euan Uglow (1932–2000)
Zagi, 1981–2
Oil on canvas, 150 × 107 cm
Tate, London

scholarship in 1953. Piero's impact is evident in paintings such as *Zagi* (fig. 30), where the pose is inspired by the figure of Saint John the Baptist in *The Baptism*. Indeed, the mathematical structure of Uglow's compositions (with traces of measurements typically left in evidence) and the muted tonalities, as well as bodies made up of shapes, are qualities that resonate with Piero's work.

The sculptor Antony Gormley remembers coming to look at Piero's *Baptism* in the National Gallery 'as a child with my father. I suppose it was my own baptism into what the space of art could be. A place that could only be imagined, and yet had this extraordinary effect on real life. I still hope to make those places and spaces myself.'[59] Of Piero's painting, Gormley has commented: 'Everything in the painting seems to be holding its breath. We, the angel, and the rest of the world are waiting for the drop of water, balancing on the point of the cockle shell held in John the Baptist's hand, to fall. So much is at stake here. The world is about to change … For me, this painting is a touchstone. It evokes the possibility that art is beyond time and the contingencies of daily life.'[60] Arguably, the work most akin to Piero's *Baptism* within Gormley's oeuvre is *Sound II* (fig. 32),

2 Transcending the Centuries

a man of fibreglass and lead that was based on a mould of his own body. Its site-specific setting of the crypt of Winchester Cathedral, where it is designed to stand in the flood waters that regularly invade the crypt, recalls Piero's Christ receiving the waters of baptism and thereby the promise of eternal life.

Moving away from Piero's figurative influences, it is notable that contemporary artists as diverse as Tess Jaray, Rachel Whiteread and Bridget Riley all reference Piero when explaining key aspects of their own creative processes.

The way that architectural space, mass, surface and light interact and act on human interlocutors has long been a preoccupation of Tess Jaray. Although abstract, minimalist and devoid of human forms, her drawings, paintings and prints engage with what she describes as the 'geometry of human relationships'.[61] When Jaray discovered Piero's paintings on a trip to Italy after graduating from the Slade School, the experience was akin to an epiphany, the effects of which have resonated in her work ever since. Her show, *From Piero and other paintings — shadows of the masters* (2023), for instance, displayed a series of new paintings, including *Flagellation I* (fig. 31), which are essentially conversations with Piero's work, and in which she challenged herself to distil the essence of Piero's art to see 'what's left when everything else is taken away'.[62]

Rachel Whiteread (born 1963) – best known for her monochrome casts of domestic spaces and everyday objects – is another contemporary artist who consciously acknowledges her debt to Piero. When Whiteread was creating *Ghost* (1990, National Gallery of Art, Washington), 'made of four tiers of stacked plaster panels bearing the impressions of the room's interior surfaces, facing outward toward the viewer', she had a postcard of Piero's *Baptism* pinned to the wall of her studio.[63] As a daily presence and source of inspiration, Whitehead observed: 'I was following some kind of solidity that existed in Piero's picture. It was an intuitive reaction, not an intellectual one.'[64] She also noted in the same article that the painting 'may tell a very particular story, but Piero's translation of it into a series of lines, colors, and shapes has transfixed me for more than thirty-five years'. While considering Piero's painting to be 'a masterpiece in early perspective', she confessed that she was also

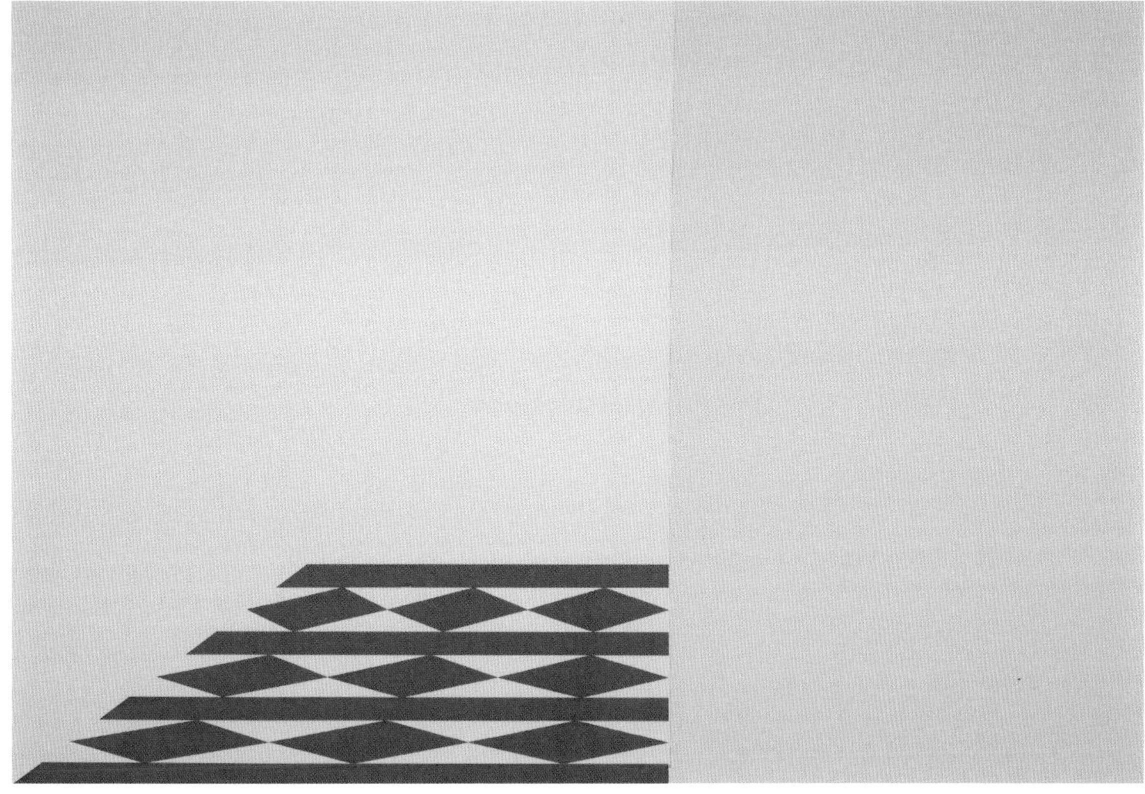

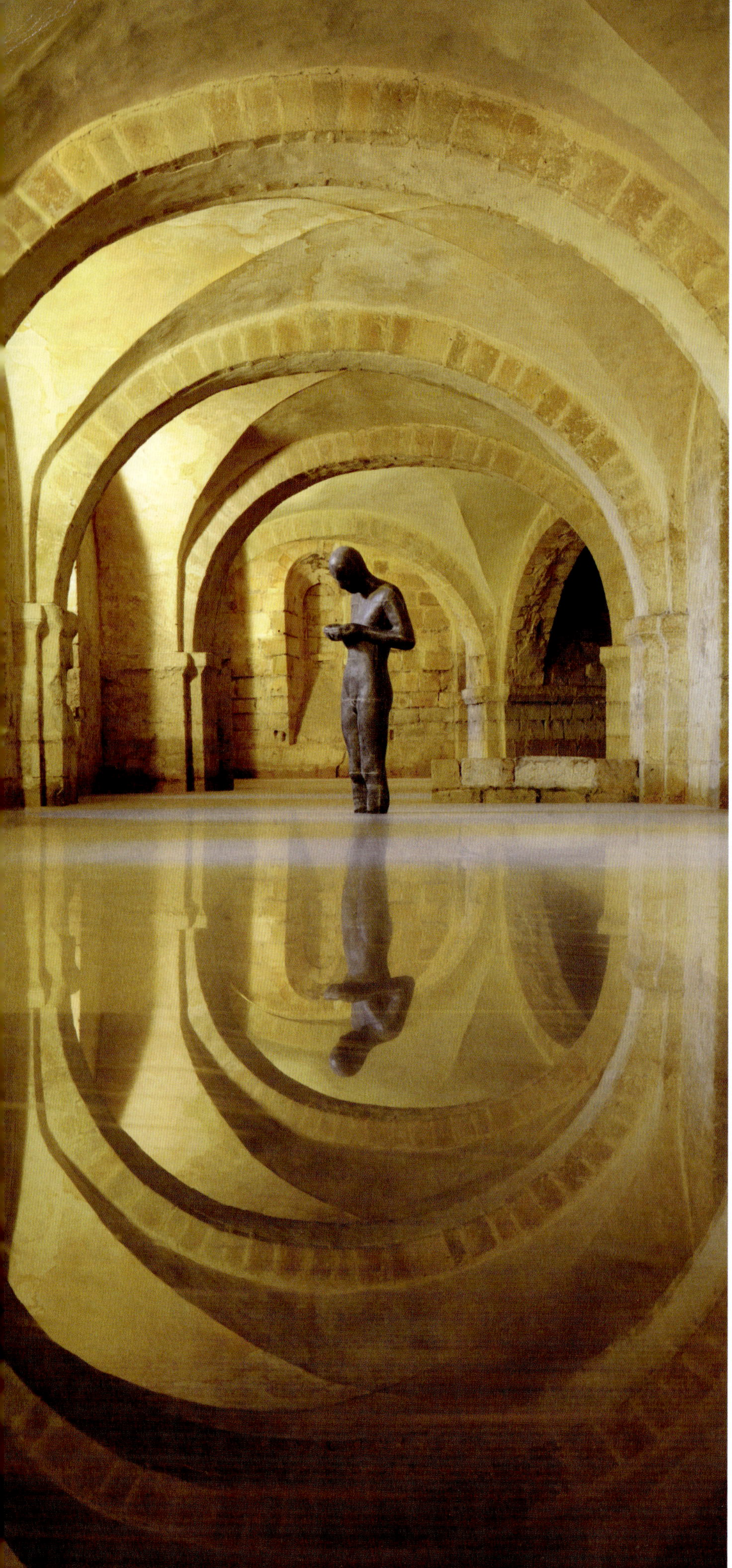

drawn to it on account of its peacefulness and piety, and because she found certain elements of it erotic, not least Christ's transparent loincloth and the strange figure undressing in the background (see figs 62 and 63).

Another painter who has long had a Piero image pinned to her studio wall for inspiration is Bridget Riley; in her case, it is his *Madonna del Parto* (1460). In her essay 'Painting Now' (1997), Riley explained the importance for her own work of Piero's paintings for their 'carefully set problems dealing with form, structure, the rhythm of planes'.[65] Her stylish, geometric abstract paintings and murals, often created using tempera, address the same concerns and the dynamism of perception through the setting up of interactions between vertical and horizontal stripes, squares, circles, ovals, triangles, rhomboids and curves. Riley's evolution in the late 1960s from a palette of black, white and greys to more intense colours partly sprang from, in her words, Piero's use of 'light and dark, and colour harmonies of breathtaking delicacy'.[66] Both *Messengers*, a vast wall painting she was commissioned to produce for the National Gallery's Annenberg Court (see Chapter 3 and Appendix 4), and *Verve*, a ceiling in the entrance hall of the British School at Rome, unveiled on 4 May 2023, combine primary colours that bring to mind the pure colour fields in Piero's *Baptism*. In *Verve*, the way in which the ceiling is mirrored in any reflective surface further recalls Piero's own exquisite reflections in the stillness of the water (fig. 33).[67]

It is an open question how future generations of artists may choose to narrate stories about Piero's art. What is predictable, however, is that just as literary interpretations of Piero continue to change, any equivalent visual responses to *The Baptism* will also remain exciting and in flux.

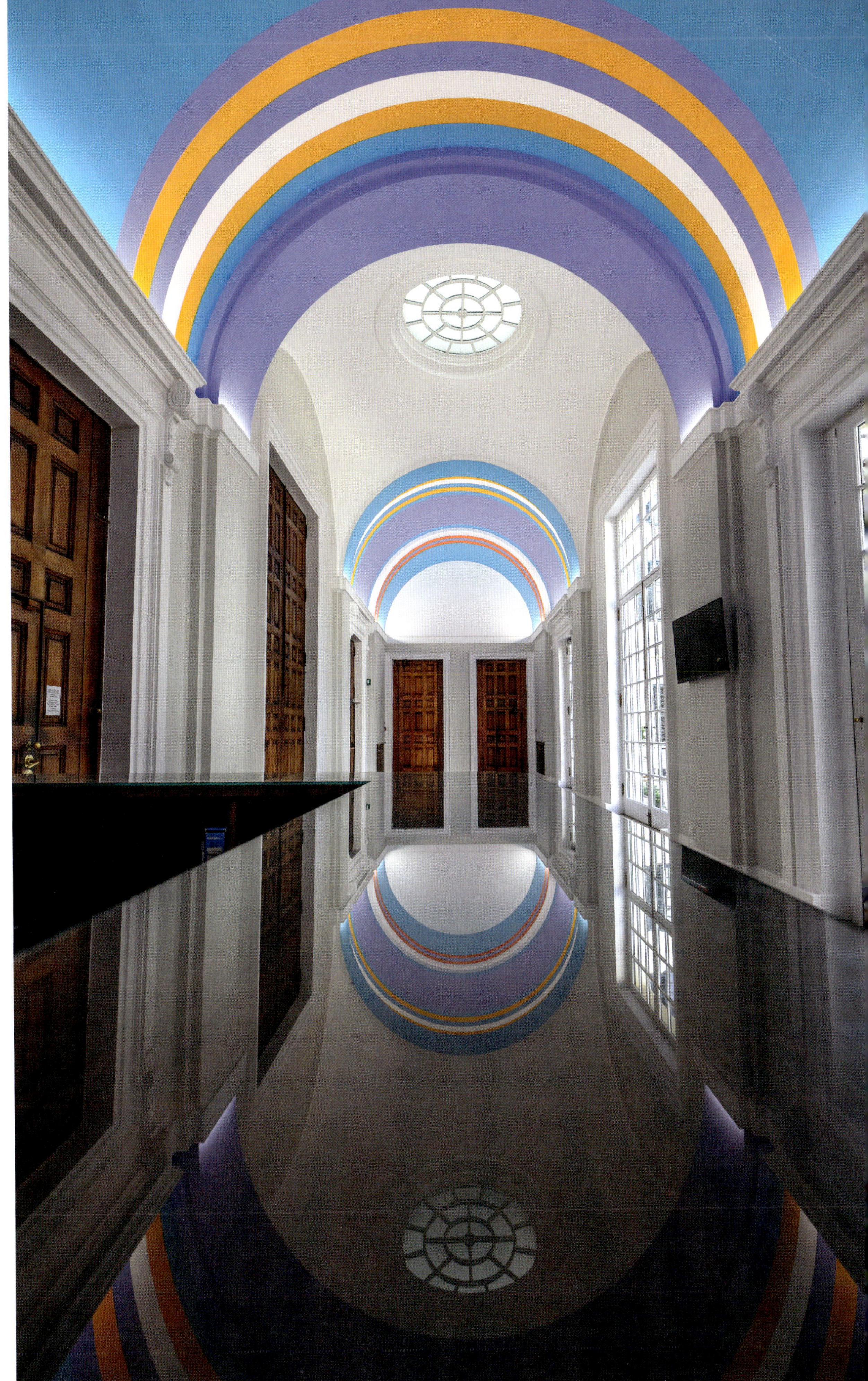

Fig. 32
Antony Gormley (born 1950)
Sound II, 1986
Lead, fibreglass and water,
188 × 60 × 45 cm
Winchester Cathedral,
Hampshire

Fig. 33
Bridget Riley (born 1931)
Verve, 2023
Ceiling painting at the British
School at Rome
Acrylic paint on plaster, in two
parts, each 660 × 250 cm
The British School at Rome

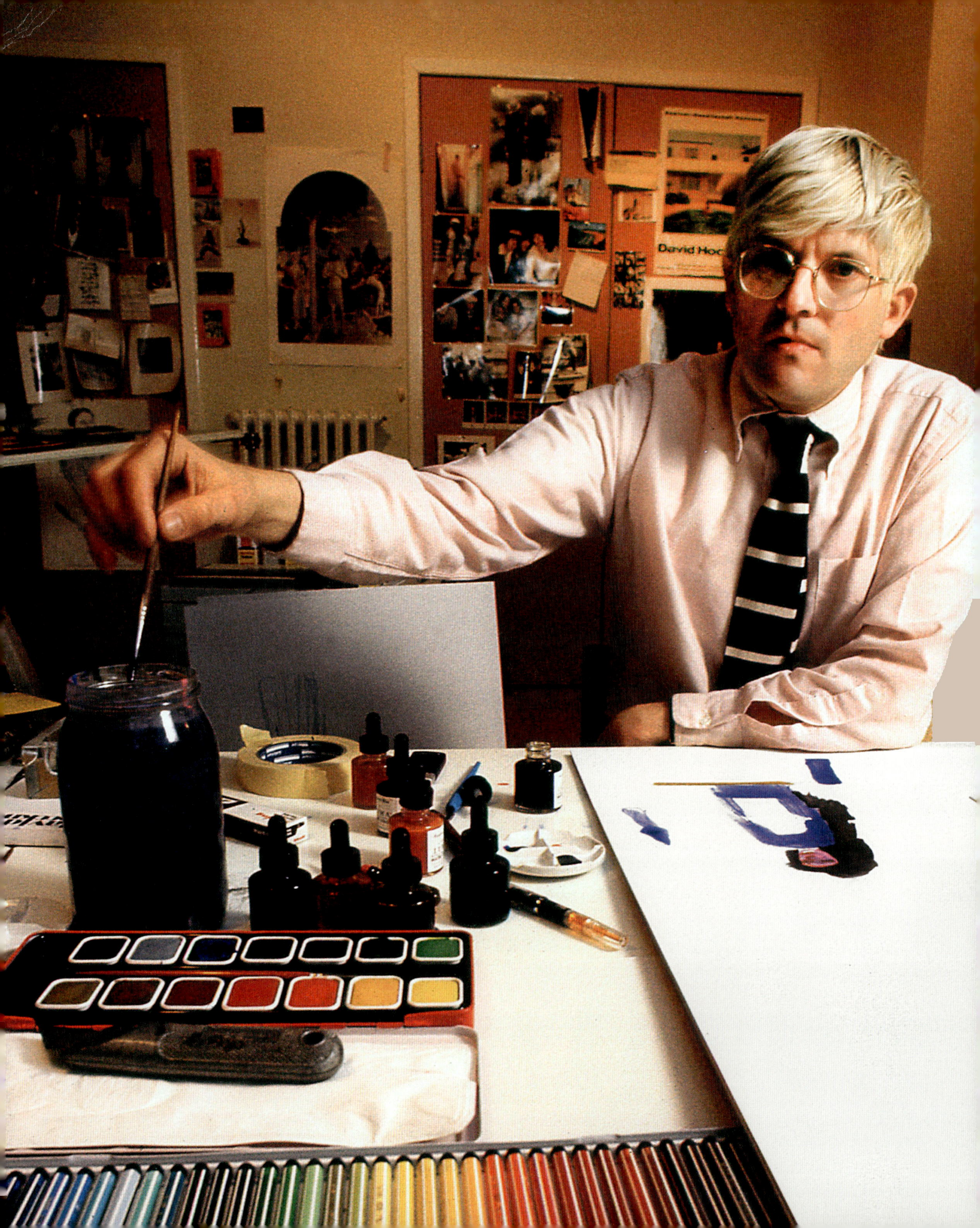

David Hoc

A 200-YEAR DIALOGUE BETWEEN LIVING ARTISTS AND THE NATIONAL GALLERY

Susanna Avery-Quash

Well, if paintings speak to you, it's happening now. So they are contemporary. They're living. The artist might have died but the pictures are still alive. They just get better and better. DAVID HOCKNEY [1]

Since its foundation in 1824, there have always been strong connections between the National Gallery and living artists. This chapter offers an overview of that complex and changing history. The first part signals the diversity of important roles that artists have played in developing and caring for the collection, and the second offers a more detailed discussion of the ways in which the Gallery has promoted artistic dialogue between living artists and its collection – and its visitors – over the last 200 years.[2]

From their years of studying the art of the past, artists were deemed to possess requisite knowledge to judge authenticity and quality, to assign works of art to artists, to distinguish originals from copies, to comment on condition and even to gauge value for money for the public purse. On these grounds, in the earliest days of the Gallery, artists were consulted as specialist advisers about potential purchases and invited to act as expert witnesses at various governmental Select Committees that investigated the Gallery, including the most influential one held in 1853, when 19 artists testified.[3] After the Gallery's management was reconstituted in 1855 – on the back of the findings of the 1853 Select Committee – the artist-cum-connoisseur Sir Charles Lock Eastlake was appointed to the new position of Director (1855–65). Remarkably, the first eight Keepers (the position in existence prior to the establishment of the directorship and retained after 1855 as a subsidiary role to that of the Director) and the first six Directors were all trained artists (see Appendix 1).[4]

Artists have also regularly served as Trustees, starting with the painter Sir Thomas Lawrence, who, having helped secure 38 pictures from the heirs of the financier and philanthropist John Julius Angerstein (1735–1823) as the foundation collection of the National Gallery, became one of six 'Gentlemen of taste' on what constituted the Gallery's first Board (see Appendix 2).[5] Since the Second World War, the Gallery has elected a single 'artist Trustee' on a regular basis, although since 2019 there have been two Trustees who are artists because Catherine Goodman joined the Board on which Dexter Dalwood was already serving as the 'artist Trustee'. Certain 'artist Trustees' have also served on the Board of Tate – and vice versa – the most recent example being Rosalind Nashashibi (Tate Liaison Trustee since 2023), a reflection of the two institutions' intertwined histories.[6]

A number of pictures in the collection have been acquired directly from living painters, in addition to those whose provenances list painters as former owners:

Anthony van Dyck's *Portrait of George Gage with Two Attendants* and Giovanni Bellini's *The Agony in the Garden*, for instance, both once belonged to Sir Joshua Reynolds, first President of the Royal Academy.[7] Among the Gallery's artist donors is Eastlake (see Appendix 5), who presented Fra Filippo Lippi's *The Annunciation* during his directorship, in 1861.[8] More recently, in 2012, Jean-Baptiste-Camille Corot's *Italian Woman* from the collection of Lucian Freud was allocated to the Gallery through the acceptance-in-lieu scheme, often thought of as a thank-you present from the painter to the UK for having welcomed his family when they arrived as refugees in 1933.[9] A large number of British pictures have likewise been donated by artists. At one end of the spectrum Eliza Bridell-Fox, a copyist at the Gallery in 1841, gave *The Woods of Sweet Chestnut above Varenna, Lake Como* by Frederick Lee Bridell, her late husband, in 1886 (Tate).[10] Of incomparably larger scale and importance is the bequest of J.M.W. Turner (1775–1851), which comprises nearly 100 finished pictures, 182 unfinished pictures, and around 19,000 sketches and watercolours by him.[11]

The celebrity status of artists such as Turner is attested to by the fact that what might be termed artistic memorabilia was once acquired by the National Gallery. Records show that three palettes were accepted that had formerly belonged to Turner, John Constable and Ford Madox Brown.[12] None of them remain in the collection, and the offers of palettes formerly belonging to Sir David Wilkie and John Phillip were refused, in the first instance on the grounds that the offer was 'not consistent with the objects of this institution'.[13] The sole remaining 'relic' is the gold medal that Constable was awarded by Charles X at the Paris Salon of 1824 for *The Hay Wain*. It used to be embedded in the frame of the painting but is now preserved in the Gallery's Contextual Collection, which consists of works of art and objects that illuminate the Gallery's history, buildings, collection and relationship with contemporary artists.

Looking at the collection in Trafalgar Square today, it is easy to forget that modern British art, as well as some modern/contemporary international art, was once very much part of it.[14] Indeed, the Angerstein collection included not only pictures by the historic British painters William Hogarth and Reynolds but also *The Village Holiday* by living Scottish painter Wilkie (fig. 34).[15] An early Select Committee of 1835, set up to investigate ways of 'extending knowledge of the Arts and principles of design among the people', concluded

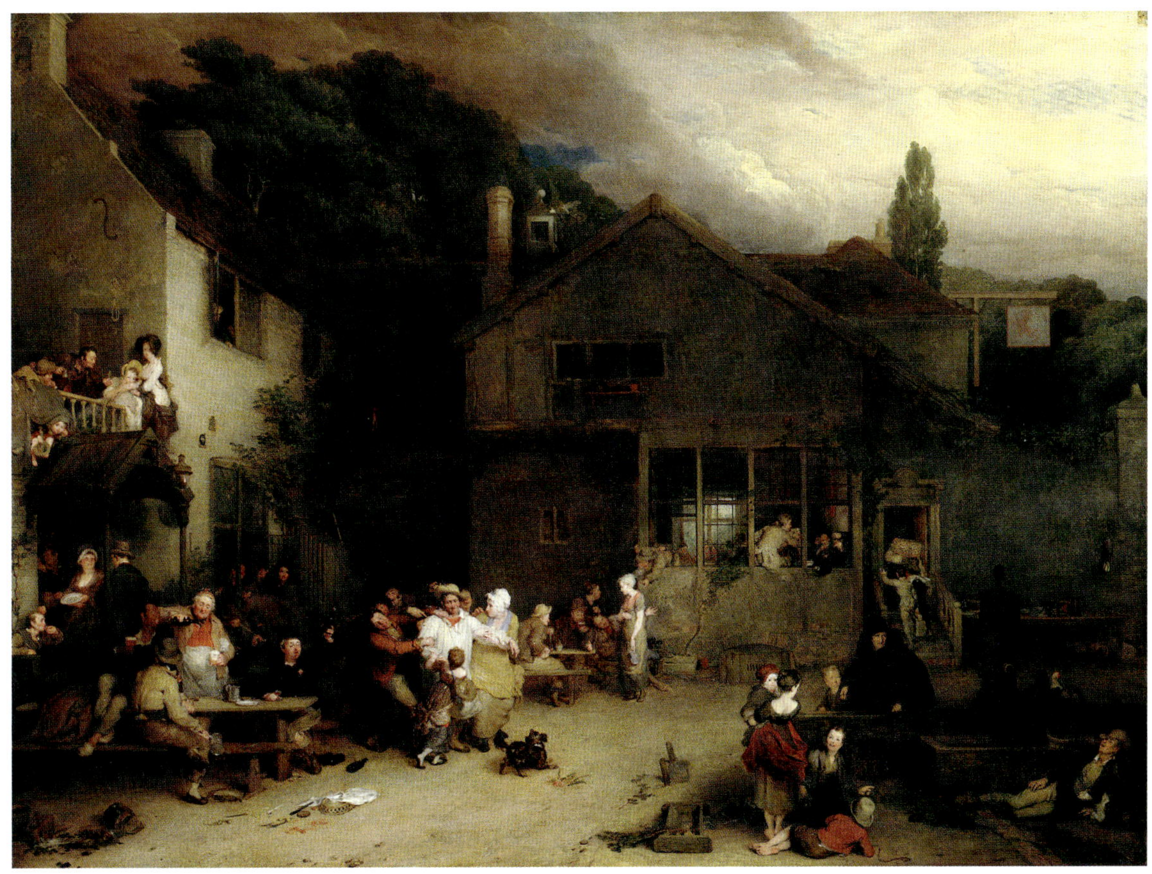

that 'some portion of the Gallery should be dedicated to the perpetuation and extension of the British School of Art. Pictures by living British artists of acknowledged merit might, after they have stood the test of time and criticism, be purchased.'[16]

This part of the collection was boosted not only by acquisitions, many of which came through funding supplied via the Chantrey Bequest,[17] but also by several very important gifts. In addition to the Turner bequest, there was the Robert Vernon gift of 1847, which comprised 157 works by 70 modern British artists, and Jacob Bell's bequest of 1859, which contained 18 modern British pictures as well as a single modern international work, Rosa Bonheur's *The Horse Fair*.[18] It was with the creation of the so-called National Gallery of British Art at Millbank in 1897 (subsequently renamed the Tate Gallery, and now Tate) that the vast majority of this part of the Gallery's collection, including nearly all of the Turners, was transferred to Millbank. The British paintings that were retained at Trafalgar Square date from the eighteenth and early nineteenth centuries and were selected as representing the greatest British pictures.[19] For most of the twentieth century, there was a lack of clarity between the sister institutions about their respective collecting remits in relation to both British and international modern art. Despite initiatives that sought to address the issue,[20] it was not until the establishment of Tate Modern in 2000 that this ongoing matter was tackled head-on. One immediate result was the agreement that Tate would loan back to the National Gallery the few nineteenth-century European paintings it possessed. Today, the general agreement is that the boundary line between the collecting remits is the early twentieth century, an understanding that has enabled the National Gallery to acquire more twentieth-century paintings. Previously, acquisitions in this area were regarded as contentious; indeed, the purchase during the 1970s by Michael Levey (Director, 1973–86) of Pablo Picasso's *Fruit Dish, Bottle and Violin* of 1914 (the Gallery's only example of twentieth-century abstraction), with two other works by Gustav Klimt and Henri Matisse, caused consternation at Tate.[21]

Fig. 34
Sir David Wilkie (1785–1841)
The Village Holiday, 1809–11
Oil on canvas, 94 × 127.6 cm
Tate, London

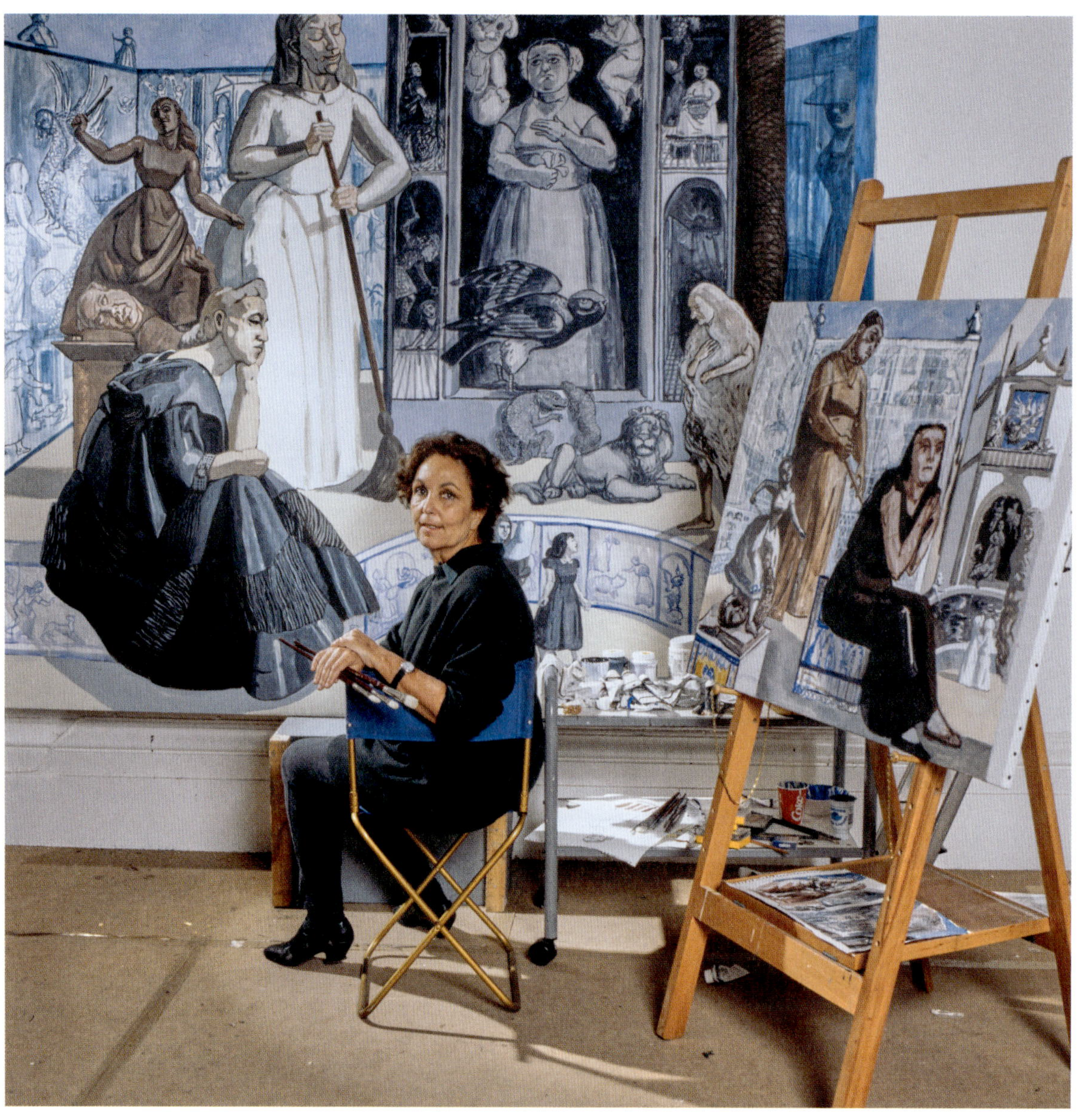

Four contemporary artists have left a permanent
trace of their work within the National Gallery's iconic
building on Trafalgar Square, designed by William
Wilkins, where the collection moved (as its third home)
in 1838 (see Appendix 4). The first artist to produce
a site-specific work was Russian-born Boris Anrep
(1883–1969), whose offer to create mosaic pavements
developed into a two-part commission (between
1928 and 1952) for four designs for the floor of the
main entrance of the Wilkins Building.[22] Anrep's designs
include personifications of the virtues and vignettes
portraying British customs and positive character
traits that he associated with his adopted country, into
which he incorporated portraits of family, friends and
celebrities. For instance, Anrep's lover, the socialite and
art patron Maud Russell, who funded the last pavement,
is represented, with amusing irony, as 'Folly'.

Portuguese-British artist Paula Rego, the Gallery's
first Associate Artist (see p. 66), was commissioned
to produce a work of art for the new Sainsbury Wing
Dining Room.[23] Executed as a large canvas extending
over two walls and installed in 1991, Rego's *Crivelli's*

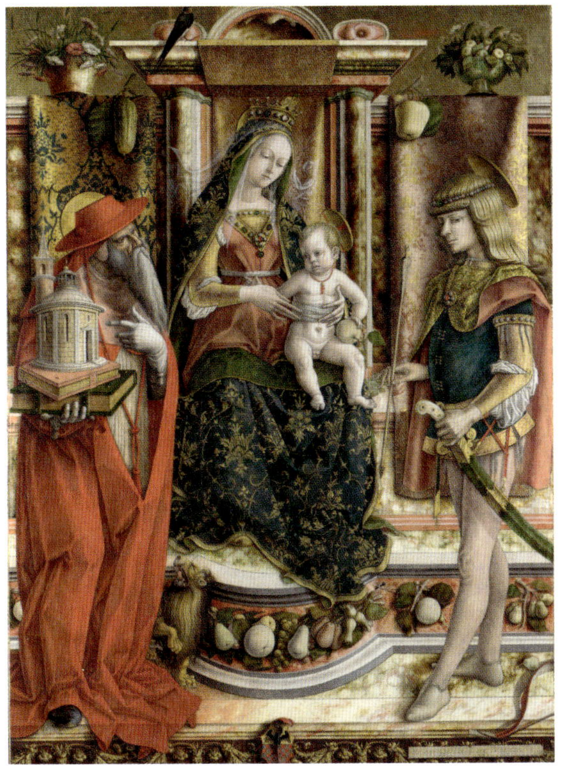

Garden explores themes central to her work, notably storytelling and overturning hierarchies to challenge the role of women in society and religion. While individual elements in *Crivelli's Garden* are inspired by paintings by Carlo Crivelli in the Gallery's collection, such as *La Madonna della Rondine (The Madonna of the Swallow)* (figs 35 and 36), some of the characters depicted in it are based on the likenesses of Gallery staff, including Erika Langmuir, then Head of Education, who was influential in encouraging Rego to learn more about the lives of female Christian saints.

Bridget Riley, another artist with a long association with the Gallery, as a Trustee and as curator of both *The Artist's Eye* exhibition of 1989 and *Bridget Riley: Paintings and Related Work* (2010–11), produced the abstract mural *Messengers*, a commission for the stairwell of the Annenberg Court, unveiled in 2019. The title is inspired by a phrase Constable used when referring to clouds as indicators of weather conditions, and it also likely alludes to the angelic bearers of other kinds of news, depicted in so many Gallery pictures, including in scenes of the Annunciation by Filippo Lippi and Crivelli.

Certain artists who visited the National Gallery have made pictorial records of some of its rooms, which serve, together with historical photographs of the building's interiors, as useful visual accounts of the displays at certain times. For instance, Emily Mary Bibbens Warren (1869–1956) produced the watercolour *View of the Entrance Hall: The North Vestibule*, while Bertha Mary Garnett (active 1882–1904) painted in oils *A Corner of The Turner Room in the National Gallery* in 1883.[24] Notably, Jewish painter Lily Delissa Joseph (born Leah Alice Solomon, 1863–1940), sister of the artist Solomon J. Solomon, and a committed member of both the women's suffrage movement and the Jewish community, produced a series of oil paintings of the interior of the National Gallery, including *The Art Gallery* (Ben Uri Gallery and Museum, London).[25] Recently, a number of artists have chosen to film at the National Gallery. For instance, Nashashibi made a film as part of her residency, a few scenes of which were shot in the galleries at Trafalgar Square, while Céline Condorelli (born 1974), the National Gallery's Artist in Residence in 2023, keen for Gallery visitors to experience art differently, used her exhibition *Pentimenti (The Corrections)* and accompanying film to encourage reflection on the way that spaces in the Gallery are navigated and utilised.[26]

THE NATIONAL GALLERY AS A TRAINING GROUND FOR ARTISTS

When the National Gallery was first conceived, artists were considered to be a principal group of beneficiaries – indeed, its establishment 'primarily as a resource for artists' made it 'unique amongst the world's great collections'.[27] Government and tastemakers, concerned in part with falling standards in design and manufacture, and in part with international competition, hoped to boost the British School of painting by making a world-class collection of pictures available to home-grown artists for study and inspiration.[28] When the Gallery opened in 1824, artists had more privileges than anyone else because two days a week – Fridays and Saturdays – were set aside specifically for them (referred to as 'Private Days', 'Students' Days' or 'Copyists' Days'), when a number of copyists using oil paints had free run of the galleries; if members of the public wanted to visit then, they had to pay.[29]

Connections between practising artists and the collection were fostered in the UK by art academies. Following earlier traditions established abroad, they regarded esteemed collections of historical paintings, as well as of antique casts and of engravings by or after historical masters, as reputable learning resources.

Fig. 36
Carlo Crivelli (about 1430/5–about 1494)
La Madonna della Rondine (The Madonna of the Swallow), after 1490
Egg tempera and some oil on wood, 150.5 × 107.3 cm
The National Gallery, London

Consequently, studying in front of such works of art became a core part of many teaching curricula. In Britain, the justification was made by Reynolds in his inaugural 'Discourse' as President of the Royal Academy of Arts in 1769. There he proclaimed that the value of 'a repository for the great examples of the Art' was that aspiring artists, by 'studying these authentick [*sic*] models', would acquire 'excellence … [in] a shorter and easier way'.[30] Reynolds also told his students that in relation to 'the great works of the great masters' they should not only 'consider them as models which you are to imitate' but also 'as rivals with whom you are to contend',[31] a challenge that has been ringing in the ears of living artists ever since.

Of all the art schools in Britain that now exist, the one associated with the Royal Academy has had a particularly long-standing and intertwined history with the National Gallery.[32] Two of its Presidents have been Directors of the National Gallery – Eastlake and Sir Edward Poynter (Director, 1894–1904). Furthermore, both institutions were housed in the same building on Trafalgar Square for 30 years from 1838. The Gallery occupied the west wing of William Wilkins's building, and the Academy its east wing, until the latter moved to its current home at Burlington House on Piccadilly, where it formally reopened in 1869. From historical records, we know the layout of the Academy's classrooms when it shared a home with the National Gallery. Life-drawing classes, for instance, took place in the central pepper-pot dome, with William Powell Frith (1819–1909) recalling: 'It was a circular room, and the model was posed on one side of it – an extended semi-circle of students working opposite. Dead silence reigned.'[33]

For the mid-nineteenth-century Royal Academy students, it must have been very convenient to have a world-class teaching collection available a stone's throw away from where their practical art classes and lectures took place, in which reference was constantly being made to the adjacent art collection.[34] Not surprisingly, certain student art rebels found inspiration in pictures that most Academicians of the time dismissed as ugly and as poor models to follow. For instance, *The Arnolfini Portrait* by Jan van Eyck (active 1422; died 1441), purchased in 1842, inspired two members of the Pre-Raphaelite Brotherhood to produce works that were heavily criticised for their backward-looking stylistic and technical tendencies: *The Girlhood of Mary Virgin* (1848–9) by Dante Gabriel Rossetti (1828–1882) and *Mariana* (1851) by Sir John Everett Millais (1829–1896).[35]

Even after the Academy moved away, its curriculum remained rooted in the Gallery's collection for many years, with copying of the historical holdings at Trafalgar Square a key component. For instance, Richard Hamilton recalled of his student days during the 1930s: 'As a student at the Royal Academy Schools I was required to attend the Gallery to make either one full-size copy or three sketch studies each year for the annual examination. I recall the pleasurable hours of deliberation before the intimate act of copying.'[36]

Many other art schools originating during the later nineteenth century likewise encouraged their students to study at the National Gallery. Certainly, students at the Slade School of Fine Art, established in 1871 as part of University College London, were expected to copy the art of the past in London museums and galleries.[37] Gwen John (1876–1939) recalled that in 1897 Henry Tonks, when Slade Professor of Fine Art, set a competition, in which his pupils had to make copies after works by Michelangelo, Raphael, Rubens or Watteau (her brother, Augustus John, was the winner).[38] Her own copy made in 1895–8 after a National Gallery picture, Gabriel Metsu's *A Woman seated at a Table and a Man tuning a Violin*, survives.[39] The same type of curriculum was in place from the start at Camberwell School of Arts and Crafts, opened in 1898 by Poynter. During the 1950s, when the teaching of art history was introduced (external lecturers included Gallery staff), visits to Trafalgar Square remained core business, with one Camberwell student remembering, 'Piero della Francesca and Ingres were our most revered Old Masters'.[40]

The National Gallery's art collection has been accessed for study purposes in two main ways: informally and by application. Today, as in former times, artists are free to wander round or draw in a sketchpad without making a booking. We know of the reactions of some of the artists to encountering the collection in this way from diaries or letters. Claude Monet (1840–1926) and Camille Pissarro (1830–1903), for example, were both in London during the Franco-Prussian War of 1870–1 and visited the National Gallery, commenting particularly favourably on Turner's *Rain, Steam, and Speed – The Great Western Railway*.[41] This was also one of the works that Vincent van Gogh (1853–1890) picked out for special praise in the Gallery's collection, together with John Constable's *The Cornfield* (1826) and an unnamed Meindert Hobbema – doubtless the celebrated *The Avenue at Middelharnis* (1689) – when he wrote to his brother Theo in 1884 about pictures worth seeing in London.[42] Several decades later, David

3 A 200-Year Dialogue between Artists and the Gallery

Bomberg, one of the first British artists to break with the figurative tradition and promote abstraction, became a regular visitor to the collection. On one occasion, in 1914, he took his wife Alice Mayes to see Michelangelo's *Entombment* and told her that 'the modern pictures … had their beginnings with the Old Masters and Michael Angelo was the chief of these'.[43]

Painters who wished to set up an easel and use oil paints in the National Gallery's rooms had to make an appointment – the same applies today. The students were looked after by the Gallery's Keeper, and a set of rules regarding their admission, established by the 1853 Select Committee, was published in the first formal Annual Report of 1856. To obtain an admission ticket, applicants had to submit a specimen of their work together with a written application. The rules stated that 'ordinary or professional copyists in oil will be permitted to pursue their studies in the Gallery for three months, after which time they will make room for those of the next list. Artists or others may, on application, be readmitted to copy after a period of three months from the expiration of the term previously granted.'[44]

Over time, working conditions improved. For instance, Charles Locke Eastlake, a nephew of the first Director, who was Keeper of the Gallery from 1878 to 1898, published new guidelines in 1878 and 1894.[45] Instead of the scrum that had previously ensued as students jostled for position in front of favourite paintings, his new scheme meant that only two artists could copy a particular work at any one time. Other improvements included the introduction of chaperons' cards so that unaccompanied female artists might feel safe while working in public, the provision of a canteen and, from 1882, the allocation of storerooms, where the students could leave their canvases between visits.

Copying became increasingly popular throughout the nineteenth century; at its peak, between 1855 and 1890, there were on average 375 copyists each year. A range of artists, mainly women, took advantage; some were professional copyists, others were amateurs pursuing a hobby (fig. 37).[46] Copyist registers in the Gallery's archive provide details of the backgrounds of those who participated (the names of their art schools and sponsors as well as their home addresses are given), while the Gallery's annual reports recorded for several decades the most popular paintings studied over the preceding 12 months.[47] One critic in 1893 noted petulantly the popularity of the British pictures: 'My footsteps echoed mournfully through the deserted rooms where the masterpieces of Cimabue and

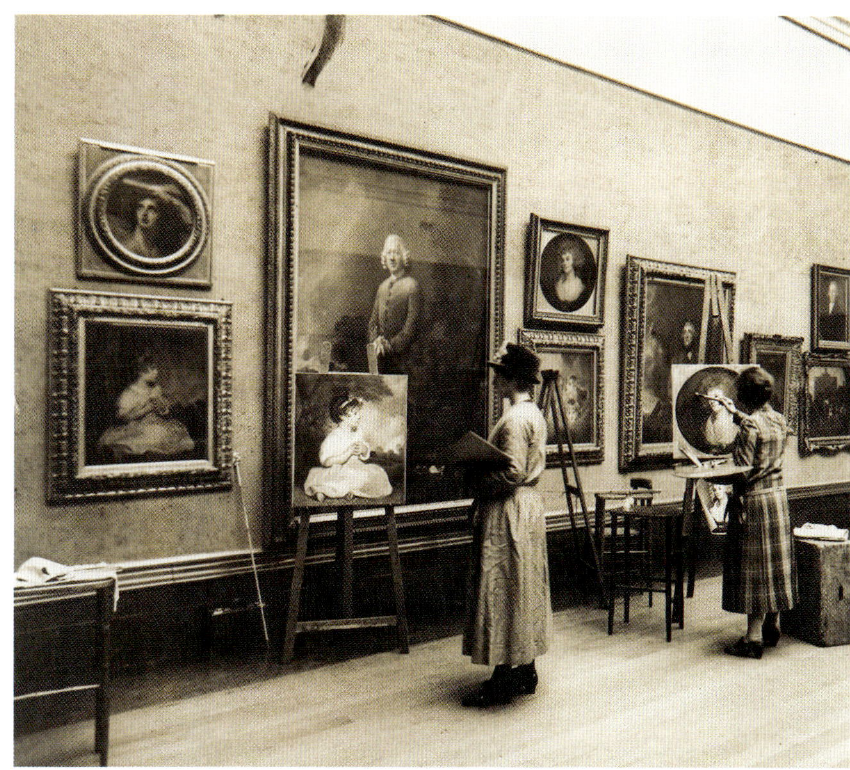

Leonardi [*sic*] da Vinci hang. I could not help thinking that if our students must waste their time and energies copying, it would be better worth their while and more elevating to their mind to study from these giants of old than copy [Sir Edwin Landseer's] "Dignity and Impudence" [now at Tate], or make hopeless attempts at the Turneresque colouring.'[48]

One female painter who copied several Gallery paintings was Christiana Herringham, who not only helped to establish the Society of Painters in Tempera in 1901, as noted in Chapter 2, but also, in 1903, along with other artists, critics and patrons including Dugald Sutherland MacColl and Roger Fry, set up the National Art Collections Fund (today Art Fund), with the goal of acquiring great works of art for public collections, two of the first being Velázquez's *'Rokeby Venus'* (1647–51) and Hans Holbein the Younger's *Christina of Denmark, Duchess of Milan* (1538).[49] Herringham was taught the value of copying by Fry, who once observed: 'The real idea behind copying is to induce one to look at a picture for a long time.'[50] In October 1897, Herringham was engaged in copying *The Virgin and Child with Saints Anthony Abbot and George* (about 1435–41) by Pisanello, while in 1909 she made a copy of

Fig. 37
Photograph showing copyists in the National Gallery, probably in Room XXV (now Gallery 9), 1928. Most of the British School paintings seen here have been transferred to Tate's collection.
The National Gallery, London

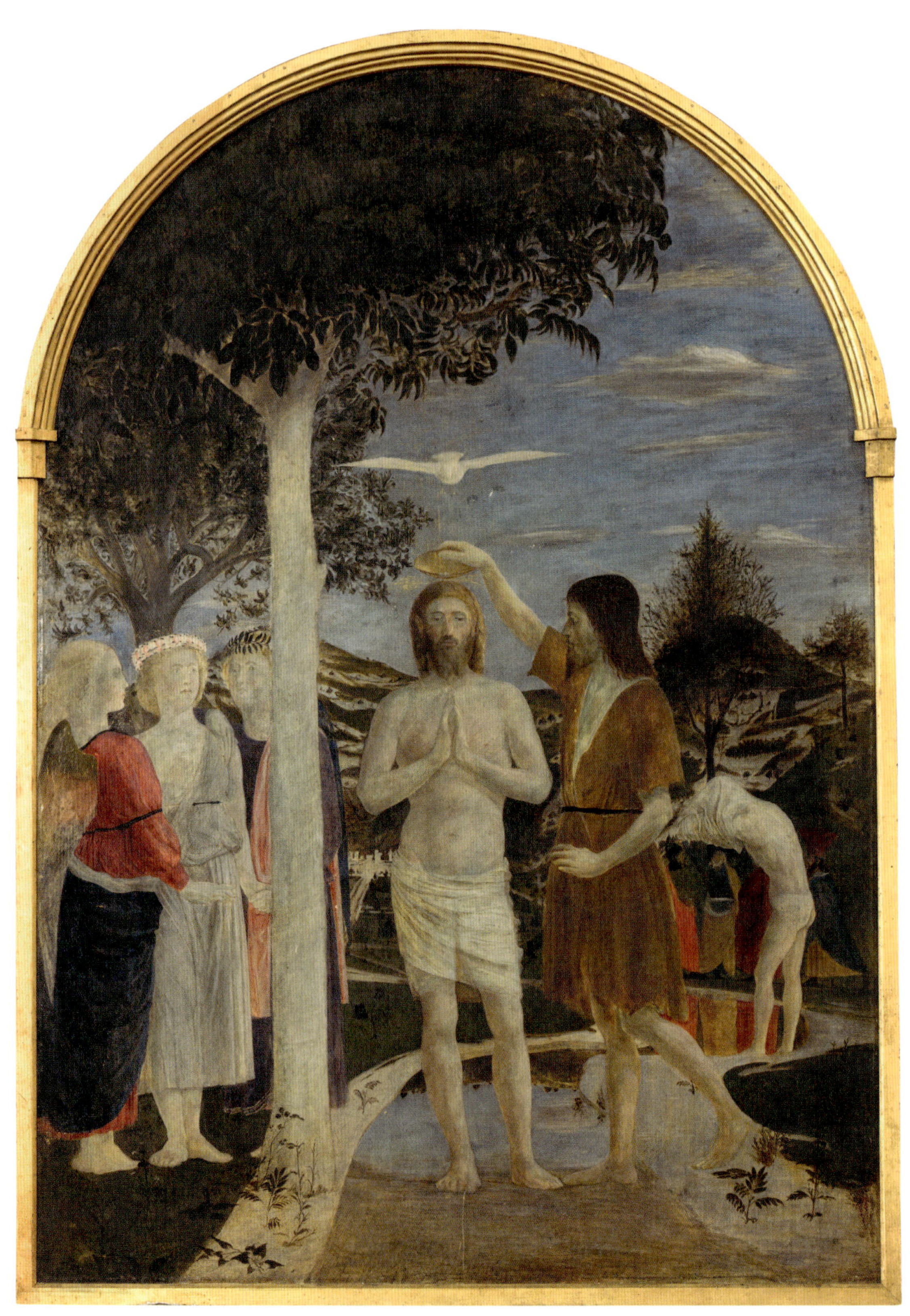

The Baptism of Christ by Piero, which she donated the same year to the Cathedral of San Sepolcro, the previous home of Piero's picture (fig. 38).[51]

During the twentieth century, the number of copyists registered on the programme started to fall, and separate student days were not reintroduced when the Gallery reopened after the Second World War. After that, numbers declined further, with the low period being 1965–80, when on average only 35–40 students signed up each year. Similarly, fewer people came to sketch. There are various explanations for the decline, including the proliferation of good-quality commercially produced reproductions and the fact that copying was, from the 1960s, no longer a requirement of art schools' curricula, a state of affairs that many lamented. David Hockney, for one, defended the tradition, telling National Gallery senior curator Alistair Smith that there should be 'daily drawing (*nulla die sine linea*)'.[52] He discussed the same topic simultaneously with the then National Gallery Director, Michael Levey, as part of an interesting and fruitful correspondence conducted when preparing his *Artist's Eye* exhibition of 1981 (fig. 39; see Appendix 11).[53] Hockney stated his belief that public art galleries should encourage copying by art students.[54] In the same letter, Hockney requested to copy a Van Gogh from the collection, but asked to do so 'in the basement', away from distracting crowds. Interestingly, Levey defended the Gallery's stance on letting the public see an artist at work, noting that this might 'sharpen the eyes of visitors … tiresome though it can be for the artist'.[55] In the catalogue that Hockney wrote to accompany his exhibition, he returned to the topic of drawing more generally, making a 'short plea for an art of depiction to be kept up'.[56] He argued that drawing is a fundamental form of human expression and a 'sharing experience', and as such 'in some way … art is our salvation'.[57] In Hockney's opinion, everyone should be given the opportunity to develop their skill in drawing, in order that people might be better equipped to connect and share, or as Hockney put it, 'to tell other people about certain experiences in a certain way'.[58]

ARTISTS AS ADVOCATES: CONNECTING OLD AND NEW ART THROUGH EXHIBITIONS

Levey's point about the public connecting with the historical collection partly through the help of a living artist is critical, and represents a vital shift in the Gallery's thinking and its acknowledgement of the need to make its collection attractive to contemporary visitors. After the Royal Academy moved out of Trafalgar Square in 1869, the tradition of dedicating space to the creation of new art ended. Once the Tate Gallery was founded in 1897, all contemporary art was transferred there, meaning that works by living artists were no longer on permanent show at Trafalgar Square. Consequently, it became increasingly hard to discern ongoing links between art of the past and that of the present. The worry then was whether the National Gallery's collection still held meaning and relevance.

I have come to the conclusion that copying is a marvellous way to learn, it was good enough for Degas, Van Gogh and almost everybody before 1920. I recommend it to young students of painting now. I even think Museums should encourage it in artists. They do have some responsibilities to artists working now, which sometimes they seem to forget. Every time I go in the Metropolitan Museum in N.Y now I get very worked up when I see the

3

notice they put up more and more 'No Photography or Sketching' This seems to me to be insulting to students of painting and very unserious. They even had it up for their own Degas exhibition which of course included some of his own copies of other pictures, — done in the days before notices like that appeared. I mean to write to them about it yet when I try I seem to be like a preacher or moralist telling them their job. If libraries started being as unserious as that though where would we be?

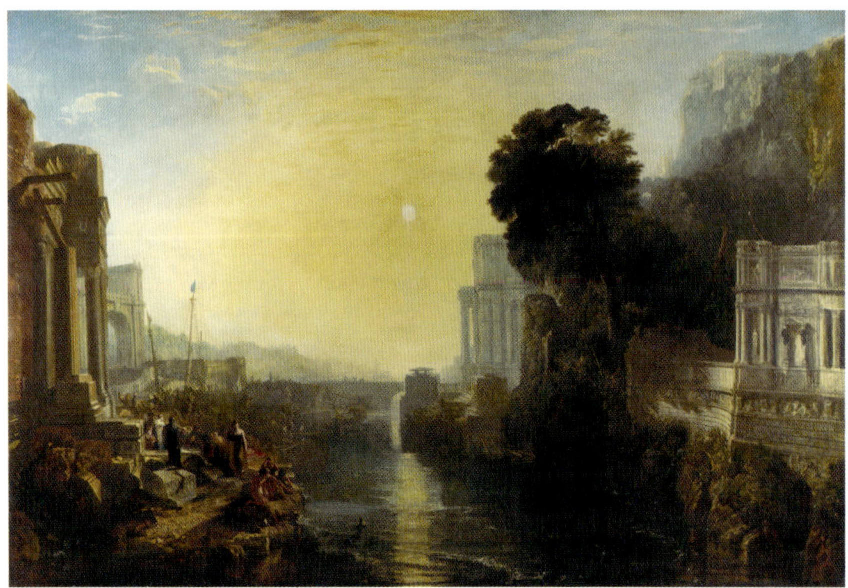

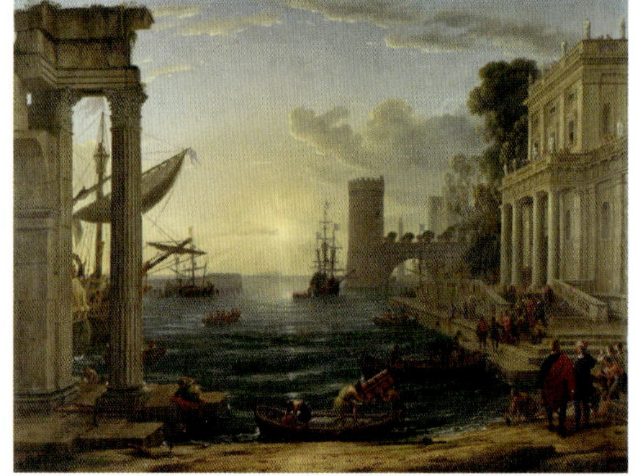

An opportunity to evaluate current thinking and to experiment with ways of bridging the perceived gap emerged during the Second World War, when the Gallery hosted its first contemporary art exhibitions. They replaced the permanent collection that had been removed for safe storage to a slate mine in Wales and gave culture-starved Londoners some visual entertainment, alongside a daily lunchtime concert organised by Myra Hess with catering provided by Lady Irene Gater. The exhibitions were the brainchild of a third woman, Lilian Browse (1906–2005), an enterprising London-based dealer in modern art.[59] *British Painting since Whistler* inaugurated her series in March 1940, while subsequent monographic exhibitions focused on the work of key twentieth-century English and Irish painters Augustus John, Walter Richard Sickert, William Nicholson, Jack Butler Yeats and Philip Wilson Steer. Kenneth Clark (Director, 1934–45), through his links with the War Artists' Advisory Committee, spearheaded another series from July 1940, which came to be known as the *War Artist Exhibitions* (see Appendix 6). These shows brought together the work of up-and-coming artists such as Henry Moore, Eric Ravilious and Stanley Spencer, as well as painters from an earlier generation, including Sir William Rothenstein and Muirhead Bone. Both series were popular and stood up well against the third type of exhibition, the *Picture of the Month* scheme, inaugurated in 1942, where one historical masterpiece such as Titian's *Noli me Tangere*[60] (sometimes accompanied by less important works) was brought

back from Wales for a short display. (Piero's *Baptism* was not among the works selected to return from Wales.)

After the war, there was a chance for more radical thinking, motivated by the need to get people back through the doors and engaged with the permanent collection. First steps were made by Clark's successor, Philip Hendy (Director, 1946–67), who challenged traditional types of display by mixing up chronologies and geographies in 'daring juxtapositions' to encourage visitors to see new artistic dialogues between unlikely conversation partners, albeit from within the permanent collection.[61] Levey made even greater strides during his later directorship, having grasped, as never before, the importance of making the case for the ongoing relevance of the collection and of finding practical solutions to 'bridge the gap between public and paintings which is particularly acute in a gallery filled with great works by dead artists'.[62]

Levey conducted his campaign essentially on two fronts, with significant help from Alistair Smith, whom he put in charge of exhibitions and the Education Department, which had been established in 1974. Firstly, as noted, Levey deliberately purchased key twentieth-century paintings, and secondly, he employed living artists, whom he realised might act as persuasive advocates for their deceased counterparts while at the same time continuing to benefit from interacting with them themselves. This 'tactic' shifted the dynamics significantly from the earlier approach, when, as discussed, the Gallery had offered its collection for the benefit of artists. Now, in effect, it was offering the collection plus artists for the benefit of the general public. Levey's collaboration with artists took place in two innovative ways: through public-facing exhibitions curated by artists, and through artists' residencies, which involved varying levels of public interaction.

ARTISTS AS CURATORS AT THE NATIONAL GALLERY

A cutting-edge exhibition series called *The Artist's Eye* was inaugurated in 1977, in which a leading artist was invited to act as curator (see Chapter 4 and Appendix 5). The brief was for the selected artist to create an exhibition that showcased a group of Gallery paintings from any part of the collection that had particular significance for them; as one critic put it, they were 'not so much a Desert Island Choice as a statement about art'.[63] Additionally, at least one example of their own work was to be shown so that the public could be introduced to a representative example of the artist-curator's oeuvre.[64] In the introduction to the catalogue for the inaugural exhibition, organised by Anthony Caro (1924–2013), Levey promoted the thinking behind the initiative: 'We urge everyone to worry less about stylistic labels, especially those dividing modern art from "old masters", and to enjoy exercising their eyes in the realm of the imagination.'[65] The same message was repeated for each show, Levey noting on another occasion that the series was a 'tacit reminder that pictures are the product of individual painters and that the art of the past and the art of the present are not – and should never be represented as being – in opposition to each other'.[66] The way a living artist saw the art of the past was intended to help visitors look freshly at those achievements. Rarely had paintings been shown at the Gallery out of chronological sequence, and only in one instance did the Gallery display two historical paintings together with two contemporary ones: the 'quartet' of pictures in question had been initiated over a century before when Turner had stated in his will that two of his pictures should be hung in perpetuity together with two works by the seventeenth-century master Claude from the foundational collection (figs 40 and 41). However, by the 1970s, this ensemble looked more like a conversation between two long-gone painters.[67]

Five exhibitions were organised between 1977 and 1981, with a second series of five taking place between 1985 and 1990. Most of the artists involved in *The Artist's Eye* series confessed to being nervous about seeing how their works would stand up against iconic

masterpieces as well as excited by the opportunity to get to know great pictures better and to encourage others to look at art, whether old or contemporary, closely and in new ways. Some used their displays, and the accompanying catalogues, to explore themes of great importance to them as artists, such as Hamilton, who staged 'an unsettling confrontation' between iconic National Gallery paintings and mechanically produced objects from contemporary life, including a television set that he had running (see fig. 59). Making the same point in a different way, Hamilton also introduced a cheap print of Van Gogh's celebrated *Sunflowers* to point out 'the degradation ... of our normal 20th century visual field'.[68]

One artist-curator who placed real Gallery paintings alongside reproductions of them was David Hockney, who titled his exhibition of 1981 *Looking at Pictures in a Room*. His starting point was his own painting, *Looking at Pictures on a Screen* (1977; see fig. 1), which showed his close friend, American art critic and curator Henry Geldzahler (1935–1994), peering at a folded screen on which were stuck poster reproductions of four Gallery pictures: *The Baptism* by Piero and a work each by Vermeer, Van Gogh and Degas (*A Young Woman standing at a Virginal*, *Sunflowers* and *After the Bath, Woman drying Herself*, respectively). Hockney's painting was displayed within the exhibition space, with the four original Gallery paintings hanging opposite. On a stage in between, Hockney introduced the original props – the screen with the posters and a chair – to re-create the original scene into which visitors were invited to step, thereby taking Geldzahler's place and putting themselves 'in the picture – literally!' (fig. 42).[69]

In this way, Hockney allowed the visitor 'to look at three versions of each picture, in his painting, in the real reproductions [four Gallery posters] on the screen and finally in the flesh'.[70] Additionally, a fourth version of each picture, as well as a carefully chosen detail from each, was produced as a series of eight postcards, placed in a pocket at the back of *Looking at Pictures in a Book* (fig. 43). In this exhibition catalogue, Hockney advocated for reproductions and the fact that they allowed the image to accompany its owner through life. While he noted that the original Piero was of a different order and had a far greater 'magic' to it than any kind of reproduction could ever have, he deliberately underscored the fact that the advantage of a reproduction was that 'you *can* take the cheap photographic copy home. You can pin it up next to your bed. You can have a look at it at night. You can wake up and have a look at it in the morning.

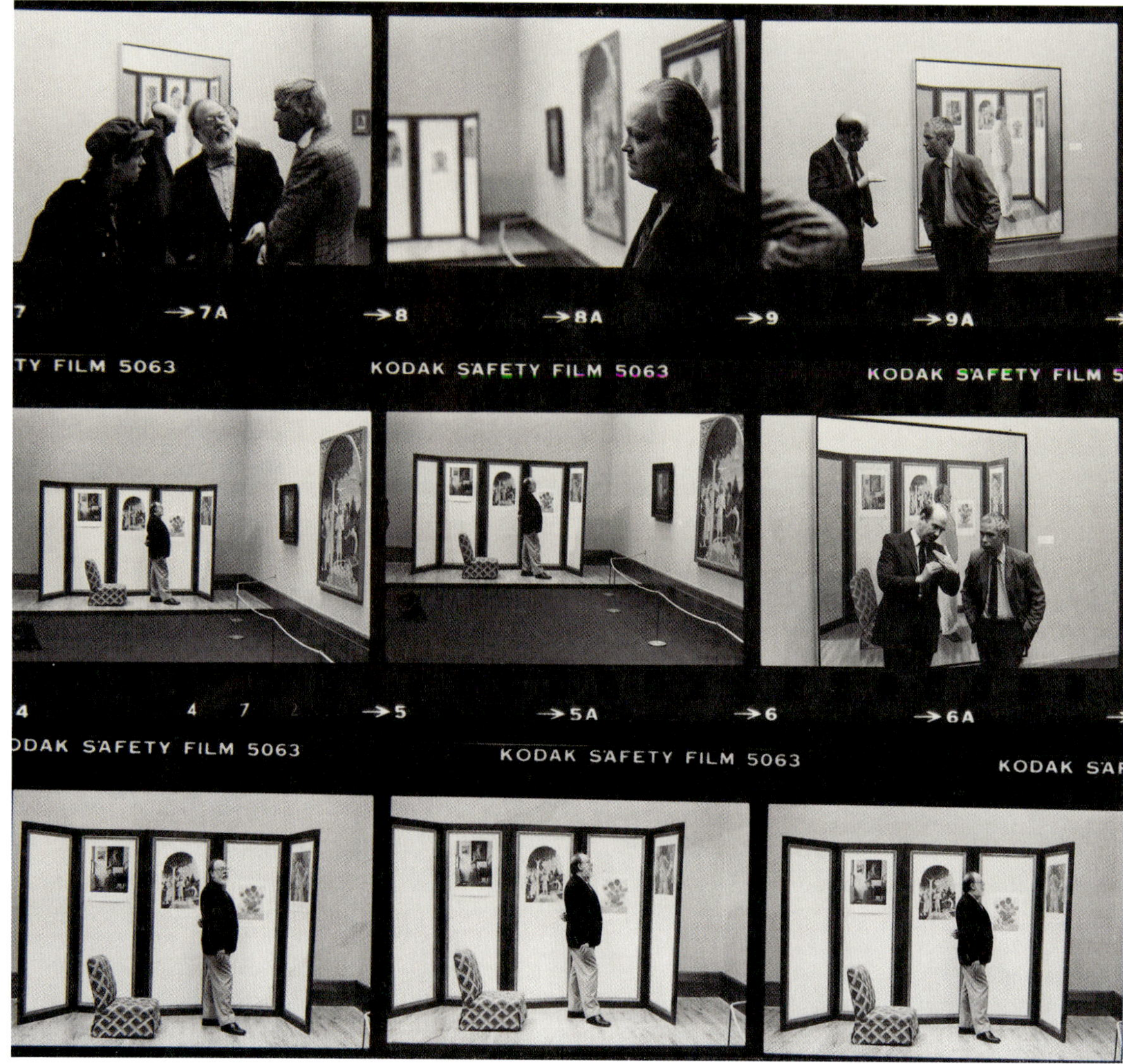

Fig. 42

Contact sheet of photographs by Alistair Smith, taken during the installation of Hockney's *Artist's Eye* exhibition, 1981. Henry Geldzahler appears in the middle and bottom rows in the pose he adopted for *Looking at Pictures on a Screen*, which Hockney (seen in 7A) struck for the exhibition poster. National Gallery Director Michael Levey is shown with the artist Howard Hodgkin in images 9A and 6A. The National Gallery, London

And it's giving off pleasure in strange ways that go on and on.'[71]

In his catalogue, Hockney took the chance to explore in depth this and other themes of the exhibition, which one critic summarised as being 'the appreciation of art through reproduction … the actual place of photography in aesthetics … and finally, the importance of "depiction" as a way of sharing experience and making it vivid to somebody else, "which is one of the great delights of art"'.[72] Producing the exhibition and catalogue were stimulating experiences for Hockney, and they developed his interest in reproduction and photography, which he continued to hone and share; indeed, he reproduced the entire text of *Looking at Pictures in a Book* in a later publication, *That's the Way I See It* (1993).

The initial five-part series was regarded by many as a success worth repeating. A common verdict of Hockney's exhibition was that it was 'the last and most effective exhibition … in the highly successful series'.[73] The critic of *The Sunday Times*, for instance, declared that Hockney had 'succeed[ed] in his purpose to get us to look closer, harder, longer … More please; foreign artists choosing next?'[74] Interestingly, on at least two different occasions, the Gallery pondered the value of 'extending the invitation to organisers other than artists', but this new avenue was never pursued because it was quickly realised that the genuinely novel and meaningful elements of the enterprise came from the involvement of influential living artists, talking engagingly about their artistic forebears.[75] William Packer from *The Financial Times* had already made the case in his review of the Hockney exhibition: 'Indeed, we would only wish that more great museums would follow [the Gallery's] example in acknowledging, as it does so gracefully, the contribution the artist can make to its work.'[76]

3 **A 200-Year Dialogue between Artists and the Gallery**

NEW WORKS INSPIRED BY NATIONAL GALLERY PAINTINGS

Half of *The Artist's Eye* artist-curators, including Caro, Freud and Hockney, were called on again to help with one of the National Gallery's two Millennium exhibitions, *Encounters: New Art from Old* (2000), which turned out to be 'hugely innovative and influential'.[77] On this occasion, the Gallery raised the stakes by inviting no fewer than 25 'great artists of our time to converse with the greatest artists of all time'.[78] The chosen artists were commissioned to produce a response to a work in the permanent collection (although no fee was paid, funding was offered towards the costs of the artists' materials). In Freud's case, for instance, he produced two paintings and an etching derived from Chardin's *The Young Schoolmistress* (about 1737), one of the paintings that had featured 13 years earlier in *The Artist's Eye* exhibition he curated, and which he often claimed had 'the most beautiful ear ever painted'.[79]

The contemporary works were displayed throughout the Gallery, the majority away from the source works. For instance, Cy Twombly's *Temeraire* paintings were displayed in the Sunley Room, Anselm Kiefer's work in Room One, while sculptures by Louise Bourgeois and Stephen Cox were installed in the Main Floor galleries, 'with the floor having to be strengthened to support the latter'.[80] In an inspired move, 'Hamilton's *Saensbury* [sic] *Wing* hung nowhere near the Saenredam church interior in the Dutch rooms but rather on the "bridge" to the Sainsbury Wing galleries, so that … you had only to turn your head to see the very architectural space it depicted, with the Cima on actual vista in the same location. Brilliant.'[81] The exception was Howard Hodgkin's version of Seurat's *Bathers*, which was hung at right angles to the original in Room 44. As Mary Hersov, Exhibitions Manager at the time, recalls: 'It became a National Gallery-wide event so the public could explore the building and its collection through different artists' perspectives.'[82]

The exhibition in 2000 was curated by the distinguished Tate curator Richard Morphet, who had just retired as Keeper of Modern Art there, a choice indicative of the National Gallery's ongoing links with Tate at key moments vis-à-vis modern and contemporary art. A hefty, multi-authored publication – the artists were not directly involved as authors – was produced, which contextualised the newly created works within each artist's oeuvre.[83] To ensure a consistency of voice across the discussion of Gallery paintings, Christopher Riopelle, Curator of Nineteenth-Century Painting at the Gallery, was tasked with writing all the introductory biographies concerning National Gallery artists. He

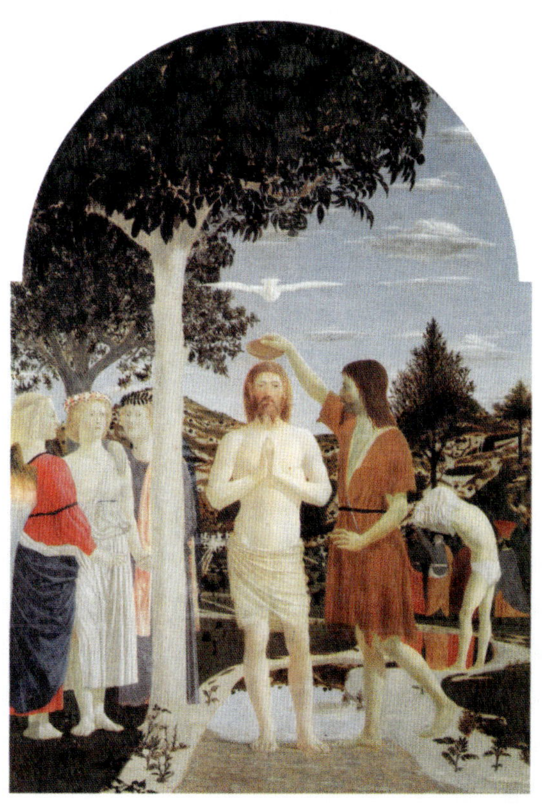

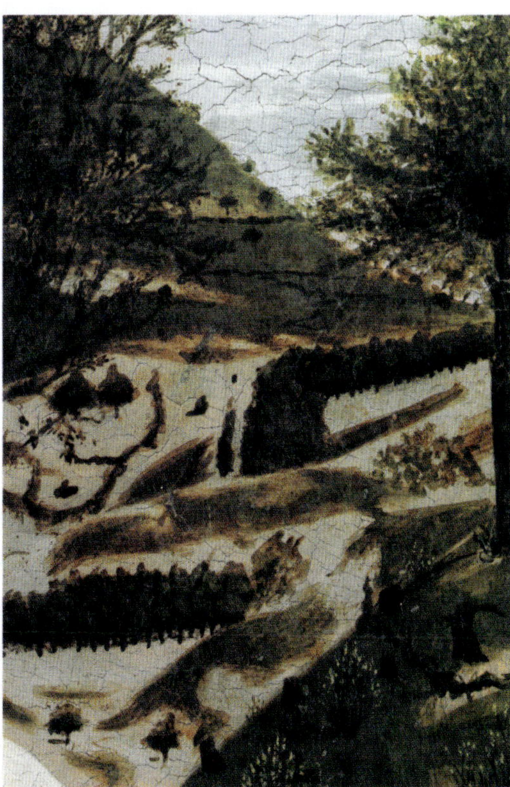

Fig. 43
Two of the eight postcards from Hockney's catalogue *Looking at Pictures in a Book*, which accompanied *The Artist's Eye* exhibition of 1981. The second postcard shows a detail of the landscape background from Piero's *Baptism*. Hockney chose to include details as postcards to encourage a longer look.
The National Gallery, London

Fig. 44 (overleaf)
David Hockney (born 1937)
12 Portraits after Ingres in a Uniform Style, 1999–2000
Pencil, crayon and gouache on 12 sheets of paper using a camera lucida, 56.2 × 38.1 cm each; 112.4 × 228.6 cm overall
Private collection

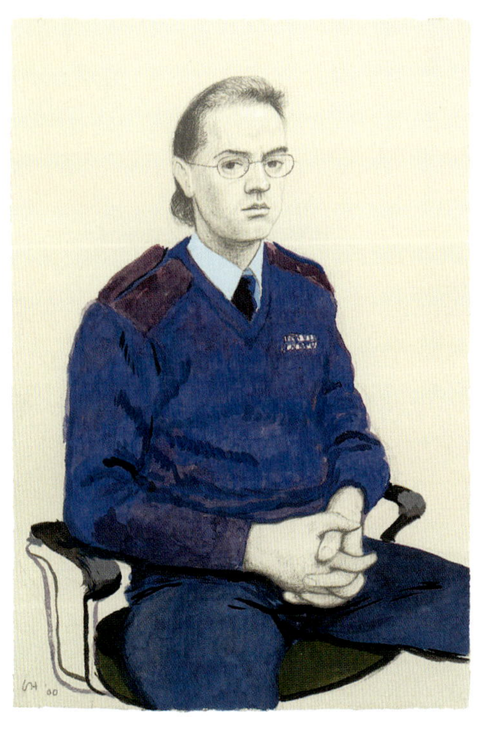
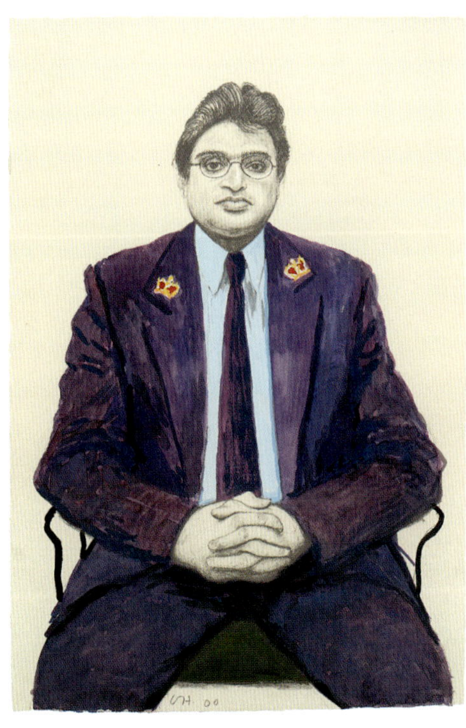
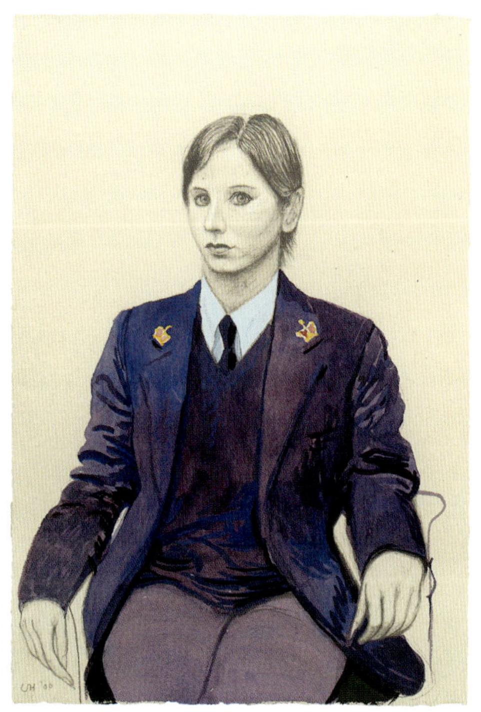
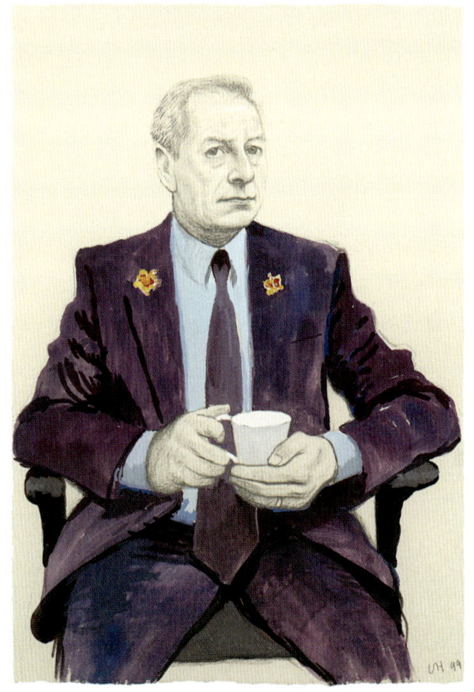
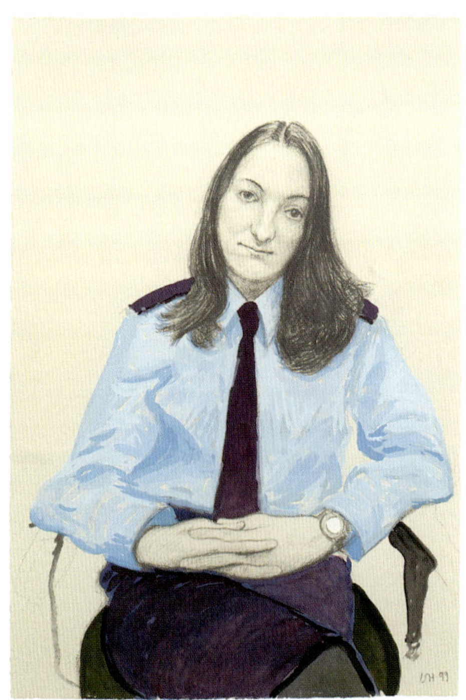
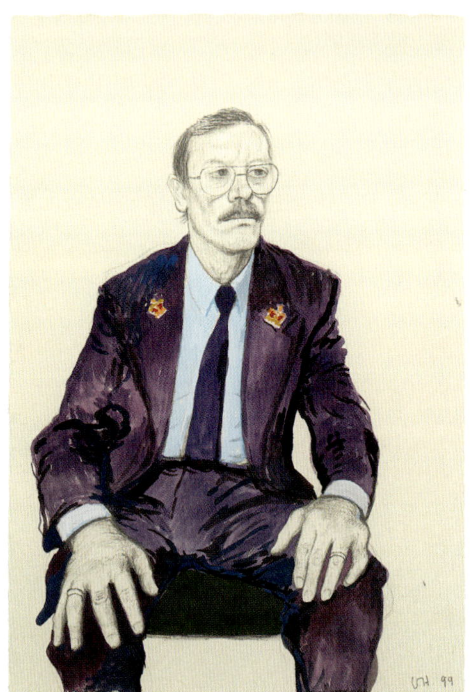

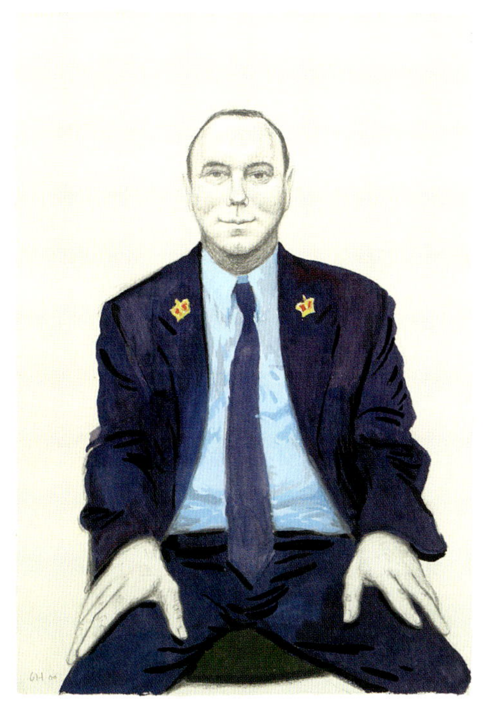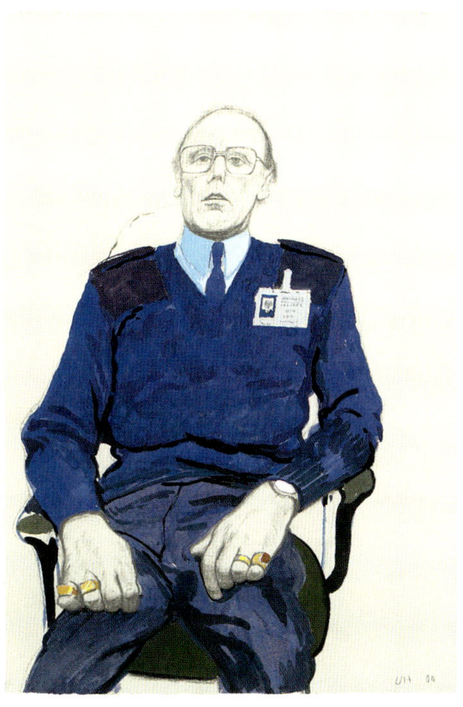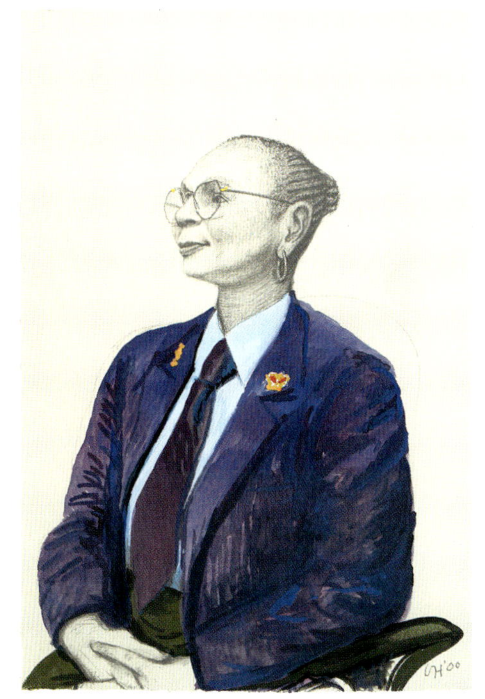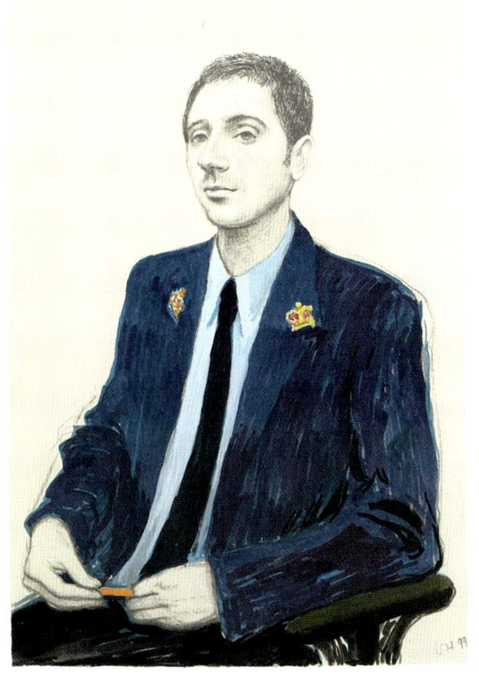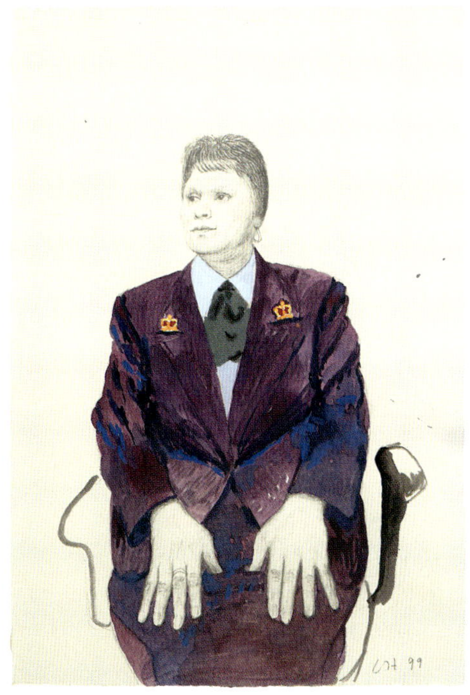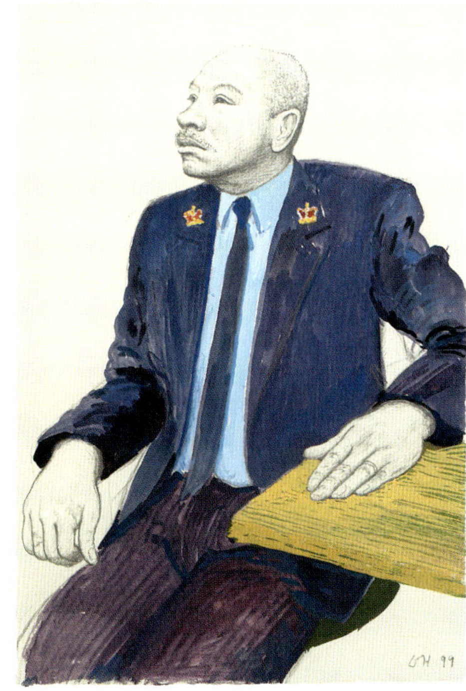

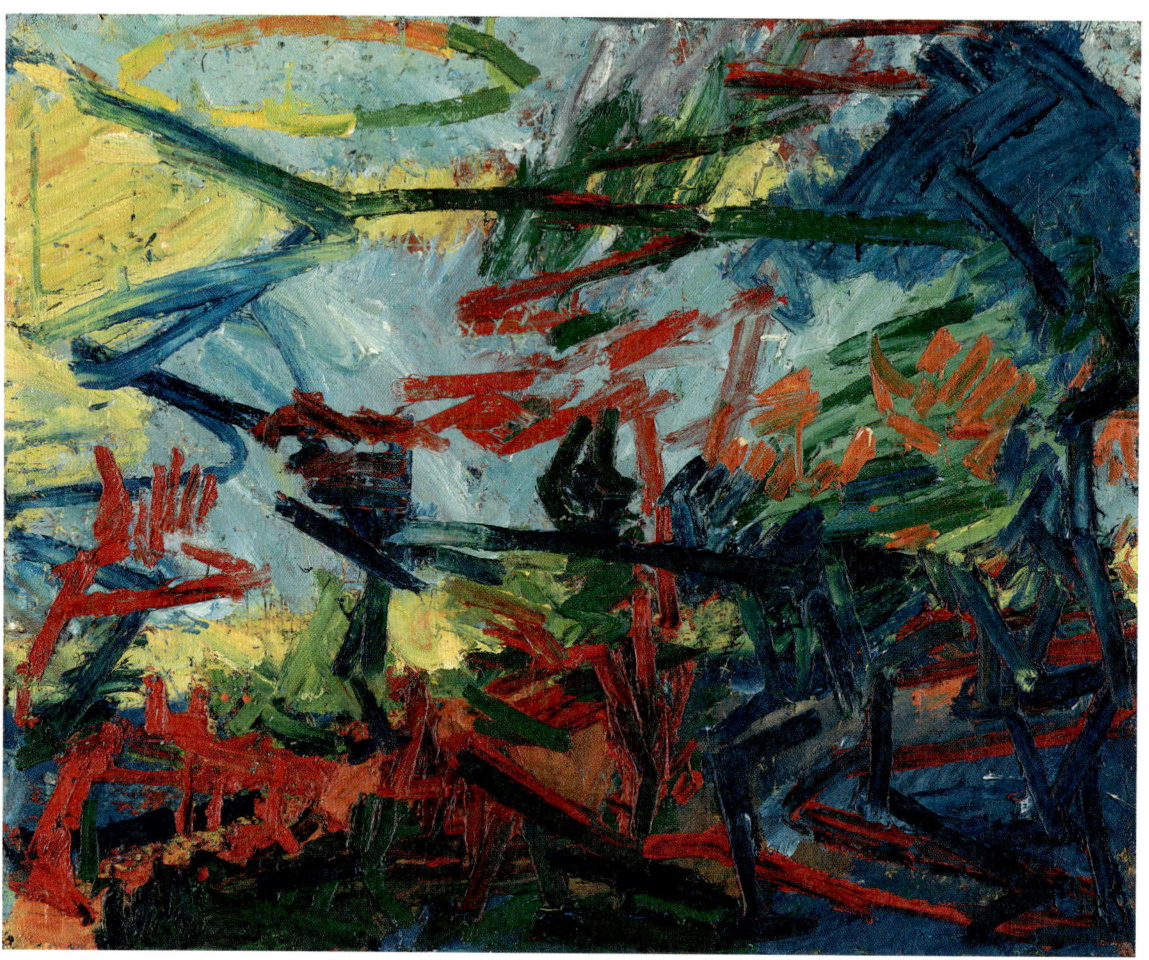

Fig. 45
Frank Auerbach (born 1931)
Bacchus and Ariadne, 1971
Oil on board, 122.3 × 153 cm
Tate, London

recalls: 'I was horrified and terrified, but it was a glorious experience as I got to work so closely not only with Morphet but with many of the artists. (Was any artist ever as witty as Howard Hodgkin?)'[84]

Hockney was one of the invited contributors to *Encounters*, and his intervention was characteristically distinctive. In fact, he adapted the brief and responded to loans he had seen at Trafalgar Square the year before in a temporary exhibition of portraits by Jean-Auguste-Dominique Ingres (1780–1867), whose level of minute detail led him to conclude that Ingres had employed a camera obscura.[85] Hockney's response was a series of 12 portraits of National Gallery room stewards, which he produced using an optical device similar to the one he conjectured Ingres had used (fig. 44).[86] Once again, time spent working on a Gallery initiative propelled Hockney's thinking. In this instance, it helped him to develop his theory that many artists used technical

apparatus, notably lenses and mirrors, to assist their image-making, including van Eyck when he produced *The Arnolfini Portrait*. His thesis would find extended expression – and in so doing, provoke controversy – in his publication *Secret Knowledge: Rediscovering the Lost Techniques of the Old Masters* (2006).[87] For this book, Hockney contacted many experts, including Susan Foister, the Gallery's Curator of Early Netherlandish, German and British Pictures, concerning both *The Arnolfini Portrait* and Hans Holbein the Younger's portraits in the collection, such as *The Ambassadors*.[88] Foister recalls that their 'very pleasant conversation [illustrated] Hockney's interest in our collection', even if their views remained different on certain matters, such as whether Holbein had used a mechanical apparatus to take the portrait drawings in the first place.[89]

In addition to *The Artist's Eye* series and *Encounters*, the Gallery started to mount, after a hiatus of several

3 A 200-Year Dialogue between Artists and the Gallery

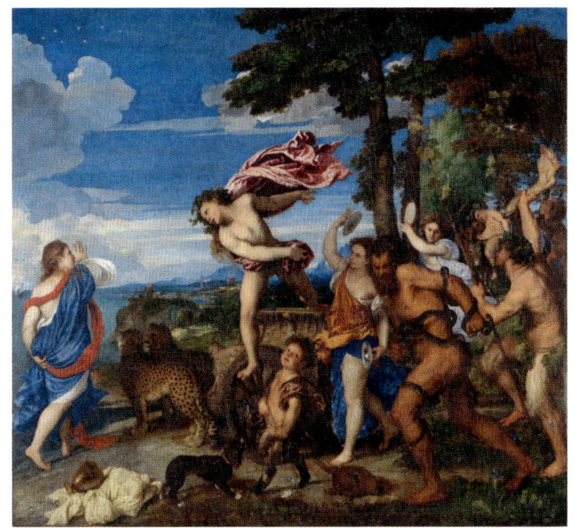

decades, numerous solo displays or exhibitions of the work of living artists, on varying scales (see Appendix 6). The intention was to launch a platform through which 'artists might interpret the collection in other ways – not verbally but through their own practice, in the production of new work'.[90] Although eclectic in subject and style, the underlying rationale of using modern art as a mouthpiece for old, especially works in the permanent collection at Trafalgar Square, has remained constant. The first such exhibition, *Frank Auerbach: Working after the Masters*, took place in 1995 and showcased Auerbach's painted versions of Gallery pictures, including Titian's *Bacchus and Ariadne* (figs 45 and 46), together with a selection from the hundreds of drawings he had made in front of the originals in Trafalgar Square (141 of these were presented to the Gallery in 2000 by the collector and dealer in modern art James Kirkman, who had also supported the mounting of the 1995 exhibition) – a practice that Auerbach had begun in his student years.[91] His debt to the National Gallery's collection was made clear when Auerbach noted: 'I've really drawn here all my life … I find it helpful and entertaining and it just reminds me, after all, that this is the family from which we spring.'[92]

This new angle on temporary art exhibitions at the National Gallery was highlighted by Neil MacGregor in his Director's Foreword to the catalogue for Auerbach's exhibition: 'To honour this part of our tradition, there is always among the Trustees a distinguished artist; and the recent *Artist's Eye* exhibitions have investigated how different artists see the changing links between past and present painting. This exhibition takes a different tack.

Rather than choose his favourites, Frank Auerbach here shows some of his transcriptions from the Collection. Spanning more than thirty years in their execution, they allow us to witness a dialogue between him and some of the greatest pictures in the Gallery.'[93] As MacGregor eloquently expressed it, seeing the Gallery's collection from the point of view of a contemporary artist was a transformative experience: 'We grasp better how the Old Masters achieved their effects and, understanding them more clearly, we are moved by them yet more deeply. Artists reveal unperceived beauties to us in art, just as they do in nature.'[94]

Often artists whose work had featured in earlier National Gallery exhibitions were asked to come back to share their latest work, and frequently it was the friendships developed with National Gallery staff over the years that helped bring certain projects to fruition, *Caro at the National Gallery: Sculpture from Painting* (1998) and *Kitaj: In the Aura of Cezanne and Other Masters* (2001–2) being cases in point. When R.B. Kitaj (1932–2007) was approached in late 1999, he was widowed, living abroad in Los Angeles and physically frail, so he was initially reluctant to participate. However, Kitaj was won over, in large measure due to the efforts of his friend Colin Wiggins, who had overseen the Associate Artist scheme for some years, as well as some of the later exhibitions as a member of the Gallery's Education Department, before being appointed Special Projects Curator between 2011 and 2016. Wiggins recalls: 'within 24 hours he got back in touch and said that he might consider making some new works. And a couple of days later he had started them, triggered by his lifelong passion for Cezanne.'[95] Kitaj even allowed a film to be made, which Wiggins organised over a two-day visit to Los Angeles.[96] In the case of Hamilton, who died in 2011, the Gallery mounted a retrospective in his honour, *Richard Hamilton: The Late Works* (2012–13).

By contrast, one of the artists newly introduced to Gallery visitors through this run of exhibitions was Leon Kossoff (1926–2019), whose exhibition in 2007, called *Drawing from Painting*, likewise showed dozens of his drawings and prints, selected from the 'probably thousands' he had produced over the previous half century. As one critic put it, the exhibits were a powerful 'testimony to a lifetime's engagement with the Gallery's collection'.[97]

Over time, the range of contemporary art exhibitions expanded to encompass new art forms. For instance, in 2005–6 the exhibition *Living in Hell and Other Stories*, which showcased work by

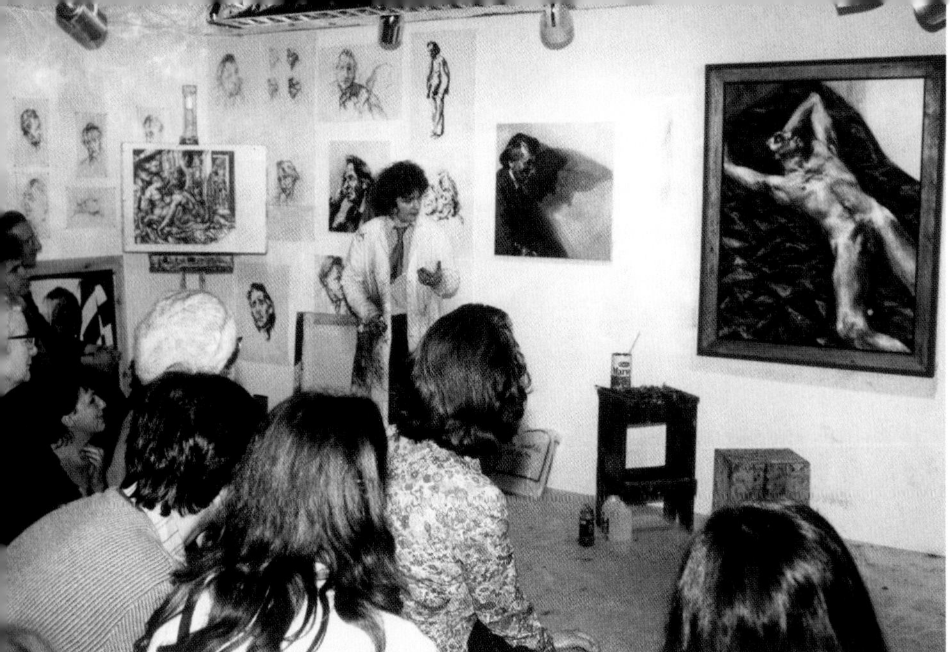

Fig. 47
Photograph showing the first Artist in Residence, Maggi Hambling (born 1945), with visitors at a public teaching session, April 1981.
The National Gallery, London

Tom Hunter (born 1965), broke new ground as the Gallery's first display of photographs based on historic paintings. Since then, the contemporary work on display has included, in addition to painting, drawing, sculpture, print-making and photography, installation art and video art, text-based work, computer-generated imagery and mixed media, dance and musical performances.

Metamorphosis: Titian 2012 was a novel episode for the Gallery, not only because of the diverse art forms it encompassed but also in its ambition to encourage, through 'spectacle and emotion', a new kind of visitor experience (and one that might hold its own amidst other activity for the London 2012 Cultural Olympiad). To celebrate the purchase in 2012 of Titian's *Diana and Callisto* (following that of *Diana and Actaeon*, another of Titian's great mythological paintings, in 2009), the Gallery brought together three artists – Chris Ofili, Conrad Shawcross and Mark Wallinger – with composers, choreographers, dancers, poets and a librettist, to produce an exhibition (including a live peep-show of sorts), three new ballets (extracts were performed in the Gallery) and a book of poetry, all of which responded to ideas of transformation in Titian's work. In the same spirit, the Gallery opened itself to 'alter and challenge conditions for experiencing works of art within the museum'.[98]

Another type of radical artist intervention was *Scratch the Surface* (2007). To mark the bicentenary of the abolition of the slave trade, Yinka Shonibare (born 1962), renowned in the 'world of revisionist museum-commissioned interventions', was invited to respond to two historic works at Trafalgar Square of sitters whose family wealth derived from slavery, including Johann Zoffany's *Mrs Oswald*. Through wit and showmanship, Shonibare raised complicated questions within the heart of the National Gallery about the UK's links with slavery and the Gallery's own connections with and responses to that history.[99]

ARTISTS INHABITING THE NATIONAL GALLERY

Another Gallery initiative that has led to displays of the work of living artists on its walls is its artist residencies. To date, there have been three different iterations. The first, the 'Artist in Residence' initiative, was devised by Alistair Smith, and it ran between 1980 and 1989, with support from the Arts Council (see Appendix 7). Although now a standard feature of many art institutions worldwide, the scheme was innovative for the art world of the day. It was, however, building on pioneering initiatives of the 1960s in which artists had enjoyed 'open brief' placements in industrial, business or governmental settings.[100] Overall, the scheme offered nine lesser-known artists working in Britain a six-month residency; to quote Colin Wiggins, 'it was never the idea to select "great artists of the future"'.[101] Notwithstanding, Maggi Hambling, who was the first National Gallery Artist in Residence, went on to have an international career, and two subsequent postholders, Jock McFadyen (born 1950) and Hughie O'Donoghue (born 1953), are now senior Royal Academicians.

The intention was to offer younger aspiring artists the chance not only to interact with the collection and show some newly created works in a self-contained display at the end of their residency, but also 'to enable the public to visit an artist in the studio and talk with them about their work and the National Gallery collection' (fig. 47).[102] Alistair Smith has explained the thinking behind his bridge-building exercise as follows: 'It had occurred to me that the visiting public would relish the opportunity to be able to talk to an artist face-to-face. It was something that I needed to do myself. I was very aware that here I was, having been serious about art for years now, and part of an institution that was dedicated to it, yet my training had been purely art-historical. I had had no more than minimal contact with practising artists. And most of my colleagues were the same. Other art forms had developed opportunities for creative individuals (musicians, writers, philosophers) to spend periods in residence in various locations. Why not art galleries? … I think that the scheme had a truly educational effect on the National Gallery staff, including curators and those that were at that time described as warders [room stewards].'[103]

3 A 200-Year Dialogue between Artists and the Gallery

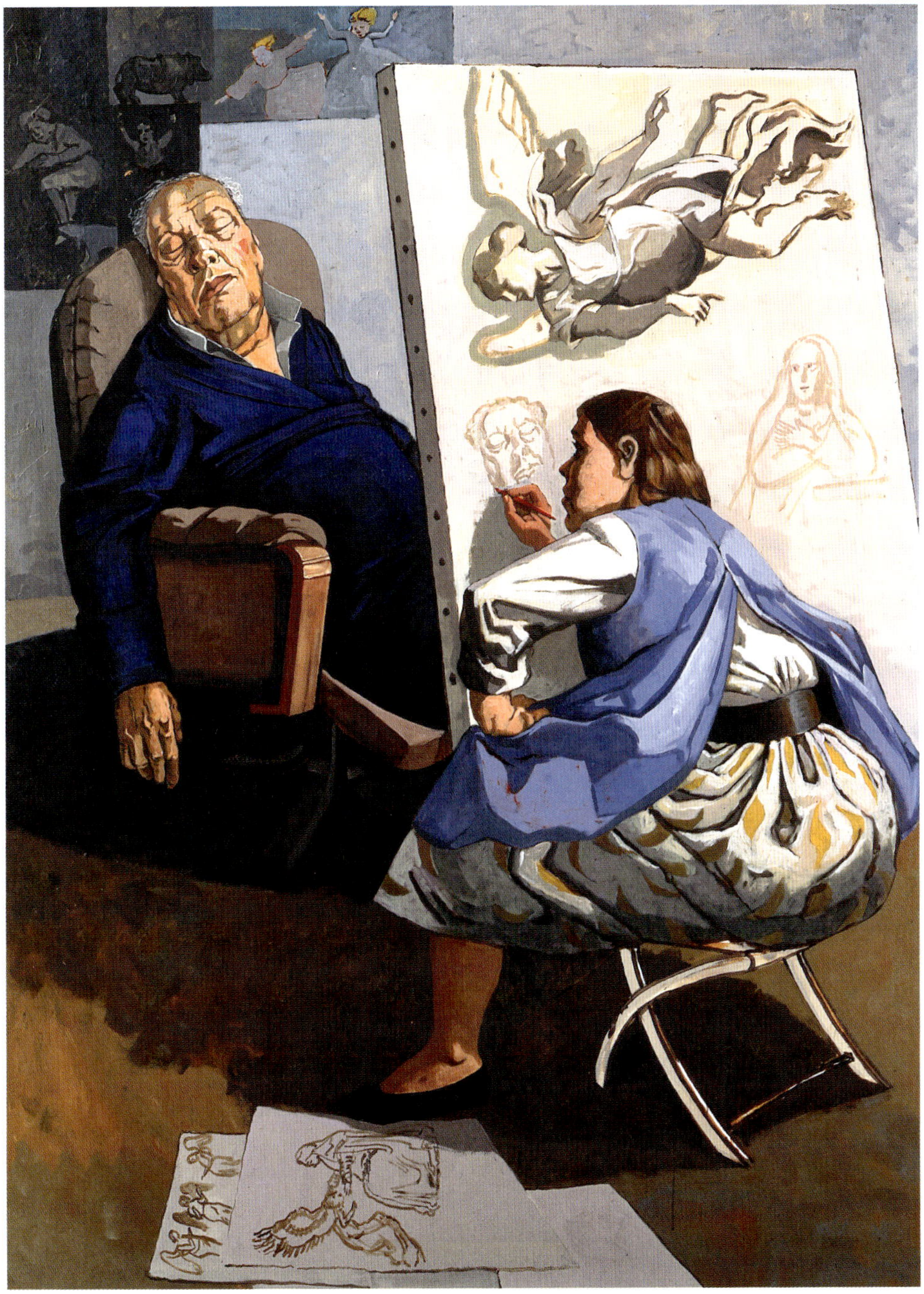

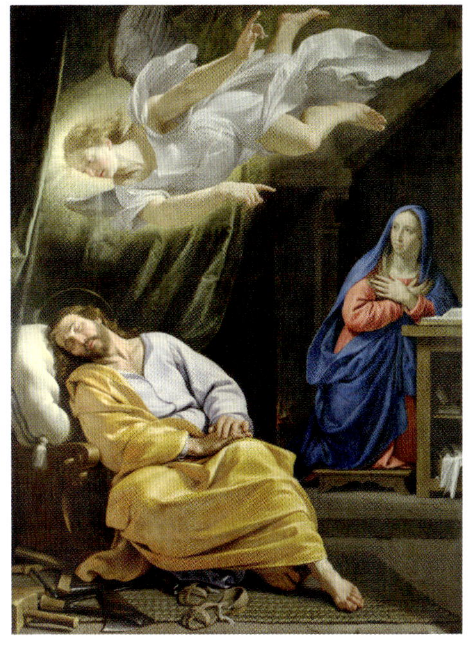

Fig. 48
Paula Rego (1935–2022)
Joseph's Dream, 1990
Acrylic on paper on canvas,
183 × 122 cm
Private collection

Fig. 49
Philippe de Champaigne
(1602–1674)
The Dream of Saint Joseph,
1642–3
Oil on canvas, 209.5 × 155.8 cm
The National Gallery, London

In 1990, Smith initiated a variant on the theme: the creation of the position of Associate Artist (see Appendix 8). The length of the residency was increased (they were initially 18 months long but ended up lasting two or three years),[104] the aim of this new series being 'to get some serious work made by an artist of already proven achievement'.[105] The Gallery invited the artists and in this iteration the field was broadened to include British-based sculptors as well as painters. An important adjustment was made during Nicholas Penny's directorship (2008–15), when an advisory committee was set up for the first time to assist with the selection process, its inaugural members being Richard Calvocoressi and Andrea Rose.

To emphasise their links with the Gallery's historic holdings, the Associate Artists were asked to create work directly related to paintings in the collection. The resulting pieces were displayed in focused monographic shows in the Bernard and Mary Sunley Room, an exhibition space opened in September 1984. As in *The Artist's Eye* exhibitions, these shows juxtaposed historic Gallery pictures with a chosen artist's work, a crucial difference being that there was now a far greater emphasis on the new.[106] The results could be thought-provoking, even subversive, none more so than the work produced by the first postholder, Paula Rego. Having turned down Smith's invitation to participate, she changed her mind and accepted it as a challenge, noting 'the National Gallery is a masculine collection and, as a woman, I think I absolutely will be able to find things there for me'.[107] Rego created paintings that she hoped would transform her deep-seated unease with the dominant Western art-historical canon by setting herself, a female painter, squarely within a lineage of male painters. For instance, in *Joseph's Dream* of 1990, partly inspired by Philippe de Champaigne's image of the same subject, Rego inserted a young woman painter sketching an older sleeping male figure, thereby subverting traditional gendered hierarchies between subject and painter (figs 48 and 49).[108] In Rego's case, some of her interactions took place in Trafalgar Square. However, she was required to give master classes to art students in several different regional centres, and the work she had created during her placement at the Gallery was exhibited in Plymouth, Middlesbrough, Manchester and Barnsley, before being displayed back at the Gallery.

The third and most recent iteration of the residency format, initiated in 2019, launched a new version of the Artist in Residence scheme, in collaboration with the Contemporary Art Society (CAS) (see Appendix 9). It is part of the Gallery's new Modern & Contemporary programme, announced on 5 May 2018 by Gabriele Finaldi (Director, 2015–present) and aligns, more generally, with the Gallery's increased promotion of national partnerships. Candidates are selected by an expert jury, looking to foster the work of mid-career artists of any nationality. Several elements of the residency are again innovative, not least the practical matter of offering the postholder, in addition to a London Living Wage, an allowance for caring responsibilities, such as childcare. A second adjustment to the standard curatorial model of artistic dialogue and institutional intervention is letting the artist decide where in the building they wish to show their work. Another novelty of the scheme is that a public legacy is created for the project since the artist conceives a work with a UK partner museum outside London in mind, which CAS pays for. In the case of Rosalind Nashashibi, the inaugural artist (2019–20), her display, *An Overflow of Passion and Sentiment*, took place in Room 30, where four of her paintings were hung alongside works she had engaged with by seventeenth-century Spanish masters, including Velázquez.[109] Nashashibi's artist film titled *Denim Sky* (2022), which was produced during her residency, was acquired by CAS for the partner museum on the project, in this instance, the Pier Arts Centre, Orkney.

Something that artists involved in Gallery residencies often comment on is the insightful conversations they have enjoyed with Gallery staff. Nashashibi, for one, noted that 'having tours with curators from different parts of the collection … was massively influential', and that as a result she 'started to feel a lot more comfortable in the museum. To actually feel settled in front of a painting and talking and learning [was] an amazing privilege!'[110]

Another flagship project of the new Modern & Contemporary programme is its Contemporary Fellowship scheme with Art Fund, which invites an internationally renowned artist of any nationality to develop a display with an associated publication, a project that is distinct from the Artist in Residence scheme because the Fellows are not allocated any specific studio space within the Gallery (see Appendix 10). Aligning with the Gallery's increased emphasis on national partnerships, the scheme collaborates with a UK-based partner outside London, inviting the chosen artist during a two-year fellowship to respond to the nation's collection of paintings (over and beyond the collection at Trafalgar Square), especially that of the partnering museum. The inaugural Contemporary Fellow (2020–22) was Nalini Malani (born 1946), an artist who has consistently experimented with various media over her five-decade career to emphasise the voices of women across different traditions to reflect on the world today. The inaugural partner was the Holburne Museum, Bath. Malani focused on details of 25 paintings across the two collections in London and Bath, which she used as a basis for a series of animations, created using an iPad, which challenged the dominance of the male gaze and colonial histories signified by the pictures' subjects. The results were projected large-scale across all four walls of the Sunley Room to create an immersive experience, which brought the historic works to life. A separate work of art was made by Malani for the Holburne.

Quite deliberately there has never been an active acquisitions policy associated with the National Gallery's work with living artists. Indeed, as noted, the current policy is instead to find appropriate homes for the works created during the Residencies and Fellowships at Trafalgar Square among UK museums and art galleries outside London. Notwithstanding, in the past, some works by living artists have entered (mainly through gifts from Artists in Residence) the Gallery's Contextual Collection (see Appendix 7). It includes, for instance, Hambling's *Portrait of Archie MacDonald*, which depicts one of the Gallery's room stewards, whom she got to know during her residency, and which she gifted at the end of her tenure (fig. 50).[111] There is also a portfolio of 10 prints by Artists in Residence that was produced in 1991, in an edition of 35, a project made possible through a donation to the Education Department and which allowed the remaining sets to be sold for the benefit of 'new schemes involving artists and art students'.[112] As one journalist pointed out, the initiative was a way for the National Gallery to demonstrate that 'it is no longer just a temple for the "elevated arts" but a living institution involved with living art and living artists'.[113]

It is fitting that the Gallery's Bicentenary celebrations for 2024–5 will include several elements that continue its long-established tradition of bringing artists, pictures and publics into a fruitful three-way dialogue.

Turner Prize-winner Jeremy Deller (born 1966) has been commissioned to create a nationwide performance work. A peer-to-peer collaboration titled 'The Triumph of Art', the project brings together different art-partner organisations and their communities

from each of the four nations of the UK: The Playhouse, a performing-arts venue in Derry/Londonderry; Duncan of Jordanstone College of Art & Design at the University of Dundee; Mostyn Gallery in Llandudno; and the Box, Plymouth. Each of these representatives of the fertile art ecology in Britain will launch an interconnected series of smaller local projects with the artist, before coming together for a combined spectacular finale on Trafalgar Square.

Inside the National Gallery, the artistic creativity of David Hockney is celebrated and shared through a focus display in Room 46. It marks a significant and abiding relationship between a living painter and the National Gallery, which, while necessarily unique (especially in its longevity), also stands in for countless others.

Looking ahead to the Gallery's third century, the institution will surely wish to continue to engage with living artists in creative ways to forge new and inspiring connections between them, the collection and visitors.

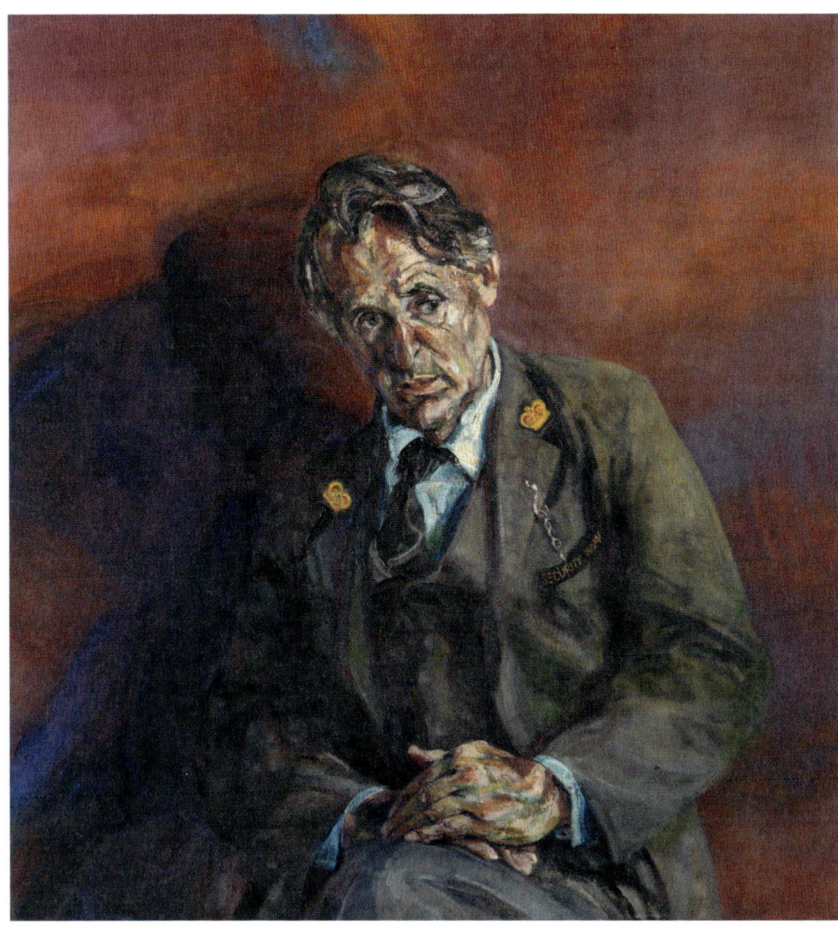

Fig. 50
Maggi Hambling (born 1945)
Portrait of Archie MacDonald,
1980–1
Oil on canvas, 105 × 100 cm
(framed)
The National Gallery, London

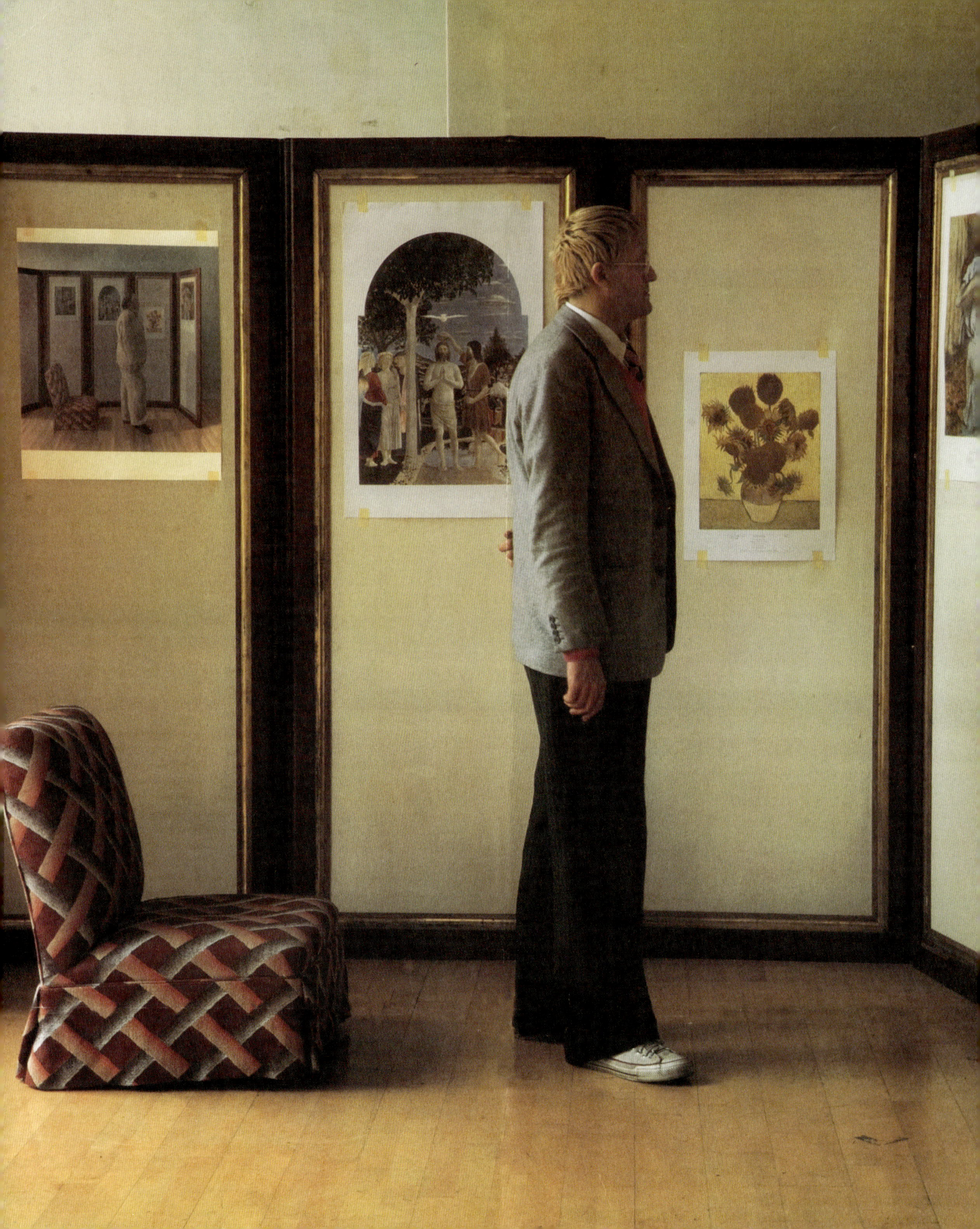

CHAPTER 4

LOOKING (BACK) AT PICTURES IN A ROOM: *THE ARTIST'S EYE* EXHIBITIONS

Susanna Avery-Quash

I'm interested in ways of looking, because people will respond. Everybody does look. It's just a question of how hard. DAVID HOCKNEY [1]

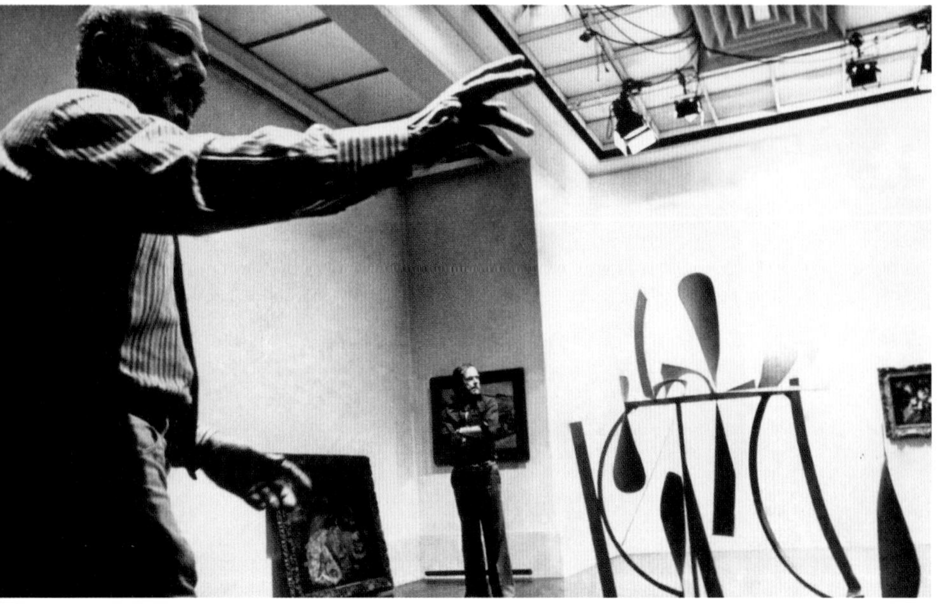

Between 1977 and 1990 the National Gallery hosted a series of 10 innovative exhibitions called *The Artist's Eye*, in which one artist on each occasion was invited to choose, display and discuss paintings from the permanent collection however they wished, alongside one or two of their own (already created) works (see Appendix 5). Living artists had played an important role at the National Gallery from its very beginnings. As discussed in Chapter 3, its early directors had been practising artists; some living artists, notably J.M.W. Turner, had planned their legacy with the Gallery in mind; and others, including Boris Anrep, had received commissions to decorate parts of the Gallery. But no artist had hitherto ever been invited to select, hang and interpret works from the collection for presentation to the public – in other words, to curate an exhibition.[2] The intention behind the initiative was to draw fresh attention to the National Gallery and to get the public excited again about its historical art collection, not least by understanding its ongoing relevance for the modern day. It was thought that an effective way of making this argument would be to marshal great living artists as advocates who could 'demonstrate how many contemporary artists [were] in touch with the past'.[3] The other aim of the series was, more generally, for visitors to access alternative ways of looking at art meaningfully. This chapter offers an overview for the first time of *The Artist's Eye* exhibition series by charting its origin and evolution, and by exploring some of the main issues arising as well as its perceived achievements and legacies. The documentation that illuminates this fascinating story is largely taken from the Gallery's rich archive, including previously unpublished and little-known correspondence between artists and National Gallery staff.[4] These primary sources have been supplemented by new conversations between the author and several Gallery staff, both past and present, who were heavily involved with the conception and execution of *The Artist's Eye* exhibition series.

ORIGINS AND AIMS

The Artist's Eye series, launched in 1977, was the brainchild of a trio of forward-thinking individuals, who enjoyed pushing boundaries in their fields. Arguably, the most important figure behind the initiative was Alistair Smith,[5] Deputy Keeper and Head of Education at the National Gallery, who had recently become the first curator to be given a brief for public outreach and 'whose own belief in the need to bridge the gap between ancient and modern art has been a significant stimulus'.[6] Then there was the dynamic Michael Levey, Director of the National Gallery since 1973, who had been introducing new ways to focus attention on the permanent collection.[7] Finally, there was Anthony Caro, a charismatic and vocal leading British abstract sculptor.

Smith has recalled that his intention behind the new initiative was not so much to promote contemporary art per se, but rather 'to attract new visitors to the Gallery' through offering 'a new way of understanding the National Gallery collection and contemporary art simultaneously'.[8] Of the evolution of his idea, he records: 'I had weekly meetings with the Director and had gradually taken on the habit of writing to him short papers on things I was responsible for, including Education … and now Exhibitions. I now wrote a paper outlining "The Artist's Eye" series and proposing Richard Hamilton (with whom I was friendly) as the first artist to be invited … the result was that Michael came back with the Trustees' approval of the first exhibition and with the Chairman [John Hale]'s suggestion that Anthony Caro be Artist's Eye Number One.'[9]

Levey's account of the origins of the initiative emphasises Caro's role in the project's development. He explained to Caro: 'We have now submitted to the Trustees a proposal whereby there should, at least occasionally, be small exhibitions here from among our own pictures selected by leading artists. I am glad to say that the Board warmly welcomed this proposal … I think you know how enthusiastic Alistair Smith and I were about this whole concept which stems very much from you … To establish a visible link with living artists is something we are eager to do, and I cannot think of a better way to initiate the project than by having the benefit and pleasure of your involvement.'[10] An initial idea of Caro's had been to bring in 'one or two modern painters to show the continuity of a painterly approach', but it was not taken up, partly due to restrictions on the space available in a one-room show and partly to keep the focus tightly centred on the work and ideas of one artist-curator at a time.[11]

Over the decade of its existence other staff became involved, including Levey's successor as Director, Neil MacGregor, and Colin Wiggins from the Education Department. Sponsorship for the series was sought to help with increasing costs, particularly those associated with transporting the artists' own works to Trafalgar Square, sometimes from abroad. Apart from the first, the subsequent eight exhibitions were all sponsored by Shell UK Limited.[12] The last one was sponsored by Marlborough Fine Art (London) Ltd, who were happy to step in, not least because they represented the chosen artist, Victor Pasmore.[13]

As for the choice of artists, Smith did not have to wait long to get his 'favourite' painter involved: Hamilton was invited to be *The Artist's Eye* Number Two.[14] The first series featured Anthony Caro (1977; fig. 51), Richard Hamilton (1978, referred to in the press release as the 'Big Daddy of Pop'), Howard Hodgkin (1979) and R.B. Kitaj (1980), and culminated in 1981 with David Hockney (he had originally been approached to curate *The Artist's Eye* of 1980). The second series comprised exhibitions organised by Francis Bacon (1985), Patrick Caulfield (1986), Lucian Freud (1987), Bridget Riley (1989) and Victor Pasmore (1990, considered the father of the abstract revolution in the UK). All the artists were British or, like Kitaj, long-time UK residents, a decision based on the fact that appointing anyone non-British 'would have brought added complications and expense'.[15] More striking still is the fact that there was only one woman chosen – Bridget Riley (fig. 52), who was, in any case, known and trusted, having just finished serving as a National Gallery Trustee from 1981 to 1988. What would seem to most today to be an extraordinary imbalance was at the time 'not given the slightest consideration'.[16]

Some of the artists had existing connections at Trafalgar Square. For one thing, many had studied the collection in their youth. As the press release for the Pasmore show noted: 'These exhibitions re-introduced the artists to the Collection where, very often, they had made transcriptions and copies in their student years.'[17] Some had served as Gallery Trustees, notably Hodgkin and Riley, which meant they were already profoundly knowledgeable about the collection. In certain cases, artists had the advantage of being part of cosy patronage circles; for instance, Pasmore had enjoyed a decades-long friendship with former Gallery Director Kenneth Clark, a fact which the latter recorded in his autobiography.[18] Some of the artists would continue to have connections with the Gallery after the end of their *Artist's Eye* exhibition. For instance, as noted, several were invited to participate in the Gallery's Millennium exhibition, *Encounters*, and Riley's monumental wall painting, *Messengers*, was unveiled in the Annenberg Court in 2019 (see Chapter 3).

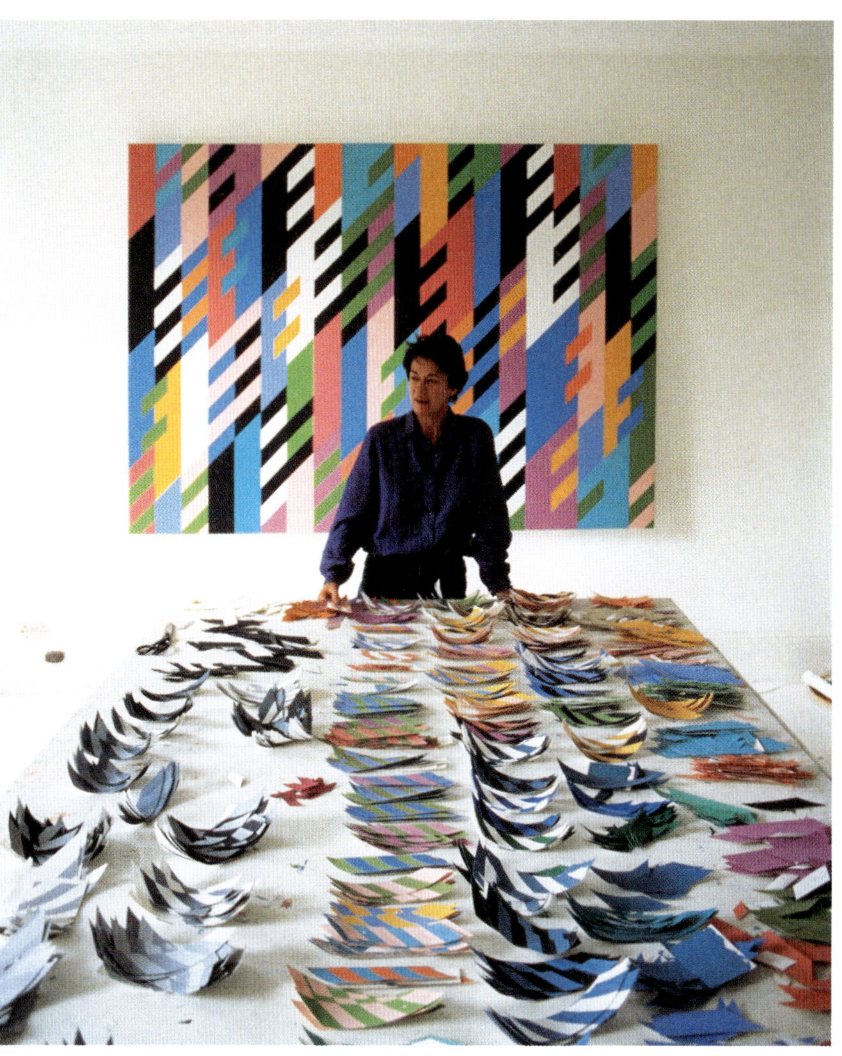

Fig. 52
Photograph showing Bridget Riley standing in front of her recently completed *Gaillard I*, a large abstract work composed of multi-coloured rectangles, which she included in her *Artist's Eye* exhibition, 1988.
The National Gallery, London

When MacGregor spoke about *The Artist's Eye* series, he noted with excitement that the artists' new pairings and clusterings 'disrupted' the type of display that prevailed elsewhere at Trafalgar Square at the time.[19] Certainly, through each *Artist's Eye* exhibition, the usual, traditional hang at Trafalgar Square was transformed in one room for a period of time. Worth recalling is just how static the arrangement of pictures was – something that was quite intentional. There were few temporary exhibitions of historical art anywhere, and often those that were mounted were monographic in nature, and showed the pictures essentially by school or date. As a result, loaning pictures from the Gallery's collection was a less intense activity than it would become. Consequently, the public got used to seeing pictures in the same places, surrounded by the same 'neighbours'.[20] *The Artist's Eye* series was a way of removing pictures from their usual homes. As MacGregor put it: 'With new neighbours, the pictures speak with new voices.'[21] It was hoped that placing works from different countries and of different dates in thought-provoking new juxtapositions would encourage viewers to look at Gallery pictures with fresh eyes.

The novelty of thinking about the collection in ways other than a traditional art historical hang (at least for a limited period of time) appealed across the board, not least to art critics. Richard Cork, for one, in relation to Caro's inaugural *Artist's Eye* exhibition of 1977, commented on the 'exhilaration' of finding 'one room at the National Gallery where the normal rigid arrangement of pictures had been abandoned, and where, for a couple of months, paintings as far apart in period and intention as Bellini's *Madonna of the Meadow* [1500–5] and Monet's *The Beach at Trouville* [1870] coexisted in the same arena simply because a fellow artist liked them'.[22] Another leading art critic, William Feaver, noted in 1989: 'I think the great charm and delight of these exhibitions – and they've been pretty consistently interesting through the series – has been the ability for the artist to overstep art history. Instead of being arranged by schools, movements, nominations and classifications, suddenly you can just wander round if you're the artist involved … and say I'll have that, that, that and that, put them together across the centuries, across the styles, across the schools, and see what the consequence is. To my mind, the most interesting ones so far have been by Francis Bacon and by Howard Hodgkin.'[23] Marina Vaizey concurred in her praise for the initiative in a later radio discussion of the

second series in 1990, when she noted: 'I think what Pasmore has done, which is thrilling, is he's chosen an amazing knockout group of paintings, and put them together in a room in a way that they have never been put together before, across the centuries …'[24]

These novel juxtapositions were important in encouraging fresh looking. In Cork's words: 'Any change of setting helps us to look again at familiar pictures which we may be in danger of taking for granted.'[25] Consequently, he was not overly concerned that within *The Artist's Eye* series contextualisation was not for once the prime concern: 'It may mix pictures together with blithe disregard for their historical origin and purpose. But this temporary mobility is preferable to the idea of a museum as a static pantheon, fostering the illusion that the unchanged contents of each room have been there ever since they were painted.'[26]

PRACTICAL OUTCOMES

The tangible outputs of the inaugural *Artist's Eye* exhibition – a new temporary display of works from the Gallery's permanent collection with one or two examples of the artist-curator's own work, accompanied by a catalogue – remained generally in play for the duration of the series. Minimal guidance was given to the invited artists concerning their choice of pictures. Levey gave the following broad outlines to Caro: 'we see it very much in terms which I might call biographical, in which the artist looks at the pictures here in terms of those that not only interest him but may have, however obscurely, played their part in the development of his own art at some time. This seems to give a coherent but not too rigid framework; it would allow for something which in principle we are very attracted by, that is a work of art or two by the artist himself being shown with such pictures as he selects from here.'[27]

The opportunity to select which pictures they liked was compared by Patrick Caulfield (1936–2005) to a child being let loose in a sweet shop![28] There were very few pictures regarded as off limits – about a dozen pictures that the Gallery preferred not to move (due to size or fragility) and any picture already committed as a loan elsewhere. Being desirous to showcase Gallery pictures and equally keen to keep expenses to a minimum, the Gallery did not offer to bring in loans, although occasionally they did so at the request of the artist. Pasmore, for instance, remained determined to include James Abbott McNeill Whistler's *Harmony in Grey and Green: Miss Cicely Alexander*, which was at the Tate Gallery. The situation led MacGregor to reflect:

'One of the problems about this series – and one of its great strengths – is the freedom which must be left to the artist to make and present his choice as he thinks best.'[29] Interestingly, the negotiations to borrow Vincent van Gogh's *Van Gogh's Chair* from the Tate Gallery in 1980 for Kitaj's *Artist's Eye* resulted in the picture being transferred permanently to the National Gallery (see fig. 16).[30]

To show the pictures at their best, the Gallery was happy to consider cleaning or re-framing any chosen work for an *Artist's Eye* exhibition.[31] For instance, for the 1979 show curated by Hodgkin, the 'somewhat neglected fragment of General Miramon' was cleaned before it was displayed together, for the first time, with the Gallery's other fragments from Manet's *Execution of Maximilian*. Hodgkin made this inspired decision – one the Gallery has retained – because he 'knew that Degas had attached them all to one canvas when he owned them. So in order to honour both Manet and Degas, he requested that the fragments be reassembled' (fig. 53).[32]

Indeed, artists were at liberty to display their selection of pictures as they pleased. Occasionally, the examples of their own work were shown among National Gallery paintings. This was the case, for instance, with Caro's massive metal and painted abstract sculpture *Orangerie*, which was shown at one end of the main exhibiting space (see fig. 51), and Hockney's *Looking at Pictures on a Screen*, the work that became the centrepiece around which the rest of his display revolved (see fig. 42), although a tapestry by Archie Brennan after Hockney's painting *Play within a Play* was displayed alone in the foyer outside.[33] More often, the modern work was displayed on its own.[34] In a single instance, the artist – Bacon – offered none of his own works for display. The Gallery tried to cover over the glaring deficit by noting that a simultaneous retrospective of the artist's work was taking place at the Tate Gallery, which gave the audience the opportunity to view Bacon's own work at the Tate and his curated work at the National Gallery.[35] A visitor survey after the event noted: 'The fact that none of Bacon's own work was featured (and this was something that almost everyone appreciated) may well have been a disappointment for many visitors, half of whom said they would like to have had the opportunity to see some of it.'[36]

Although the small Board Room (the space occupied today by the Portico Entrance shop) was selected as the venue for the inaugural *Artist's Eye*

exhibition, as well as by Kitaj and Hockney for their shows, two took place in the Special Exhibitions Room in the North Galleries (then known as the 'New Extension'; now Room 18), while the second series was hosted entirely in the new Sunley Room. Some of the resulting arrangements were particularly novel, which encouraged visitors to think more about display choices

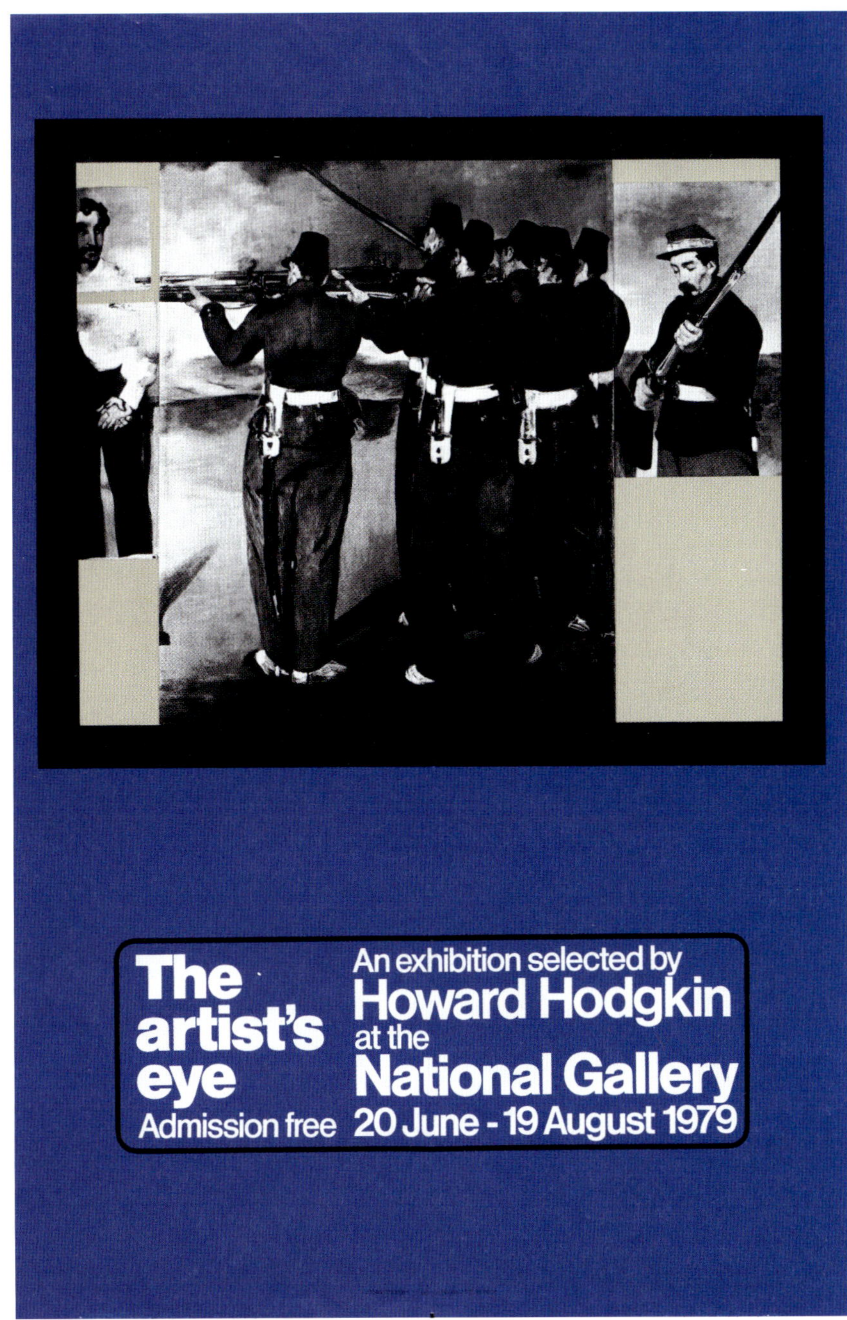

Fig. 53
Poster designed by Howard Hodgkin for his *Artist's Eye* exhibition, 1979.
Paper, 76 × 50.5 cm
The National Gallery, London

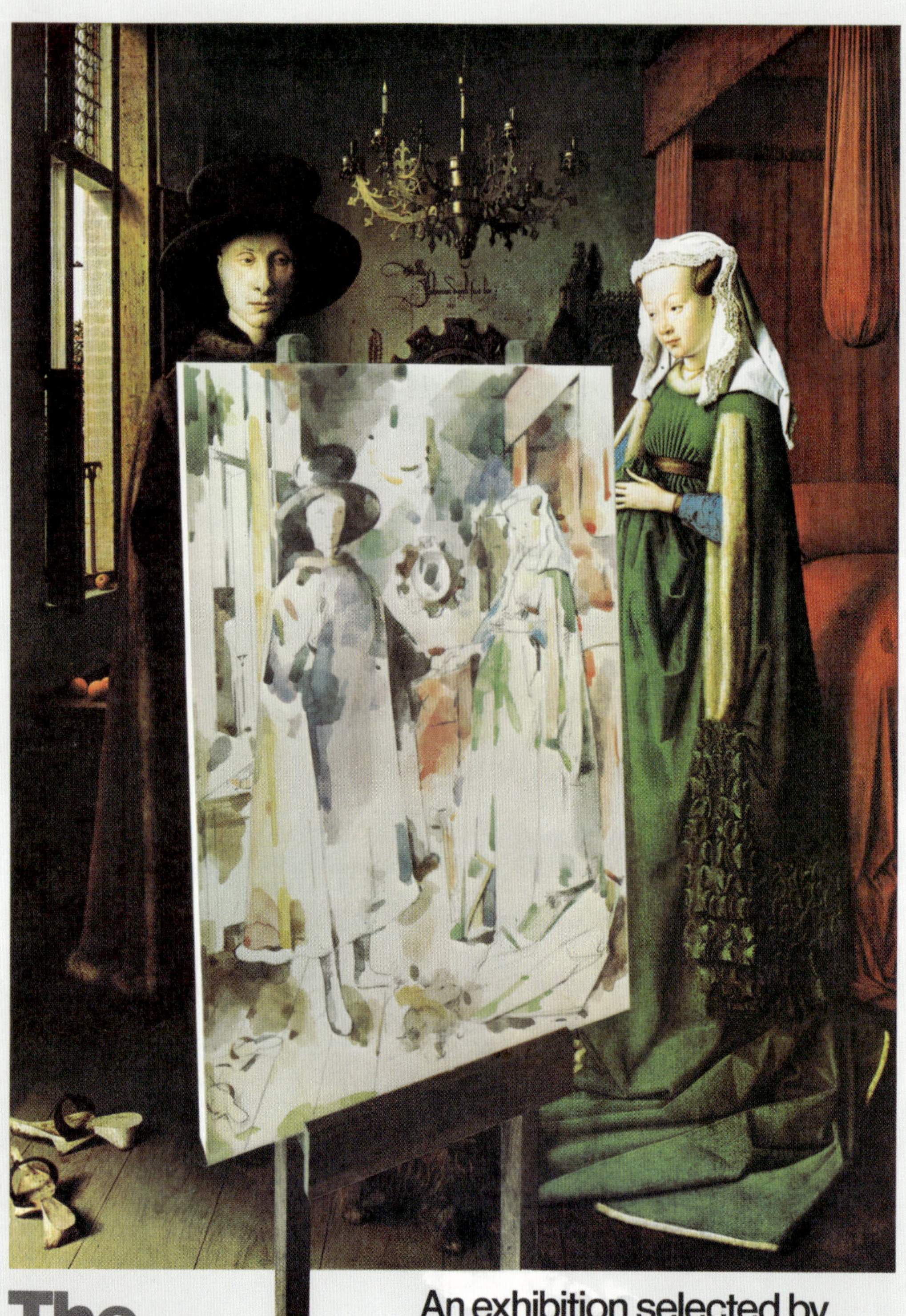
The
artist's
eye
Admission free
An exhibition selected by
Richard Hamilton
at the
National Gallery
5 July-31 August 1978

Fig. 54
Poster designed by Richard
Hamilton for his *Artist's Eye*
exhibition, 1978.
Paper, 76 × 50.5 cm
The National Gallery, London

Fig. 55
Poster designed by David
Hockney for his *Artist's Eye*
exhibition, 1981.
Paper, 76 × 50.5 cm
The National Gallery, London

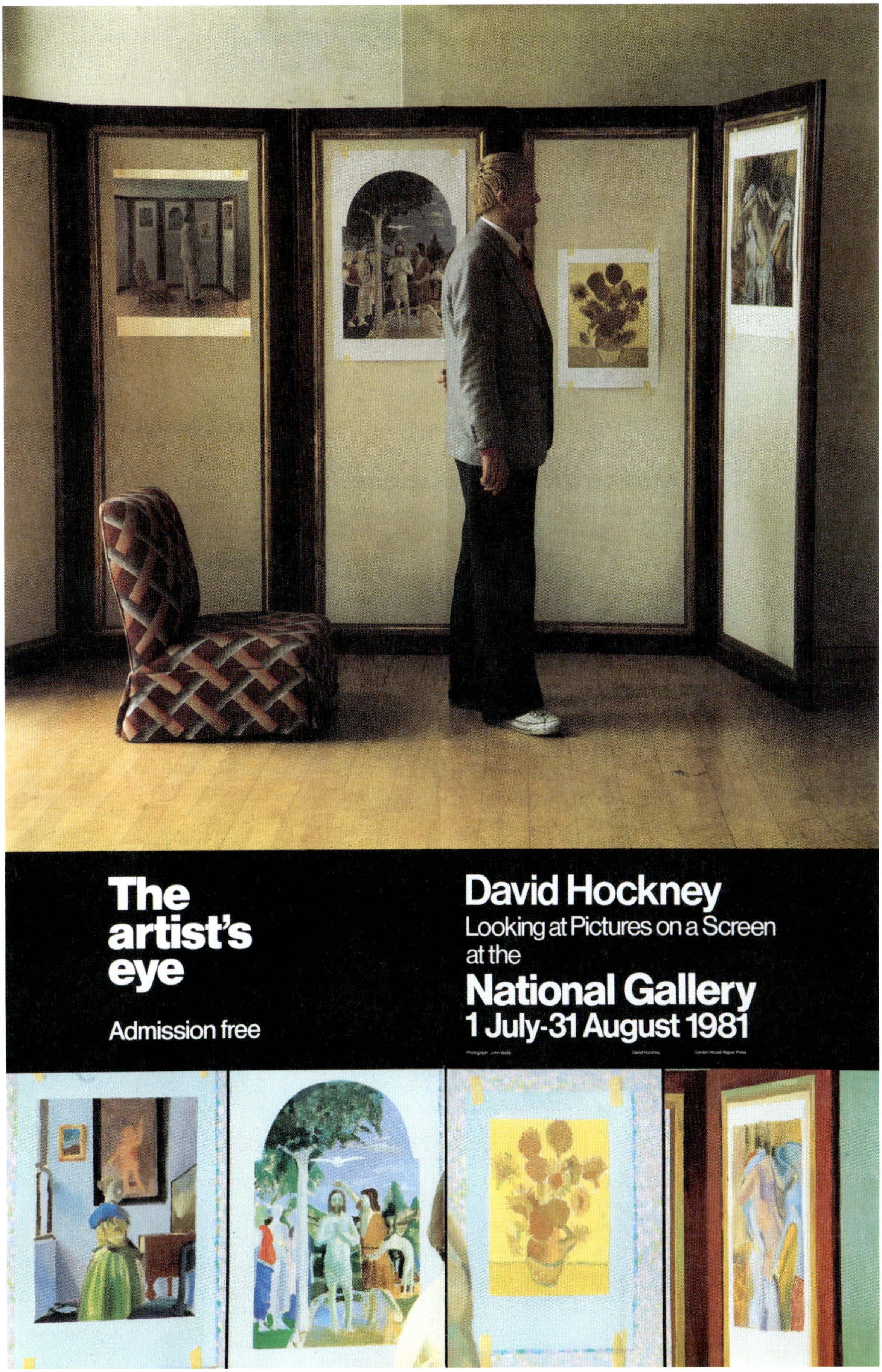

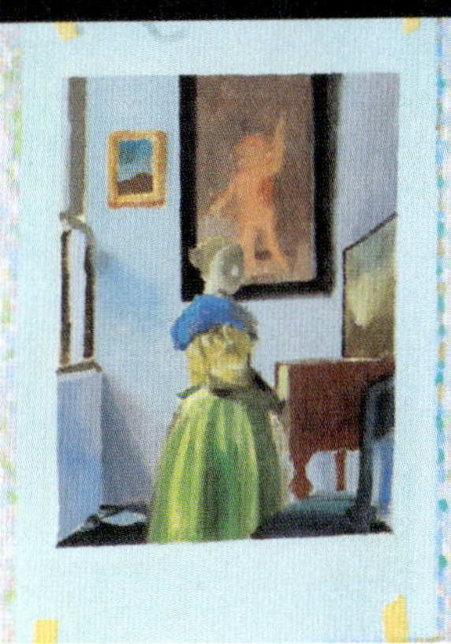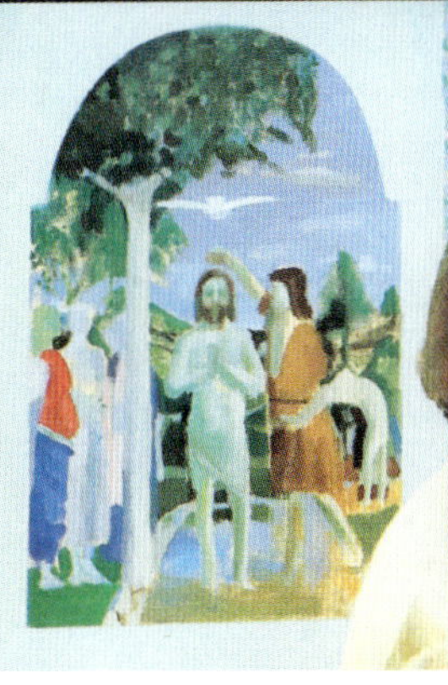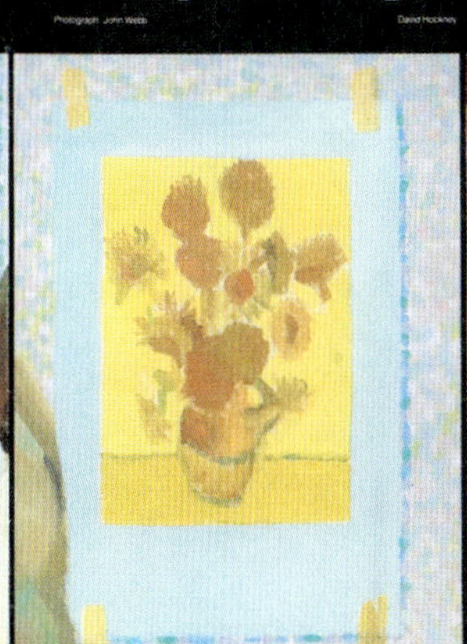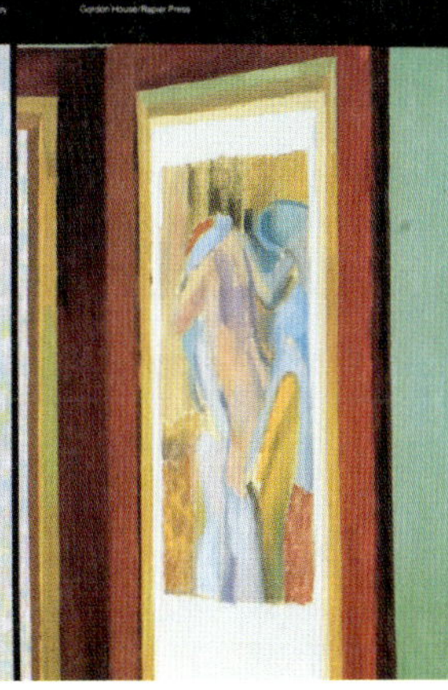

The
artist's
eye

Admission free

David Hockney
Looking at Pictures on a Screen
at the
National Gallery
1 July-31 August 1981

at the Gallery. Kitaj, for example, crammed his 34 selected Gallery works into one small room, admitting that he was following the example of Claude Monet, who liked 'living with his pictures in three stacked tiers'.[37] Artists could also act as their own designers and request additions in terms of 'screens, lights or other aids to display' or, if they did not wish to be so actively involved, they could ask that this element be undertaken by either a designer at the Department of the Environment or a commercial designer.[38] Pasmore played an active role in relation to choosing the wall colours for his *Artist's Eye*, writing: 'Many thanks for the colour samples. I'm thinking now of the possibility of painting each wall a different colour to suit the particular pictures allotted to it. For instance, pale bluish grey for Seurat and [Piero della] Francesca, dark green for Ingres and Leonardo, dark brown for Constable, Rembrandt and Ruysdael, etc.'[39]

Likewise, to help promote and explain *The Artist's Eye* series, the artist-curators were given the option of being involved in the designing of its graphics, poster and leaflet. As Smith told Hamilton: 'We do have people that we use regularly, but you may prefer others, or may prefer to design these yourself.'[40] Hamilton responded to this open brief by creating a special exhibition poster that included his own watercolour copy after van Eyck's *Arnolfini Portrait* overlaid on a photograph of the original. Hamilton's copy is seen in progress, set up on the easel, with his colour tests visible in the margins (fig. 54). The poster was reproduced as the cover of the catalogue, even though van Eyck's painting was not ultimately included in the exhibition. The couple pose for the portrait as if for a twentieth-century wedding photographer. Likewise, Hockney put much effort into designing a special poster (fig. 55), signed copies of which were put on sale.[41]

A fundamental part of the artist's contribution was the production of texts to elucidate their choice of Gallery pictures and of their own work(s) of art and any relationship between them. This first-person narrative was very rare at the time and challenged the usual dominance of the institutional voice. The participating artists were encouraged to write labels by their Gallery contacts, who reassured them 'that the public greatly benefits from such insights'.[42] The inaugural exhibition was accompanied by a pamphlet containing an interview with Caro, although the subsequent exhibitions all had proper catalogues, where the artist could 'explain [their] selection, as far as that is possible, and include comments on particular paintings'.[43] As Smith informed Pasmore: 'In the past, the public has been particularly interested in this text, which, of course, is normally very different from the usual art historically based exhibition catalogue[s] which are produced here.'[44]

Certain of the artists took a great deal of effort over their exhibition catalogues, including David Hockney, as discussed in Chapter 3, of whose catalogue Smith recalled, 'I was rather surprised when Hockney wrote such a lengthy and committed text, but then he is always thinking, and talking, so that translated onto the page quite readily.'[45] To Riley, whose *Artist's Eye* followed Freud's, Smith explained: 'Neil [MacGregor] is very concerned that a fairly lengthy text be supplied for the catalogue, either written by yourself, or in the form of an interview, or written by an author you respect.'[46] Reassurance was received from Riley, who was determined to create a 'lucid and accessible' text that would 'examine the use of colour in the paintings and take up the theme of the "Artist's Eye" on two levels: how these artists in the past looked at the work of other artists, and how modern artists have continued this process'.[47] She chose as her interlocuter Robert Kudielka, Professor of Aesthetics at Berlin University. She also suggested working with Roger Huggert to design the catalogue, given that they had worked together previously on her Arts Council book *Working with Colour*, so she knew he was 'sensitive to her requirements and careful about budgets'.[48]

Further explanatory material was produced in the form of films.[49] For instance, Caro's project was shown in the *Aquarius* series on London Weekend Television, where the sculptor discussed great paintings of the past and their relevance to him. Occasionally, external films were hired in, such as an Arts Council film that was used to explain more about Hamilton as an artist, but more often films were made in-house by the Gallery's newly established Audio-Visual Department. The public responded well to these films, doubtless because, as Marina Vaizey pointed out when commenting on this aspect of Riley's *Artist's Eye*, 'people love videos, they love the television … Bridget Riley actually gave almost a lecture, a wonderful lecture about colour and composition in terms of what she was choosing.'[50] Some of the exhibitions also had an in-person lecture series, such as that titled 'Reinterpretations of the Past', which accompanied Pasmore's *Artist's Eye* in 1990.

However, certain artists, namely Bacon and Freud, were averse to any form of words being used, wishing the pictures to speak directly to the viewers without any

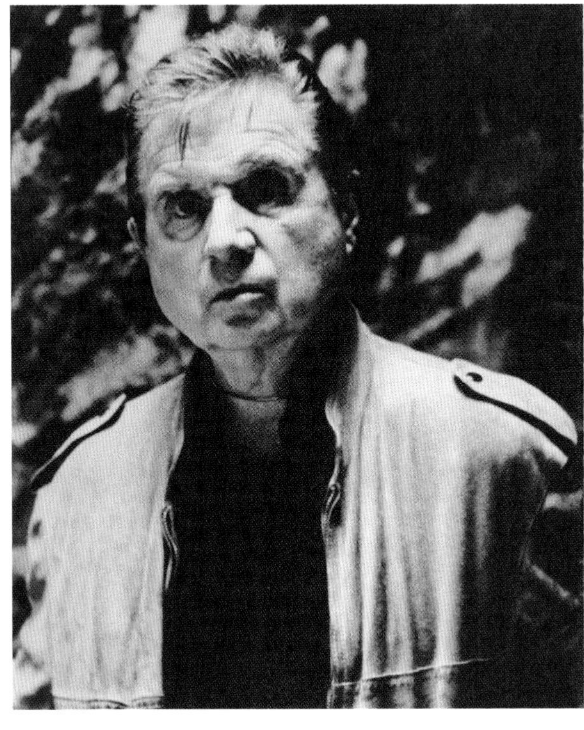

mediation. Bacon declared: 'I am not writing a foreword
– I have often tried to talk about painting but writing or
talking about it is only an approximation as painting is
its own language and is not translatable into words' (fig.
56).[51] The Gallery did its best to encourage words out
of him, but in the end it accepted the famous painter's
principled decision to remain silent. In a press release
of 23 August 1985, the Gallery explained: '[Bacon]
adheres resolutely to the philosophy that any painting
worth its salt should speak for itself. Consequently his
selection of National Gallery paintings, too, is self-
explanatory – a statement without words. This is perhaps
a measure of his singlemindedness and his reverence for
the Old Masters.'[52]

The Gallery came up against the same issue two
years later with Freud. Once again, its urging of Freud
to help 'improve the general communication level of
the exhibition' was not heeded.[53] As Freud explained
to Gallery staff, 'Art education is primarily a process of
educating the Eye … An explanatory text would both
question this instinct and the power of paintings to
speak for themselves … I hope the pictures will do a
bit of explaining by the way they are hung.'[54] Even the
Director and Chair of Trustees failed to persuade him 'to
allow the odd sentence of comment to be added after
the photographs in the catalogue of the exhibition'.[55]

Perhaps in the spirit of communication, however,
Freud did complete a drawing after one of his choices,
Turner's *Sun rising through Vapour*, which appeared
on the front of the catalogue, where it could readily
be compared to a detail from Turner's original painting
reproduced inside.

It was the lack of exhibition labels and extrinsic
commentary about the paintings in Freud's *Artist's
Eye* exhibition of 1987 that led to a particularly lengthy
exchange with one disgruntled member of the public,
who ended up writing to the Chair of Trustees to express
his hope 'that any individual, however eminent, shall not
in future be permitted to have an artist's name and title
taken off his paintings in order to allow his own view of
things to be guessed at'.[56] MacGregor was happy to
defend Freud's radical decision: 'These were deliberate
preferences, and I think it is obvious what advantages he
hoped would flow from unlabelled pictures: the whole
exercise is, after all, a visual one. We are providing hand
lists for visitors who want to know who painted what and
explaining to them more fully that the absence of labels
is not an oversight but part of the way in which Lucian
Freud is presenting his choice of pictures. And some
visitors applaud.'[57] In a similar vein, Smith defended
Freud's decision to the exhibition's sponsor, noting that
'it does seem that the public are very much interested in

Fig. 56
Opening spread from Francis
Bacon's catalogue for his *Artist's
Eye* exhibition, 1985.
The National Gallery, London

the exhibition and are relishing the opportunity to look at the paintings afresh, without the normal labels'.[58]

CHOICE OF PICTURES AND RANGE OF APPROACHES: ARTISTS AS CONNOISSEURS, ART HISTORIANS, CURATORS

The Artist's Eye series had originally been conceived as artists choosing their 'favourite' works that 'played their part in the development of [their] own art at some time'.[59] However, most artists preferred to make choices that spoke to areas of special interest to them. In Freud's exhibition, he chose seven paintings by Rembrandt (or attributed to Rembrandt), which was the largest number of works by any single artist not only in his exhibition,[60] but within the series as a whole. *The Baptism of Christ* by Piero della Francesca was clearly a firm favourite, being chosen by both Hockney and Pasmore while Caro had originally considered featuring it.[61] Interestingly, on analysing the artists' choices, there are certain historical painters and even particular works by those painters that were repeatedly selected, Seurat's *Bathers* and Ingres's *Madame Moitessier* being among the favourites, while Rembrandt and Cezanne were probably the painters' painters par excellence.[62]

One artist whose *Artist's Eye* included fewer acknowledged masterpieces was Caulfield, who selected half of his display from works in the so-called 'Lower Floor Galleries',[63] a decision that amused fellow artist Pasmore, who, looking back on it, referred to it as a 'selection centred on works relegated to the basement'.[64] By contrast, Pasmore's extensive show, which took place four years later, in 1990, was mainstream, so much so that one critic commented with evident disappointment that his choice 'was of course very familiar' and that 'there were no surprises' in it.[65]

Surprises were what *The Artist's Eye* series was supposed to be all about. Indeed, Levey spoke of the 'double pleasure' of the series: 'encountering often very famous and familiar pictures in a fresh context and learning more perhaps about art generally through the eye of the artist who has chosen and exhibited them in this personal way'.[66] The artists themselves were eager to choose pictures and display them in such a way as to make people stop and stare – even if in practice they did not always succeed. Caro set the tone when he noted in draft answers produced for the pamphlet accompanying his *Artist's Eye*: 'What I think we tend to do in England is … to actually anesthetize people in the face of the paintings! People are only too ready to take the sting out of art.

What I think this show could perhaps do is to make people look again and entirely.'[67]

Reviewing the series as a whole, it is possible to see several different patterns emerging in terms of the artists' approaches. Some, most obviously Bacon and Freud, might be said to have acted as artist-connoisseurs, predominantly interested in selecting, hanging and presenting the paintings on aesthetic lines, a rationale that they seem to have regarded as self-explanatory. Freud, for instance, chose to hang his selection of pictures close together, without labels and with as little artificial light as possible (fig. 57).

In other cases, artists involved in the series acted more like traditional art historians, offering their own particular lens through which to view and make sense of the tradition of Western European painting. In the case of Pasmore and Riley, they presented their shows in chronological order and produced lengthy theses to argue how artists learned certain things from each other and built on a particular tradition. Pasmore saw the National Gallery's collection in terms of a constant revolution of artistic ideas, keen to demonstrate that the radicalism of abstract art was only the logical next step of artistic innovation that had been equally revolutionary in its own day. MacGregor commented on the personal nature of that thesis in his Director's Foreword to the catalogue: 'This is a personal interpretation of the European tradition and also very much the view of an insider, of someone who played an active role in that "modern revolution" to which Pasmore refers in his introduction, working alongside and exchanging ideas with, among others, Picasso, Moore, Hepworth and Nicholson.'[68] Some of the critics did not agree with Pasmore's approach, nor share his viewpoint. Marina Vaizey, for one, noted: 'in a funny kind of way [Pasmore] is doing a kind of potted art history … He's kind of slotting it into pigeon holes to show a progressive evolution – development – of art, which I happen not to believe in …'[69]

Riley had originally hoped to have a larger exhibition devoted to her topic, but MacGregor persuaded her to utilise the opportunity afforded by an *Artist's Eye* exhibition to test out her grand theory within a smaller pilot project. Consequently, she used her exhibition space (fig. 58) and – even more so – her accompanying catalogue to make a case for how the artists under discussion had each used colour 'as an element of construction … Titian, Veronese, El Greco, Rubens, Poussin and Cezanne … These artists do not exactly form a tradition, but they connect with each other in many ways … All of them however have one thing in common: they were interested in what it means to "build" a painting in plastic terms.'[70] Riley offered little in the way of comment on the figurative content of the pictures she chose, something that certain critics, including Gillian Tindall, wished she had addressed at least in passing.[71]

Yet another grouping may be discerned in which certain artists – Hamilton, Hodgkin and Hockney – acted as curators employing the exhibition itself as an artistic form, when they introduced carefully chosen props into their exhibition spaces to reinforce the arguments they were seeking to make. As Hamilton put it, he introduced 'props in [his] staging, as a device to stimulate response to the main performers [the paintings]'.[72] He made the exhibition space of his *Artist's Eye*, the second in the series in 1978, white through employing a muslin ceiling and white board walls.[73] Into this space, as noted in Chapter 3, he introduced objects from domestic everyday life, including chairs, an easel, a running TV and an ironing board, to highlight 'the vulnerable status of easel pictures in late 20th-century society',[74] which had witnessed a proliferation of mass-produced items that cost less and took less time to appreciate than unique and complex paintings (fig. 59).[75] As Alistair Smith has noted, the props and their placing in the ensemble were chosen with great care. Intended to be sat upon, the chairs nonetheless were 'famous masterpieces of design (by Charles Eames and Mies van der Rohe)' and they 'joined the masterpieces on the wall in a setting recalling a fabulous super-super millionaire's sitting room [while] a witty comparison with Van Gogh's humble farmhouse chair was made through the inclusion in the exhibition of a reproduction of *Van Gogh's Chair*'.[76]

In a different vein, Hodgkin, in the third *Artist's Eye* exhibition in 1979, raised subtle questions about display practices at the National Gallery by showing some of his chosen pictures in ways more akin to how they were probably hung by previous owners – the ways that, as a Gallery Trustee, he had always been keen to try out. Hodgkin explained: 'I have long wanted to look up at the Tiepolo ceiling; to see the fragments of Manet's *Execution of the Emperor Maximilian* reassembled; to be able to look at Velazquez' mysterious picture of *Philip IV hunting Wild Boar* without frame or glass; to see Delacroix's *Baron Schwiter* standing as nearly as possible on the ground; to see what Renoir's dancing girls looked like behind a row of potted plants',[77] the latter idea, for instance, carried out to evoke the dining room of former owner Maurice Gangnat's Paris apartment (fig. 60).

Fig. 57
Photograph showing Lucian Freud's *Artist's Eye* exhibition in the Sunley Room, 1987. The National Gallery, London

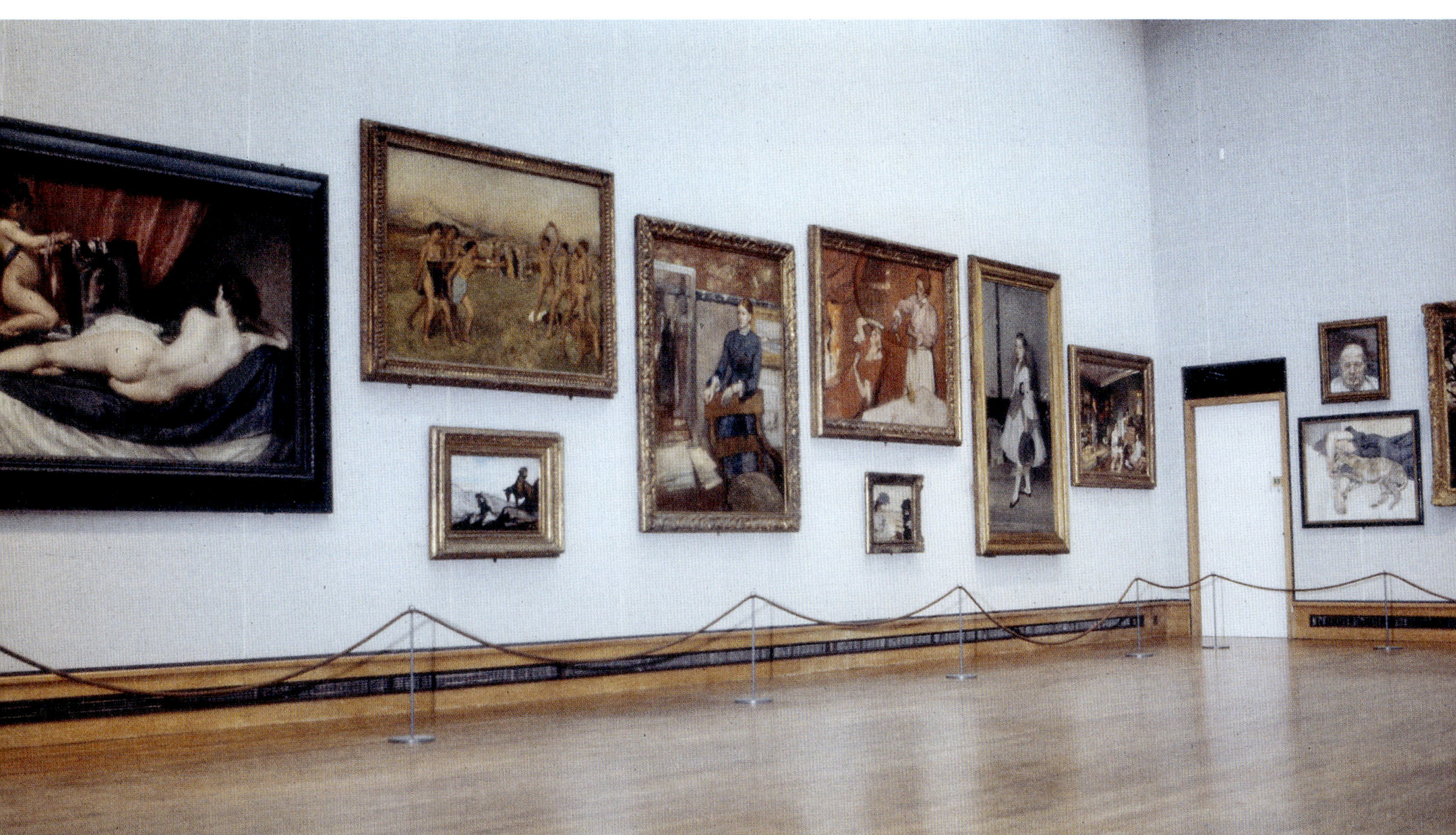

As for Hockney's *Artist's Eye* of 1981, as pointed out in Chapter 3, he brought in the very same objects he had depicted in *Looking at Pictures on a Screen*, including the screen that had once been in his studio (for models to undress or dress behind). This meant that he could recreate the painting physically in the Gallery space, humorously reflecting on the mimesis of art and allowing visitors to participate in the same joyful act of looking at art that he had captured his friend Henry Geldzahler engaged with in the original painting.

LEITMOTIFS OF *THE ARTIST'S EYE* SERIES: CONTINUITY OF ART OVER TIME AND THE VALUE OF SLOW LOOKING

Through its artist advocates and their 'disruptive' hangs in *The Artist's Eye* exhibitions, two particular messages were continually relayed by the Gallery to its visitors, namely the continuity between the art of the past and present and the pure and life-enhancing joy that spending proper time with art could bring the viewer. Both elements were seen as interconnected in subtle ways, this interplay conveyed by Levey when announcing the first *Artist's Eye* exhibition in 1977: 'The chief [aim] is a continuity in the visual arts simply because they are visual: primarily objects made to be looked at, for pleasure.'[78]

The notion of continuity was repeated throughout the rest of the series, perhaps most strongly in Levey's preface to the catalogue accompanying the second exhibition, organised by Hamilton: 'The National Gallery welcomes particularly the link which these exhibitions proclaim between art of the past and the artist of the present. They are a reminder in their quiet way that Rembrandt, for example, was once living and "modern" in relation to, say, Raphael. And perhaps we too easily forget that a century ago (before the establishment of the Tate Gallery) living painters' work was part of the National Gallery Collection, along with work by the established old masters. So loudly has the 20th century trumpeted its "break" with the past in painting, and yet we find distinguished living painters – and other visual artists – are far from indifferent to the achievements of their fellow-creators in previous centuries.'[79]

The Gallery was particularly keen to underscore continuities between the work of Pasmore and its permanent collection, because the artist had 'gone abstract'. In its press release, Pasmore's selection of pictures was noted as addressing 'itself as has his life, to the relationship between figurative painting and abstraction. He has selected paintings by Piero della Francesca and Seurat, Rembrandt and Douanier [Henri] Rousseau, among others. He is to include two major

Fig. 58
Photograph showing Bridget Riley's *Artist's Eye* exhibition in the Sunley Room, 1989.
The National Gallery, London

Fig. 59
Photograph showing Richard Hamilton's *Artist's Eye* exhibition in the Special Exhibition Room, 1978.
The National Gallery, London

Fig. 60
Photograph showing props used by Howard Hodgkin in *The Artist's Eye* exhibition in the Special Exhibition Room, 1979.
The National Gallery, London

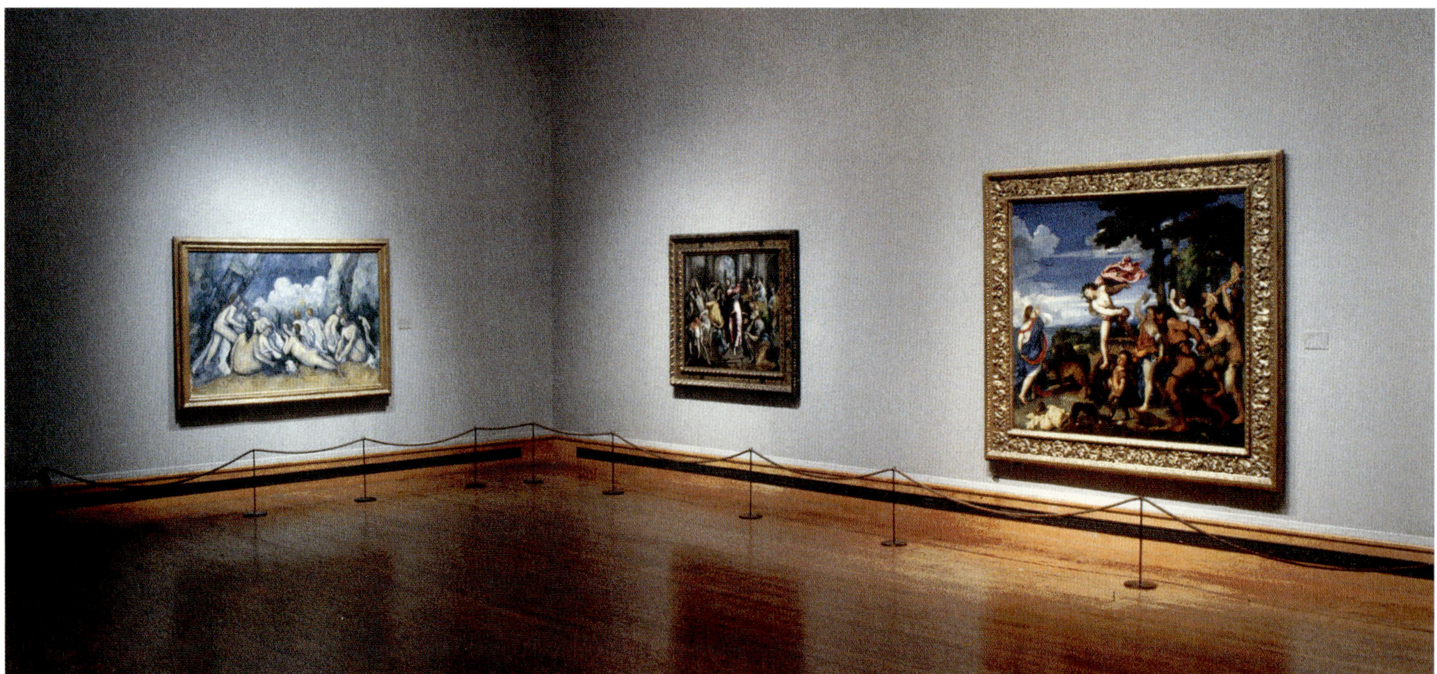

4 Looking (Back) at Pictures in a Room

works of his own in the exhibition, one of which records his admiration for Picasso, whom, he tells us, he was detailed to meet off the train from France at Victoria Station in the 1930s. Pasmore has lived the history of art in a way that few others have.'[80] This is the impression that Colin Wiggins got from working alongside Pasmore on the exhibition; he recalls him being 'full of amazing memories, referring to Picasso as "Pablo" and telling stories about going on holiday with Max Ernst'.[81] In his exhibition catalogue, Pasmore pointed out numerous connections that different artists had made with one another over space and time. One of the most carefully chosen relationships he underscored was the impact that Piero had had on Seurat's thinking and working practices (fig. 61).

Critics were equally quick to understand and appreciate this desired outcome for the series and often discussed it in their reviews. For instance, Michael Billington praised Pasmore's ability to 'make connections',[82] noting that he found the juxtaposition of apparently very different pictures stimulating: 'I thought connections were made through the way the pictures were hung and through juxtapositions … you start to look at the painting with a fresh eye. He … connects the famous Seurat painting *The Bathers* … with Piero della Francesca, and you begin to see what he means. There is something about the placement of the figures in a landscape in both paintings, about the way the figures achieve particularity and generality, that makes a lot of sense.'[83]

The second leitmotif of *The Artist's Eye* series as a whole concerned the value of slow looking, and how this invaluable life-lesson might best be shared. This entailed taking the time to focus on one painting and to look carefully and for a sustained period of time, so as to allow for a growing appreciation of the work's making and meaning, its details and subtle nuances, elements so often overlooked on a gallery visit when a lack of time or the desire to see everything often prevented such an approach. This fundamental ambition was stated by MacGregor when answering a public enquiry: 'Our concern, after the pictures' physical safety, is to encourage visitors to look as closely and as long as possible. The *Artist's Eye* exhibition is part of this strategy, and one which has proved itself to be of great value.'[84]

The artists involved in *The Artist's Eye* series also advocated close, long looking. Hockney constantly drew attention to the epiphanic joy resulting from such deep engagement, explaining to Smith that he had

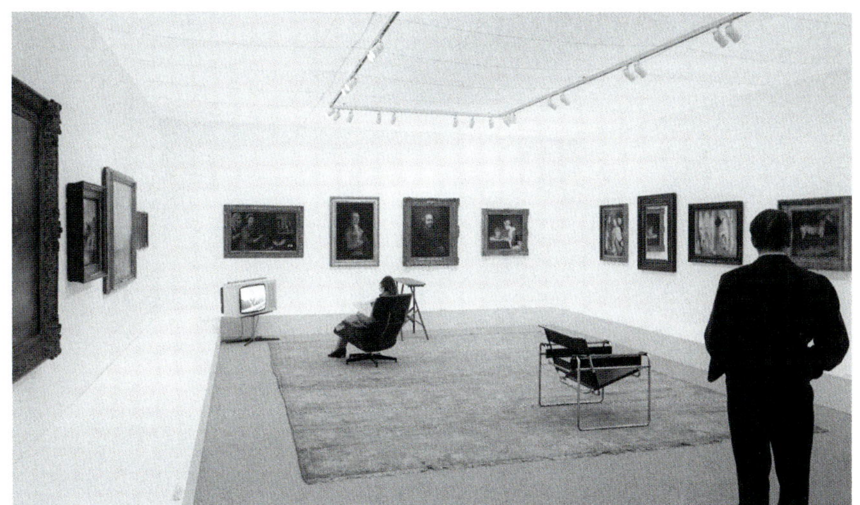

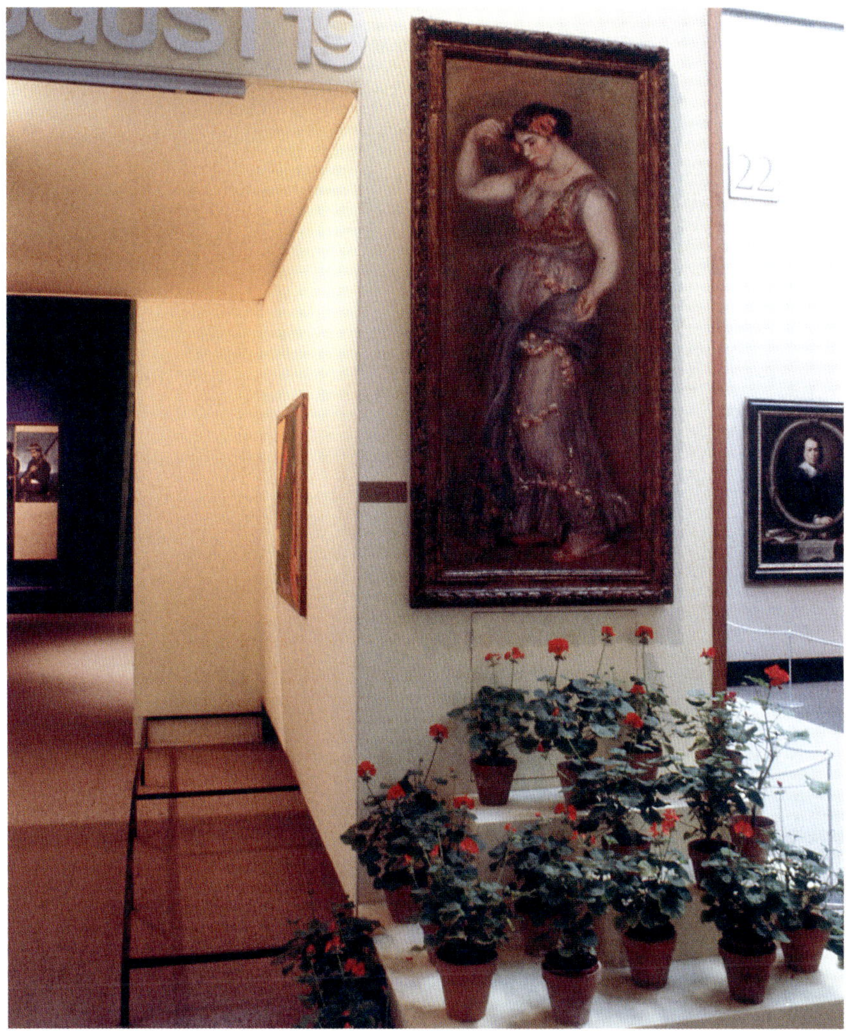

PIERO DELLA FRANCESCA
active 1439; died 1492

The Baptism of Christ

The rediscovery of Piero is a relatively recent
development dating from the late nineteenth
century, and was initiated mainly by Charles
Blanc, Director of the Ecole des Beaux-Arts in
Paris, where Seurat was a student. For Seurat,
Piero offered the possibility of creating a new
kind of classicism, based on Impressionism.

However, the classicism of Piero, unlike that of
Uccello, is not abstract. In *The Baptism of Christ*,
not only are the figures individual and human,
but the landscape in which they are set, with its
light, space and colour, is full of sentiment and
personal sensibility. Moreover, odd surprises,
such as the man removing his shirt, transform
what could have been a purely academic
exercise into a romantic and personal image.

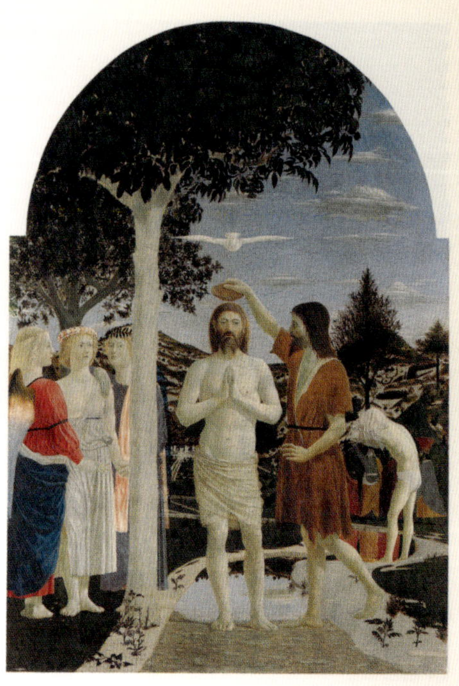

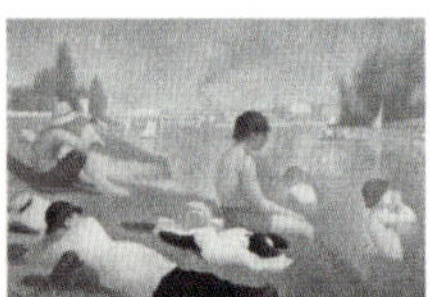

Fig. 1   Seurat, *Bathers at Asnières*.

GEORGES-PIERRE SEURAT
1859–1891

Bathers at Asnières

What is unique and remarkable about this
picture, a great masterpiece in the Renaissance
tradition of painting, is that it was painted when
Seurat was only twenty-three years old, an age
at which the average artist, however skilful,
is still an immature student.

One explanation of this extraordinary achievement may be that it was the work of two people –
on the one hand, Seurat himself, the unique
artist who created the visual image, and, on the
other, his teacher at the Ecole des Beaux-Arts,
Charles Blanc, who provided the intellectual
maturity.

Blanc was an exceptionally erudite teacher
and academician as well as author of a famous
treatise on painting. What links him directly
to this painting is his revival of Piero della
Francesca, from whose work *Bathers at Asnières*
surely drew its supreme inspiration.

Cézanne said that his own aim was to do Poussin
again from nature. So it might be claimed that
Seurat is here repeating Piero in terms of
Impressionism.

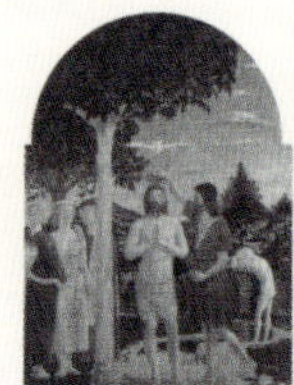

Fig. 15   Piero della Francesca,
The Baptism of Christ.

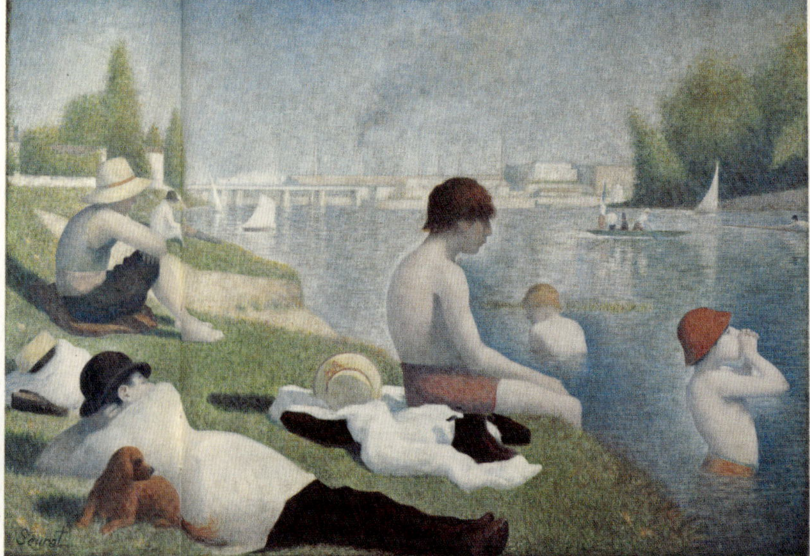

once prescribed to a disconsolate friend that visiting a particular Picasso exhibition to spend time with the pictures would be a panacea, since, as Hockney explained, 'just the joy, the inspiration, it would make you come alive'.[85] Hockney likewise encouraged a longer look in his *Artist's Eye* catalogue, which he wittily titled *Looking at Pictures in a Book*. When introducing *Looking at Pictures on a Screen*, the work he selected from his own oeuvre as the focal point of the exhibition, he stated: 'It was about the pleasure of looking.' And, in a similar vein, of the four National Gallery paintings depicted in his own painting, the originals of which he displayed alongside his work, he said he had chosen them because they 'gave me enormous pleasure'.[86] He hoped that the visitor might step into the shoes of Henry Geldzahler, the sitter in his painting, and 'identify with him and his pleasure because you were doing exactly the same, looking at [art]'.[87] In a paragraph about Piero's *Baptism* and the magic that both the original and reproductions of it gave off, Hockney noted: 'Sometimes the more you look at it, you notice different things.'[88] Developing the theme, he later quoted lines from a poem by the poet and Anglican clergyman George Herbert (1593–1633), 'The Elixir'. Hockney liked the lines because they spoke about how contemplation led to greater understanding, that it 'open[ed] up incredible ways of looking': 'A man that looks on glasse / on it may stay his eye / Or if he pleaseth, through it pass / and then the heav'n espie'.[89] In terms of getting the most out of the four National Gallery pictures selected for his *Artist's Eye* exhibition, Hockney suggested visitors should 'look at [them] for half an hour' because 'the longer you look, the richer they get'.[90] At the end of this particular *Artist's Eye*, Levey commented to Hockney: 'I feel sure that the exhibition had the stimulating effect you wished and we welcomed. It will have made many people look <u>and</u> think about paintings – and all the more thanks to your shrewd comments in the accompanying booklet.'[91]

Certain critics happily picked up on the theme of close looking and thanked *The Artist's Eye* for giving tips about how to learn to look longer and therefore better and deeper. Billington, for instance, pointed out how useful he found artists' comments to be concerning details in the pictures under review as a way of helping visitors in the Gallery to get to know particular pictures better and thereby feel a deeper connection with and appreciation for its permanent collection. As he put it: 'I mean you start to look at the detail of the painting in a way you would not in its normal hanging in the National Gallery.'[92] One detail that, as many had done before him, Pasmore picked up on in Piero's *Baptism* was the man disrobing in the background, which he used to make a larger point about Piero's distinctive brand of Classicism, which he thought was anything but abstract: 'In *The Baptism of Christ*, not only are the figures individual and human, but the landscape in which they are set, with its light, space and colour, is full of sentiment and personal sensibility. Moreover, odd surprises, such as the man removing his shirt, transform what could have been a purely academic exercise into a romantic and personal image' (fig. 62).[93] It was other details in the painting that Hockney picked up on. In his exhibition catalogue, he discussed Piero's depiction of the dove and its sense of extraordinary 'still' movement (fig. 63),[94] while he chose part of the background landscape to reproduce as one of the eight postcards – four of which were details – which accompanied his exhibition catalogue (see fig. 43). In his opinion, even postcards could 'giv[e] off real vibrations like the painting, of the sheer delight'.[95]

Something that assisted with a longer look was the smallness of the exhibition space, in which the visitor could focus properly on a restricted number of images without being distracted by too many other great works of art, competing for attention. The critic Jeremy Treglown noted of the works in *The Artist's Eye* series: 'they are in a manageable number. I think, like many people, I find big galleries like the National Gallery … very hard to digest' – so he was relieved 'to go into this beautifully selected room of … paintings of world importance'.[96]

REACTIONS TO *THE ARTIST'S EYE* SERIES

Visitor numbers for *The Artist's Eye* exhibitions were always respectable, sometimes even astonishingly high. While Caro's inaugural show attracted 130,169 visitors and Hockney's just over 163,000, the most visited show was Pasmore's (290,738 visitors). In terms of critical reception, a whole spectrum of reactions was evoked. Even the most visited show elicited heated as well as warm-hearted responses. Pasmore himself diplomatically acknowledged, when writing to Gallery colleagues, that the press reviews he had seen were 'a nice mixture of praise and abuse, knowledge and ignorance, understanding and misunderstanding, which of course is just what is needed if you want to attract public interest'.[97]

The most favourable press commentary concerned the way in which *The Artist's Eye* series had clearly

Fig. 61
Pages 8–9 and 42–3 from Victor Pasmore's catalogue for his *Artist's Eye* exhibition, 1990, discussing the artistic dialogue between Seurat and Piero. The National Gallery, London

demonstrated that there was more than one way to approach and appreciate art and that opening up picture galleries to specialist interpretation of other kinds than just the curatorial one, including the eye of the artist, was a wholly worthwhile exercise. Cork ended his review article of 1981 concerning the first four *Artist's Eye* exhibitions with a rousing endorsement of the enterprise: 'By using their "eyes" so keenly, the artists who were invited to select the series have all helped us "see" the work they chose in new ways.'[98]

Thinking about what the artists involved in the series gained from the experience, many noted that what had been the most enjoyable aspect was what Caro called 'the learning experience … from close contact with the pictures in the National Gallery'.[99] He and others expressed gratitude for the chance, however daunting, testing or humbling,[100] to show examples of their own work at the National Gallery and near iconic historic paintings. Additionally, most of the artists noted that they found organising an *Artist's Eye* show creative and inspiring, even fun. Some commented too that they were delighted to have helped open people's eyes to the Gallery's collection in new ways. For instance, Caro spoke with evident joy of the effect of his *Artist's Eye* exhibition: 'The best thing that I had said to me was that it showed someone a new way to look at paintings – I reckon that that's exactly what it was about.'[101]

The Artist's Eye series was brought to a close largely because National Gallery staff believed it had served its purpose admirably.[102] Indeed, its novelty was evident from the start, Levey telling Caro at the close of the inaugural *Artist's Eye* in 1977 that he felt the initiative 'was an important breakthrough. I apologise for this rather ugly word but all of us feel the exhibition, which took considerable courage on your part to do, has been a significant step … Simply to have a living artist participating in some sort of public way in this building has been invaluable.'[103] As Alistair Smith put it in 2023, when reflecting on *The Artist's Eye* series and what has happened in the art world since: 'there have been great changes in thinking about the contemporary and its relation to the historic, and *The Artist's Eye* exhibitions played a part in that – and that's had real benefits for the visual arts public'.[104]

The pioneering approach of calling on living artists to select and discuss works in the Gallery's collection in relation to their own artistic practice lives on. It inspired similar initiatives elsewhere, including Grayson Perry's *Unpopular Culture* (2008–10) and exhibitions of the British Council Collection curated by Jeremy Deller and Alan Kane (*My Yard*, 2009) and the late Paula Rego (*My Choice*, 2011–12).[105]

As discussed, under the directorship of Gabriele Finaldi, in May 2018, the Gallery Trustees agreed to an ambitious Modern & Contemporary Programme.[106] Tasked with using exhibitions and displays, commissions and residencies to explore 'counter-intuitive facets of the collection and the history of art', the current programme aims to feature living artists and their works more prominently than ever before. Its 'Unexpected Views' series, in which contemporary artists talk about their favourite works from the collection, is perhaps the most obvious successor of *The Artist's Eye* series, even if, as a discursive, event-based initiative, it is produced in a format that is more frequent, diverse and manageable for the Gallery than its predecessor. The 'Unexpected Views' programme offers a monthly conversation that takes place in public between Gallery curators and leading cultural practitioners. The focus is an important National Gallery painting, and the interlocuters explore its relevance to the artist's work in particular, to contemporary artistic practice in general, and to other, even bigger current social and cultural issues. It is hoped that the three-way engagement between a living artist and the general public through an historic painting will be conducted in a manner that is 'critical, counter-intuitive and joyful'.[107] Just like *The Artist's Eye* before it, this recent Gallery initiative aims to enhance, for public benefit, the Gallery's traditional, art historical point of view by providing time and space for a multitude of refreshing and inspiring artists' perspectives.

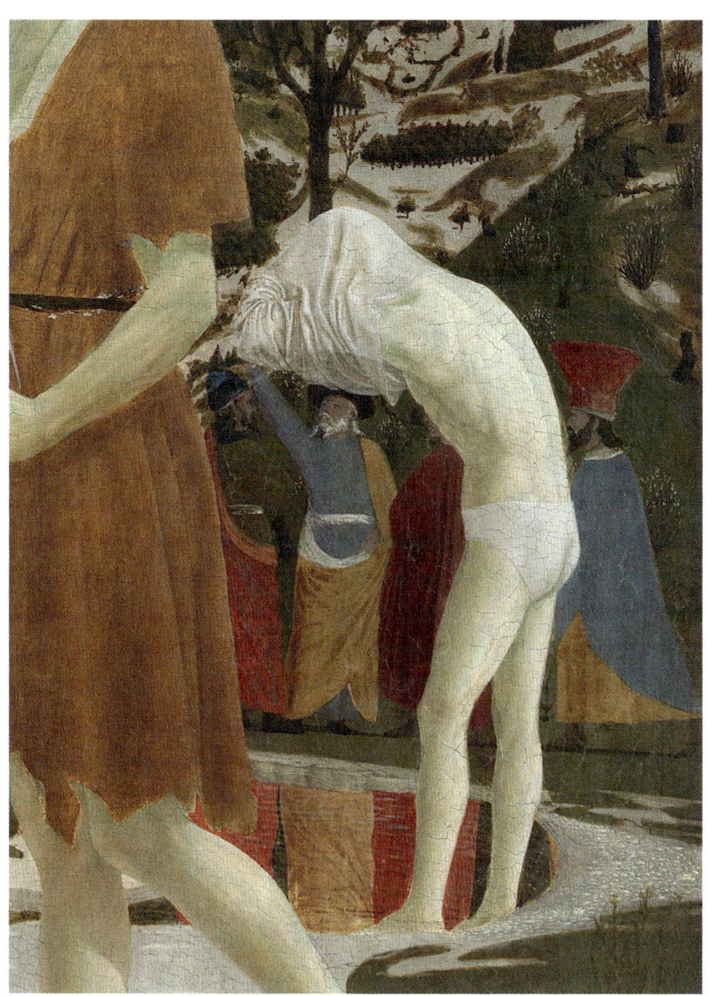 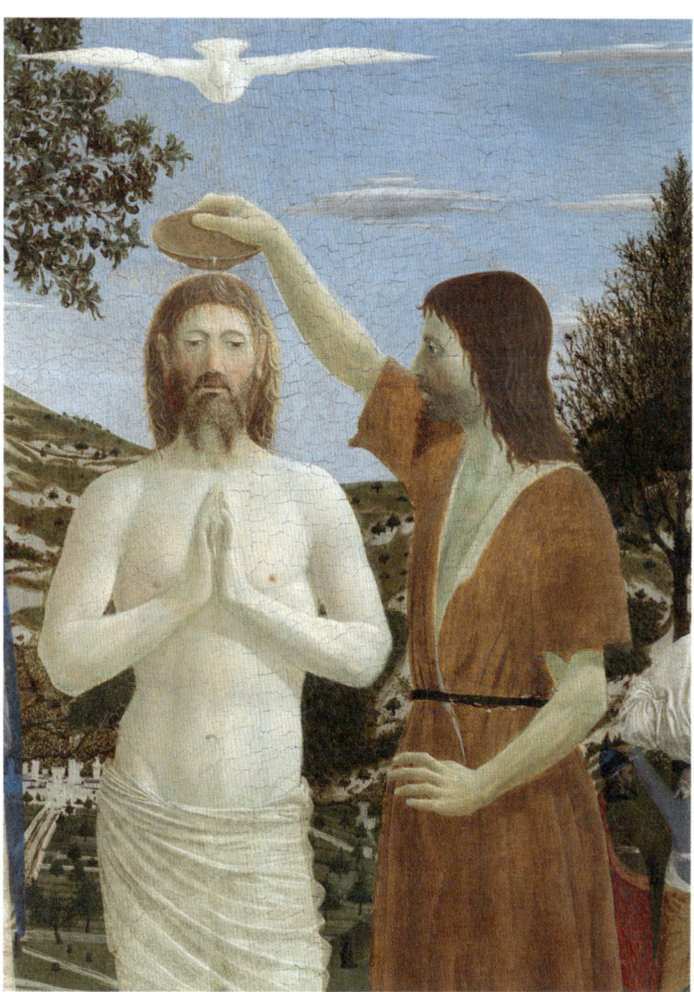

Fig. 62
Detail showing the disrobing figure from Piero's *Baptism* (fig. 2).

Fig. 63
Detail showing the dove and Christ in his loincloth from Piero's *Baptism* (fig. 2).

APPENDICES

(For National Gallery works, further information can be sourced via the Gallery's website, using the NG number.)

APPENDIX 1

ARTIST KEEPERS OF THE NATIONAL GALLERY

William Seguier (1772–1843): served 1824–43

Sir Charles Lock Eastlake, PRA (1793–1865): served 1843–7

Thomas Uwins, RA (1782–1857): served 1847–55

Ralph Nicholson Wornum (1812–1877): served 1855–77

Charles Locke Eastlake (1836–1906): served 1878–98

Hawes Harison Turner (1851–1939): served 1898–1914

Charles Henry Collins Baker (1880–1959): served 1914–34

Edwin Glasgow (1874–1955): served 1934–36

ARTIST DIRECTORS OF THE NATIONAL GALLERY

Sir Charles Lock Eastlake, PRA (1793–1865): served 1855–65

Sir William Boxall, RA (1800–1879): served 1866–74

Sir Frederic William Burton, RHA (1816–1900): served 1874–94

Sir Edward John Poynter, Bt, PRA (1836–1919): served 1894–1904

Sir Charles Holroyd (1861–1917): served 1906–16

Sir Charles John Holmes (1868–1936): served 1916–28

WORKS BY OR AFTER ARTIST KEEPERS/DIRECTORS AT THE NATIONAL GALLERY (Contextual Collection items bear the prefix 'H'; National Gallery Archive items bear the prefix NGA.)

After Thomas Uwins (1782–1857), *Family carrying Fruit*, early to mid-nineteenth century, engraving on paper (H25)

Sir Charles Lock Eastlake (1793–1865), *After Titian, Martyrdom of Saint Peter Martyr*, 1830, oil on paper on canvas (H201)

Sir Charles Lock Eastlake (1793–1865), *Cypresses*, about 1817, oil on paper laid on canvas (H203)

Sir Charles Lock Eastlake (1793–1865), *Italian Pines*, about 1817, oil on paper laid on canvas (H204)

After Sir Charles Lock Eastlake (1793–1865), *Greek Fugitives*, 1833, engraving on paper (H23)

Ralph Nicholson Wornum (1812–1877), a handful of paintings and sketches of family members (part of the Ralph Nicholson Wornum Papers, NGA, NGA2/5/*)

Possibly Sir William Boxall (1800–1879), *Portrait of a Man* and *Portrait of a Woman*, about 1830 (NG6352, NG6353)

Sir Charles Holroyd (1861–1917), *Portrait of Nancy Holroyd*, late nineteenth century, etching on paper (H44)

PORTRAITS OF ARTIST KEEPERS/DIRECTORS AT THE NATIONAL GALLERY (Contextual Collection items bear the prefix 'H'; National Gallery Archive items bear the prefix NGA.)

John Jackson (1778–1831), *William Seguier*, 1830 (NG6022)

Sir Francis Grant (1803–1878), *Sir Charles Lock Eastlake*, pen and ink drawing, 1853 (H202)

Ralph Nicholson Wornum (1812–1877): *Self Portrait of Ralph Nicholson Wornum at the Age of Sixty-One*, 1873 (NGA, NGA2/5/7)

Sir William Boxall (1800–1879), *Self Portrait at the Age of about Nineteen*, about 1819 (NG6482)

Alphonse Legros (1837–1911), *Edward Poynter*, 1905 (NGA, NG67/12/3)

Alphonse Legros (1837–1911), *Sir Charles Holroyd*, etching on paper (H7)

Alphonse Legros (1837–1911), *Sir Charles Holroyd*, pencil on paper (H46)

Unknown artist, *Charles Henry Collins Baker*, 1920s–1930s (NGA, NG67/2/1)

APPENDIX 2

ARTISTS WHO HAVE SERVED AS TRUSTEES OF THE NATIONAL GALLERY

Sir George Beaumont, 7th Baronet (1753–1827): served 1824–7

Sir Thomas Lawrence, PRA (1769–1830): served 1824–30

Sir Martin Archer Shee, PRA (1769–1850): served 1831–50

Sir Charles Lock Eastlake, PRA (1793–1865): served 1850–55

George James Howard, 9th Earl of Carlisle (1843–1911): served 1881–1911

John Postle Heseltine (1843–1929): served 1893–1929

Sir William Llewellyn, GCVO, PRA (1858–1941): served 1933–40

Lord Paul Ayshford Methuen, 4th Baron Methuen, RA, PRWA (1886–1974): served 1938–45

Sir Muirhead Bone (1876–1953): served 1941–8

William Coldstream, CBE (1908–1987): served 1948–63

Henry Moore (1898–1986): served 1954–74

Andrew Forge (1923–2002): served 1967–72

John Piper (1903–1992): served 1967–78

Martin Froy (1926–2017): served 1972–9

Howard Hodgkin (1932–2017): served 1978–85 (previously, 1974–6, Tate Liaison Trustee)

Bridget Riley (born 1931): served 1981–8

Michael Andrews (1928–1995): served 1988

Euan Uglow (1932–2000): served 1990–5

Philip Hughes (born 1936): served 1996–9
Christopher Le Brun, PRA (born 1951): served 1996–2003
John Lessore (born 1939): served 2003–11
Lisa Milroy (born 1959): served 2015–17
Dexter Dalwood (born 1960): served 2015–19
Catherine Goodman (born 1961): served 2019–present
Rosalind Nashashibi (born 1973): served 2023–present
(Tate Liaison Trustee)

APPENDIX 3
ARTIST DONORS OF PAINTINGS CURRENTLY IN THE NATIONAL GALLERY (For works gifted by Gallery
Artists in Residence of their own work, see Appendix 7.)

Joseph Mallord William Turner (1775–1851): unless otherwise stated, the paintings are by Turner himself: *Calais Pier* (NG472), *Sun rising through Vapour* (NG479), *Dido building Carthage* (NG498), *Ulysses deriding Polyphemus – Homer's Odyssey* (NG508), *The Parting of Hero and Leander* (NG521), *The Fighting Temeraire* (NG524), *Rain, Steam and Speed – The Great Western Railway* (NG538), *Margate (?), from the Sea* (NG1984), *The Evening Star* (NG1991), After Guercino, *A Bearded Man holding a Lamp* (NG5537). All Turner Bequest, 1856 (the majority of the Turner Bequest has been transferred to Tate)

Sir Charles Lock Eastlake (1793–1865): Fra Filippo Lippi, *The Annunciation*, presented in 1861 (NG666)

George Frederic Watts (1817–1904): probably by Girolamo Macchietti, *A Knight of S. Stefano*, presented in 1861 (NG670)

Charles Fairfax Murray (1849–1919): Pietro Lorenzetti and Workshop, *Saint Sabinus before the Roman Governor of Tuscany*, presented in 1882 (NG1113)

George Frederic Watts (1817–1904): unknown French artist, *Profile Portrait of a Young Man*, presented in 1885 (NG1190)

Charles Haslewood Shannon (1863–1937): Piero di Cosimo, *The Fight between the Lapiths and the Centaurs* (NG4890); Master of the Mansi Magdalen, *Judith and the Infant Hercules* (NG4891), both bequeathed in 1937

Lucien Pissarro (1863–1944): Camille Pissarro, *Portrait of Félix Pissarro*, 1881 (L722), *The Little Country Maid*,1882 (L723) and *The Pork Butcher*,1883 (L724), all bequeathed in 1944 and on loan from Tate

Executors of W. Graham Robertson (1866–1948): Bartolomé Esteban Murillo, *Christ healing the Paralytic at the Pool of Bethesda* (NG5931), presented through the Art Fund in memory of W. Graham Robertson, 1950

Eliot Hodgkin (1905–1987): Jean-François de Troy, *The Capture of the Golden Fleece* (NG6512), presented by Mr and Mrs Eliot Hodgkin through the Art Fund, 1987

Lucian Freud (1922–2011): Jean-Baptiste-Camille Corot, *Italian Woman, or Woman with Yellow Sleeve* (*L'Italienne*) (NG6620), accepted in lieu of Inheritance Tax by HM Government from the estate of Lucian Freud and allocated to the National Gallery, 2012

Sean Scully (born 1945): Sean Scully, *Landlines and Robes*, 2018, 10 aquatints, presented in 2020 (GROUP158, comprising H243–H254)

APPENDIX 4
ARTIST COMMISSIONS FOR THE NATIONAL GALLERY

Boris Anrep (1883–1969): *The Labours of Life*, 1928; *The Pleasures of Life*, 1929; *The Awakening of the Muses*, 1933; and *The Modern Virtues*, 1952, mosaics, Portico Entrance. Commissioned by the National Gallery, the final one supported by Maud Russell, 1952 (GROUP166, H239–242)

Paula Rego (1935–2022): *Crivelli's Garden*, 1990–1, acrylic on canvas, for the Sainsbury Wing Dining Room (GROUP137, H12.1–5)

Bridget Riley (born 1931): *Messengers*, 2019, mural, Annenberg Court. Commissioned by the National Gallery, supported by Rothschild & Co., 2019 (H205)

Gerald Laing (1936–2011), *Sir Paul Getty K.B.E., 1932–2003*, 1996. Commissioned by the National Gallery in honour of Sir Paul Getty K.B.E., benefactor of the Gallery, 1997 (H192)

APPENDIX 5
***THE ARTIST'S EYE*: FIRST SERIES, 1977–81** (The
date of *The Artist's Eye* exhibition, any works by the artist displayed and a list of National Gallery paintings and other loans chosen by the artist-curator are listed in the order in which they were discussed in the accompanying exhibition catalogue. Entries concerning Gallery paintings have been updated to reflect current inventory numbers, attributions and dates.)

Anthony Caro (1924–2013): *The Artist's Eye: Anthony Caro* (1 June–24 July 1977) (Board Room)
Caro's list of Gallery paintings is taken from a press release of 31 May 1977 – no list of exhibited works was reproduced in his exhibition pamphlet.

Anthony Caro, *Orangerie*, 1969
Antonello da Messina, *Christ Crucified* (NG1166)
Giovanni Bellini, *Madonna of the Meadow* (NG599)
Paul Cezanne, *Hillside in Provence* (NG4136)
Gustave Courbet, *Still Life with Apples and a Pomegranate* (NG5983)
Edouard Manet, *Eva Gonzalès* (NG3259)
Edouard Manet, 'A non-commissioned officer holding his rifle', a fragment from *The Execution of Maximilian* (NG3294)
Claude Monet, *The Beach at Trouville* (NG3951)
Rembrandt, *Saskia van Uylenburgh in Arcadian Costume* (NG4930)
Titian, *Noli me Tangere* (NG270)

Richard Hamilton (1922–2011): *The Artist's Eye: Richard Hamilton* (5 July–31 August 1978) (Special Exhibition Room)
Richard Hamilton, *My Marilyn*, 1965
Pisanello, *The Virgin and Child with Saints Anthony Abbot and George* (NG776)
Dirk Bouts, *Portrait of a Man (Jan van Winckele?)* (NG943)
Piero del Pollaiuolo, *Apollo and Daphne* (NG928)
Andrea Mantegna, *The Agony in the Garden* (NG1417)
Hieronymus Bosch, *Christ Mocked (The Crowning with Thorns)* (NG4744)
Imitator of Pieter Bruegel the Elder, *Landscape: A River among Mountains* (NG1298)
Diego Velázquez, *Kitchen Scene with Christ in the House of Martha and Mary* (NG1375)
Nicolas Poussin, *Landscape with a Man killed by a Snake* (NG5763)
Pieter Saenredam, *The Interior of the Grote Kerk at Haarlem* (NG2531)
Rembrandt, *Self Portrait at the Age of 63* (NG221)
Jean-Siméon Chardin, *The Young Schoolmistress* (NG4077)
Thomas Gainsborough, *John Plampin* (NG5984)
Francisco de Goya, *Don Andrés del Peral* (NG1951)
Jean-Louis-André-Théodore Géricault, *A Horse frightened by Lightning* (NG4927)
J.M.W. Turner, *The Evening Star* (NG1991)
Gustave Courbet, *Still Life with Apples and a Pomegranate* (NG5983)
Paul Cezanne, *The Grounds of the Château Noir* (NG6342)
Odilon Redon, *Ophelia among the Flowers* (NG6438)

Howard Hodgkin (1932–2017): *The Artist's Eye: Howard Hodgkin* (20 June–19 August 1979) (Special Exhibition Room)
Howard Hodgkin, *Dinner at Smith Square*, 1975–9
Howard Hodgkin, *Mr and Mrs E.J.P.*, 1978–9
Eugène Delacroix, *Louis-Auguste Schwiter* (NG3286)
Pierre-Auguste Renoir, *Dancing Girl with Tambourine* (NG6317)
Pierre-Auguste Renoir, *Dancing Girl with Castanets* (NG6318)
Giovanni Battista Tiepolo, *An Allegory with Venus and Time* (NG6387)
Diego Velázquez, *Philip IV hunting Wild Boar (La Tela Real)* (NG197)
Gherardo di Jacopo Starnina (Master of the Bambino Vispo), *The Beheading of Saint Margaret (?)* (NG3926)
Andrea Mantegna, *The Introduction of the Cult of Cybele at Rome* (NG902)
Edouard Manet, *The Execution of Maximilian* (NG3294)
Carel Fabritius, *A View of Delft, with a Musical Instrument Seller's Stall* (NG3714)
Edouard Vuillard, *The Mantelpiece (La Cheminée)* (NG3271)
Laurent de La Hyre, *Allegory of Grammar* (NG6329)
Moghul School, *Mihrdukht aims her Arrow at the Ring*, about 1570 (Private collection)

R.B. Kitaj (1932–2007): *The Artist's Eye: R.B. Kitaj* (21 May–20 July 1980) (Board Room)
R.B. Kitaj, *The Orientalist*, 1976–7
R.B. Kitaj, *Marynka*, 1979
Greco-Roman, *A Young Woman* (NG3931)
Greco-Roman, *A Man with a Wreath* (NG3932)
Duccio, *The Annunciation* (NG1139)
Duccio, *The Transfiguration* (NG1330)
Ambrogio Lorenzetti, *A Group of Four Poor Clares* (NG1147)
Robert Campin, *A Man* (NG653.1)
Robert Campin, *A Woman* (NG653.2)
Sassetta, *Saint Francis meets a Knight Poorer than Himself and Saint Francis's Vision of the Founding of the Franciscan Order* (NG4757)
Sassetta, *Saint Francis renounces his Earthly Father* (NG4758)
Workshop of Rogier van der Weyden, *A Man Reading (Saint Ivo?)* (NG6394)
Piero della Francesca, *Saint Michael* (NG769)
Hans Memling, *Saint John the Baptist* (NG747.1)
Andrea Mantegna, *The Agony in the Garden* (NG1417)

Giovanni Bellini, *The Agony in the Garden* (NG726)
Sandro Botticelli, *Portrait of a Young Man* (NG626)
Raphael, *The Dream of a Knight* (NG213)
Hans Baldung Grien, *Portrait of a Man* (NG245)
Lucas Cranach the Elder, *Cupid complaining to Venus* (NG6344)
Titian, *The Death of Actaeon* (NG6420)
Michelangelo Merisi da Caravaggio, *The Supper at Emmaus* (NG172)
Diego Velázquez, *Kitchen Scene with Christ in the House of Martha and Mary* (NG1375)
Rembrandt, *The Lamentation over the Dead Christ* (NG43)
Rembrandt, *A Woman bathing in a Stream (Hendrickje Stoffels?)* (NG54)
Rembrandt, *Self Portrait at the Age of 34* (NG672)
Rembrandt, *Ecce Homo* (NG1400)
Francisco de Goya, *Don Andrés del Peral* (NG1951)
Unknown French artist (formerly ascribed to Eugène Delacroix), *Portrait of a Man (Victor Considerant?)* (NG3686)
Hilaire-Germain-Edgar Degas, *Beach Scene* (NG3247)
Hilaire-Germain-Edgar Degas, *Young Spartans Exercising* (NG3860)
Hilaire-Germain-Edgar Degas, *After the Bath, Woman drying herself* (NG6295)
Vincent van Gogh, *Van Gogh's Chair* (NG3862)
Vincent van Gogh, *Long Grass with Butterflies* (NG4169)
Paul Cezanne, *An Old Woman with a Rosary* (NG6195)
Paul Cezanne, *Bathers (Les Grandes Baigneuses)* (NG6359)

David Hockney (born 1937): *The Artist's Eye: David Hockney* (1 July–31 August 1981) (Board Room)

Archie Brennan, *Play within a Play* (tapestry after Hockney's painting of that title of 1963), 1970
David Hockney, *Looking at Pictures on a Screen*, 1977
Colour postcard reproduction of Edouard Vuillard, *Portrait of Toulouse-Lautrec*, in an ornate gold frame
Johannes Vermeer, *A Young Woman standing at a Virginal* (NG1383)
Piero della Francesca, *The Baptism of Christ* (NG665)
Vincent van Gogh, *Sunflowers* (NG3863)
Hilaire-Germain-Edgar Degas, *After the Bath, Woman drying herself* (NG6295)

***THE ARTIST'S EYE*: SECOND SERIES, 1985–90**

Francis Bacon (1909–1992): *The Artist's Eye: Francis Bacon* (23 October–15 December 1985) (Sunley Room)

No work by Bacon was displayed.
Masaccio, *The Virgin and Child* (NG3046)
Michelangelo, *The Entombment (or Christ being carried to his Tomb)* (NG790)
Diego Velázquez, *Philip IV of Spain* (NG745)
Diego Velázquez, *The Toilet of Venus ('The Rokeby Venus')* (NG2057)
Probably by Rembrandt, *Portrait of Margaretha de Geer, Wife of Jacob Trip* (NG5282)
Rembrandt, *Portrait of Margaretha de Geer, Wife of Jacob Trip* (NG1675)
Francisco de Goya, *Don Andrés del Peral* (NG1951)
Jean-Auguste-Dominique Ingres, *Madame Moitessier* (NG4821)
J.M.W. Turner, *Rain, Steam, and Speed – The Great Western Railway* (NG538)
Edouard Manet, *The Execution of Maximilian* (NG3294)
Georges Seurat, *Bathers at Asnières* (NG3908)
Georges Seurat, *Horses in the Water*, about 1883 (Private collection on extended loan to the Courtauld Gallery, London)
Georges Seurat, *The Angler*, about 1884 (Private collection, on extended loan to the Courtauld Gallery, London)
Georges Seurat, *Fisherman in a Moored Boat*, about 1882 (Private collection, on extended loan to the Courtauld Gallery, London)
Vincent van Gogh, *A Wheatfield, with Cypresses* (NG3861)
Vincent van Gogh, *Van Gogh's Chair* (NG3862)
Paul Cezanne, *The Grounds of the Château Noir* (NG6342)
Hilaire-Germain-Edgar Degas, *After the Bath, Woman drying herself* (NG6295)

Patrick Caulfield (1936–2005): *The Artist's Eye: Patrick Caulfield* (4 June–10 August 1986) (Sunley Room)

Patrick Caulfield, *Lunchtime*, 1985
Théodore Rousseau, *Landscape with Stormy Sunset* (NG2635)
Narcisse-Virgilio Diaz de la Peña, *The Storm* (NG2632)
Alfred Stevens, *Storm at Honfleur* (NG3966)
J.M.W. Turner, *The Evening Star* (NG1991)
Camille Pissarro, *Fox Hill, Upper Norwood* (NG6351)
Style of Gustave Courbet, *Landscape* (NG4182)
Jean-Baptiste-Camille Corot, *The Roman Campagna, with the Claudian Aqueduct* (NG3285)
Dutch artist (?), *A White House among Trees* (NG3140)
Albrecht Altdorfer, *Landscape with a Footbridge* (NG6320)

Paul Cezanne, *Avenue at Chantilly* (NG6525)

Paul Cezanne, *The Painter's Father, Louis-Auguste Cezanne* (NG6385)

Johannes van der Aack, *An Old Woman seated sewing* (NG1397)

Nicolaes Maes, *A Woman scraping Parsnips, with a Child standing by her* (NG159)

Diego Velázquez, *Kitchen Scene with Christ in the House of Martha and Mary* (NG1375)

Unknown Spanish artist, *A Man and a Child eating Grapes* (NG2526)

Jean-Siméon Chardin, *The Young Schoolmistress* (NG4077)

Pieter de Hooch, *The Courtyard of a House in Delft* (NG835)

Pieter de Hooch, *A Musical Party in a Courtyard* (NG3047)

Adriaen Brouwer, *Tavern Scene* (NG6591)

Edouard Manet, *Corner of a Café-Concert* (NG3858)

Camille Pissarro, *The Boulevard Montmartre at Night* (NG4119)

Carel Fabritius, *A View of Delft, with a Musical Instrument Seller's Stall* (NG3714)

Carel Fabritius, *A Young Man in a Fur Cap and a Cuirass (probably a Self Portrait)* (NG4042)

Possibly by Francesco Granacci, *Portrait of a Man in Armour* (NG895)

Jacob van Oost the Elder, *Portrait of a Boy aged 11* (NG1137)

Peter Paul Rubens, *Portrait of Susanna Lunden(?) ('Le Chapeau de Paille')* (NG852)

Dosso Dossi, *A Man embracing a Woman* (NG1234)

Dirk Bouts, *Portrait of a Man (Jan van Winckele?)* (NG943)

Pieter Saenredam, *The Interior of the Grote Kerk at Haarlem* (NG2531)

Vincenzo Catena, *Saint Jerome in his Study* (NG694)

Workshop of Quinten Massys, *Saint Luke painting the Virgin and Child* (NG3902)

Paul Cezanne, *The Stove in the Studio* (NG6509)

Philippe Rousseau, *Still Life with Oysters* (NG3829)

Jan van de Velde, *Still Life: A Goblet of Wine, Oysters and Lemons* (NG1255)

Lucian Freud (1922–2011): *The Artist's Eye: Lucian Freud* (17 June–16 August 1987) (Sunley Room)
Lucian Freud, *The Painter's Brother Stephen*, 1985–6
Lucian Freud, *Double Portrait*, 1985–6
Georges Seurat, *Bathers at Asnières* (NG3908)

Jean-Auguste-Dominique Ingres, *Angelica saved by Ruggiero* (NG3292)

Jean-Auguste-Dominique Ingres, *Madame Moitessier* (NG4821)

Diego Velázquez, *The Toilet of Venus ('The Rokeby Venus')* (NG2057)

Peter Paul Rubens, *Samson and Delilah* (NG6461)

Honoré-Victorin Daumier, *Don Quixote and Sancho Panza* (NG3244)

Hilaire-Germain-Edgar Degas, *Young Spartans Exercising* (NG3860)

Hilaire-Germain-Edgar Degas, *Hélène Rouart in her Father's Study* (NG6469)

Hilaire-Germain-Edgar Degas, *Combing the Hair ('La Coiffure')* (NG4865)

Claude Monet, *The Beach at Trouville* (NG3951)

James Abbott McNeill Whistler, *Harmony in Grey and Green: Miss Cicely Alexander*, 1872–4 (Tate, N04622)

Edouard Vuillard, *Madame André Wormser and her Children* (NG6488)

John Constable, *Cenotaph to the Memory of Sir Joshua Reynolds, erected in the grounds of Coleorton Hall, Leicestershire by the late Sir George Beaumont, Bt.* (NG1272)

John Constable, *Salisbury Cathedral from the Meadows*, about 1830 (Private collection)

John Constable, *The Hay Wain* (NG1207)

J.M.W. Turner, *Sun rising through Vapour: Fishermen cleaning and selling Fish* (NG479)

Paul Cezanne, *The Painter's Father, Louis-Auguste Cezanne* (NG6385)

Rembrandt, *Portrait of Hendrickje Stoffels* (NG6432)

Jean-Siméon Chardin, *The Young Schoolmistress* (NG4077)

Probably by Rembrandt, *Portrait of Margaretha de Geer, Wife of Jacob Trip* (NG5282)

Rembrandt, *Portrait of Margaretha de Geer, Wife of Jacob Trip* (NG1675)

Probably by Rembrandt, *An Old Man in an Armchair* (NG6274)

Rembrandt, *Saskia van Uylenburgh in Arcadian Costume* (NG4930)

Rembrandt, *The Lamentation over the Dead Christ* (NG43)

Rembrandt, *A Woman bathing in a Stream (Hendrickje Stoffels?)* (NG54)

Frans Hals, *A Family Group in a Landscape* (NG2285)

Frans Hals, *Young Man holding a Skull (Vanitas)* (NG6458)

Bridget Riley (born 1931): *The Artist's Eye: Bridget Riley* (28 June–31 August 1989) (Sunley Room)

Bridget Riley, *Gaillard I*, 1989

Titian, *Bacchus and Ariadne* (NG35)

Paolo Veronese, *The Adoration of the Kings* (NG268)

El Greco, *Christ driving the Traders from the Temple* (NG1457)

Peter Paul Rubens, *Minerva protects Pax from Mars ('Peace and War')* (NG46)

Nicolas Poussin, *The Adoration of the Shepherds* (NG6277)

Nicolas Poussin, *The Triumph of Pan* (NG6477)

Paul Cezanne, *Bathers ('Les Grandes Baigneuses')* (NG6359)

Victor Pasmore (1908–1998): *The Artist's Eye: Victor Pasmore* (4 July–7 October 1990) (Sunley Room)

Victor Pasmore, *A Crime of Ideas* (after *The Charnel House* by Picasso) , 1989

Piero della Francesca, *The Baptism of Christ* (NG665)

Paolo Uccello, *Niccolò Mauruzi da Tolentino at the Battle of San Romano* (NG583)

Sandro Botticelli, *'Mystic Nativity'* (NG1034)

Leonardo da Vinci, *The Virgin with the Infant Saint John the Baptist adoring the Christ Child accompanied by an Angel ('The Virgin of the Rocks')* (NG1093)

Titian, *The Death of Actaeon* (NG6420)

El Greco, *Christ driving the Traders from the Temple* (NG1457)

Claude, *Landscape with Narcissus and Echo* (NG19)

Jan van de Velde, *Still Life: A Goblet of Wine, Oysters and Lemons* (NG1255)

Rembrandt, *Portrait of Margaretha de Geer, Wife of Jacob Trip* (NG1675)

Jacob van Ruisdael, *A Pool surrounded by Trees, and Two Sportsmen coursing a Hare* (NG854)

John Constable, *The Hay Wain* (NG1207)

J.M.W. Turner, *Margate (?), from the Sea* (NG1984)

Jean-Auguste-Dominique Ingres, *Madame Moitessier* (NG4821)

Jean-François Millet, *The Winnower* (NG6447)

Possibly after Gustave Courbet, *Young Ladies on the Banks of the Seine (Summer)* (NG6355)

James Abbott McNeill Whistler, *Harmony in Grey and Green: Miss Cicely Alexander*, 1872–4 (Tate, N04622)

Edouard Manet, *Corner of a Café-Concert* (NG3858)

Georges Seurat, *Bathers at Asnières* (NG3908)

Paul Cezanne, *Hillside in Provence* (NG4136)

Vincent van Gogh, *Sunflowers* (NG3863)

Henri Rousseau, *Surprised!* (NG6421)

APPENDIX 6
NATIONAL GALLERY EXHIBITIONS FEATURING THE WORK OF CONTEMPORARY ARTISTS

(excluding *The Artist's Eye* exhibition series and Artist Residency exhibitions, for which see above and below)

British Painting since Whistler (March 1940) (exh. cat.): Augustus John (1878–1961), Duncan Grant (1885–1978), Graham Sutherland (1903–1980), Gwen John (1876–1939), Henry Moore (1898–1986), Jacob Epstein (1880–1959), John Singer Sargent (1856–1925), Paul Nash (1889–1946), Wyndham Lewis (1882–1957), Stanley Spencer (1891–1959), Ivon Hitchens (1893–1979), Vanessa Bell (1879–1961), William Coldstream (1908–1987), William Nicholson (1872–1949), Winifred Nicholson (1893–1981), among many others

British War Artists (July 1940): Charles Cundall (1890–1971), Eric Kennington (1888–1960), William Rothenstein (1872–1945), Anthony Gross (1905–1984), Eric Ravilious (1903–1942), Raymond McGrath (1903–1977), R.V. Pitchforth (1895–1982), Evelyn Dunbar (1906–1960), Edward Ardizzone (1900–1979), Barnett Freedman (1901–1958), Edward Bawden (1903–1989), Muirhead Bone (1876–1953)

Drawings of Augustus John R.A. & some drawings of the past 50 years (19 November 1940–23 March 1941) (exh. cat.): Augustus John (1878–1961), Keith Baynes (1887–1977), Aubrey Beardsley (1872–1898), Muirhead Bone (1876–1953), Hercules Brabazon (1821–1906), Frank Brangwyn (1867–1956), Frederick Brown (1851–1941), Rodney J. Burn (1899–1984), David Young Cameron (1865–1945), Charles Conder (1868–1909), Philip Connard (1875–1958), Jacob Epstein (1880–1959), Ian Fairweather (1891–1974), Mark Gertler (1891–1939), Harold Gilman (1876–1919), Charles Ginner (1878–1952), Duncan Grant (1885–1978), Walter Greaves (1846–1931), Archibald S. Hartrick (1864–1950), Frances Hodgkins (1869–1947), Charles Holmes (1868–1936), James D. Innes (1887–1914), Francis Edward James (1849-1920), Gwen John (1876–1939), Edmond Kapp (1890–1978), Henry Lamb (1883–1960), Dugald Sutherland MacColl (1859–1948), William Frederick Mayor (1866–1916), James McBey (1883–1959), Ambrose McEvoy (1877–1927), Bernard Meninsky (1891–1950), Lord Methuen

(1886–1974), Thomas Monnington (1902–1976), John Nash (1893–1977), Paul Nash (1889–1946), Algernon Newton (1880–1968), William Orpen (1878–1931), Glyn Philpot (1884–1937), H.E. de Plessis (1894–1978), James Pryde (1866–1941), Eric Ravilious (1903–1942), Alfred William Rich (1856–1921), William Roberts (1895–1980), John Singer Sargent (1856–1925), Charles Shannon (1863–1937), Walter Richard Sickert (1860–1942), John Skeaping (1901–1980), Matthew Smith (1879–1959), Stanley Spencer (1891–1959), Philip Wilson Steer (1860–1942), Edward Stott (1855–1918), Graham Sutherland (1903–1980), Henry Tonks (1862–1937), Ethel Walker (1861–1951), James Abbott McNeil Whistler (1834–1903)

A Whistler and Early Twentieth-Century Oils (1941) (exh. cat.): James Abbott McNeil Whistler (1834–1903), Philip Wilson Steer (1860–1942), Charles Shannon (1863–1937), Francis Dodd (1874–1949), William Rothenstein (1872–1945), David Muirhead (1867–1930), Walter Richard Sickert (1860–1942), Augustus John (1878–1961), Philip Connard (1875–1958), Henry Tonks (1862–1937), Frederick Brown (1851–1941), Annie L. Swynnerton (1844–1933), Beatrice Bland (1864–1951), William Nicholson (1872–1949), John Singer Sargent (1856–1925), Walter Greaves (1846–1931), William Orpen (1878–1931), Gwen John (1876–1939), Charles Ricketts (1866–1931), Dugald Sutherland MacColl (1859–1948), Wilfrid Gabriel de Glehn (1870–1951), George Clausen (1852–1944), Charles Sims (1873–1928), Gerald Brockhurst (1890–1978), John Lavery (1856–1941)

Six Water Colour Painters of Today (1941) (exh. cat.): Ethel Walker (1861–1951), John Nash (1893–1977), David Jones (1895–1974), Paul Nash (1889–1946), Frances Hodgkins (1869–1947), Edna Clarke Hall (1879–1979)

Walter Richard Sickert (1941) (exh. cat.): Walter Richard Sickert (1860–1942)

War Artist Exhibitions (1941): no catalogue appears to have been produced for this exhibition

Nicholson and Yeats (January 1942) (exh. cat.): William Nicholson (1872–1949), Jack Butler Yeats (1871–1957)

War Artist Exhibitions (1942) (exh. cat.): Muirhead Bone (1876–1953), Paul Nash (1889–1946), Edward

Bawden (1903–1989), John Piper (1903–1992), Graham Sutherland (1903–1980), William Dring (1904–1990), Eric Kennington (1888–1960), Kenneth Rowntree (1915–1997), Michael Ford (1920–2005), Edward Ardizzone (1900–1979), Feliks Topolski (1907–1989), Henry Moore (1898–1986), Stanley Spencer (1891–1959), Eric Ravilious (1903–1942), Richard Eurich (1903–1992), Anthony Gross (1905–1984), R.V. Pitchforth (1895–1982), John Armstrong (1893–1973), Charles Ginner (1878–1952), Carel Weight (1908–1997), Barnett Freedman (1901–1958)

Memorial Exhibition of the Work of Philip Wilson Steer, organised by the Tate Gallery at the National Gallery (1943): Philip Wilson Steer (1860–1942)

War Artist Exhibitions (1943): no catalogue appears to have been produced for this exhibition

War Pictures at the National Gallery (1944) (exh. cat.): Henry Moore (1898–1986), Paul Nash (1889–1946), Edward Bawden (1903–1989), John Piper (1903–1992), Graham Sutherland (1903–1980), William Dring (1904–1990), Eric Kennington (1888–1960), Charles Ginner (1878–1952), Edward Ardizzone (1900–1979), Feliks Topolski (1907–1989), Muirhead Bone (1876–1953), Charles Cundall (1890–1971), Patrick Carpenter (active 1939–46), Eric Ravilious (1903–1942), John Platt (1886–1967), Richard Eurich (1903–1992), R.V. Pitchforth (1895–1982), John Armstrong (1893–1973), Stanley Spencer (1891–1959), Henry Lamb (1883–1960), Anthony Gross (1905–1984), Walter Russell (1867–1949)

War Artist Exhibitions (1945): no catalogue appears to have been produced for this exhibition

Paul Klee, organised by the Tate Gallery at the National Gallery (11 December 1945–17 February 1946) (exh. cat.): Paul Klee (1879–1940)

The Works of James Ensor, organised by the Arts Council of Great Britain at the National Gallery (27 February–31 March 1946) (exh. cat.): James Ensor (1860–1949)

Frank Auerbach and the National Gallery: Working after the Masters (19 July–17 September 1995) (exh. cat.): Frank Auerbach (born 1931)

Caro at the National Gallery: Sculpture from Painting (25 February–4 May 1998) (exh. cat.): Anthony Caro (1924–2013)

Henry Moore and the National Gallery (3 April– 31 May 1998) (exh. cat.): Henry Moore (1898–1986)

Encounters: New Art from Old (14 June–17 September 2000) (exh. cat.): Frank Auerbach (born 1931), Balthus (1908–2001), Louise Bourgeois (1911–2010), Anthony Caro (1924–2013), Patrick Caulfield (1936–2005), Francesco Clemente (born 1952), Stephen Cox (born 1946), Ian Hamilton Finlay (1925–2006), Lucian Freud (1922–2011), Richard Hamilton (1922–2011), David Hockney (born 1937), Howard Hodgkin (1932–2017), Jasper Johns (born 1930), Anselm Kiefer (born 1945), R.B. Kitaj (1932–2007), Leon Kossoff (1926–2019), Christopher Le Brun (born 1951), Claes Oldenburg (1929–2022), Paula Rego (1935–2022), Antoni Tàpies (1923–2012), Cy Twombly (1928–2011), Euan Uglow (1932–2000), Coosje van Bruggen (1942–2009), Bill Viola (born 1951), Jeff Wall (born 1946)

Kitaj: In the Aura of Cezanne and Other Masters (7 November 2001–10 February 2002) (exh. cat.): R.B. Kitaj (1932–2007)

Bill Viola: The Passions (22 October 2003–4 January 2004) (exh. cat.): Bill Viola (born 1951)

Tom Hunter: Living in Hell and Other Stories (7 December 2005–2 March 2006) (exh. cat.): Tom Hunter (born 1965). Hunter's *Murder: Two Men Wanted*, 2003, was bought with funds provided by Michael and Jane Wilson, 2007 (H199)

Tim Gardner: New Works (17 January–15 April 2007) (exh. cat.): Tim Gardner (born 1973)

Leon Kossoff: Drawing from Painting (14 May–1 July 2007) (exh. cat.): Leon Kossoff (1926–2019)

Scratch the Surface (20 July–30 November 2007): Yinka Shonibare (born 1962)

Alison Watt: Phantom (12 March–29 June 2008) (exh. cat.): Alison Watt (born 1965)

Kienholz: The Hoerengracht (18 November 2009– 21 February 2010) (exh. cat.): Edward Kienholz (1927–1994) and Nancy Reddin Kienholz (1943–2019)

Modern Perspectives: Clive Head (13 October– 28 November 2010): Clive Head (born 1965)

Bridget Riley: Paintings and Related Work (24 November 2010–22 May 2011) (exh. cat.): Bridget Riley (born 1931)

Modern Perspectives: Ben Johnson (8 December 2010–23 January 2011): Ben Johnson (born 1946)

Metamorphosis: Titian 2012 (11 July–23 September 2012) (exh. cat.): Chris Ofili (born 1968), Conrad Shawcross (born 1977), Mark Wallinger (born 1959)

Richard Hamilton: The Late Works (10 October 2012–13 January 2013) (exh. cat.): Richard Hamilton (1922–2011)

Seduced by Art: Photography Past and Present (31 October 2012–20 January 2013) (exh. cat.): Tina Barney (born 1945), Richard Billingham (born 1970), Nicky Bird (born 1960), John Blakemore (born 1936), Maisie Broadhead (born 1980), Julia Margaret Cameron (1815–1879), Helen Chadwick (1953–1996), Tacita Dean (born 1965), Luc Delahaye (born 1962), Rineke Dijkstra (born 1959), Ori Gersht (born 1967), Nan Goldin (born 1953), Beate Gütschow (born 1970), Craigie Horsfield (born 1949), Tom Hunter (born 1965), Sarah Jones (born 1959), Karen Knorr (born 1954), Richard Learoyd (born 1966), Dave Lewis (born 1962), Simon Norfolk (born 1963), Martin Parr (born 1952), Corinna Schnitt (born 1964), Jem Southam (born 1950), Thomas Struth (born 1954), Maud Sulter (1960–2008), Sam Taylor-Wood (born 1967), Jeff Wall (born 1946), Bettina von Zwehl (born 1971)

Maggi Hambling: Walls of Water (26 November 2014–15 February 2015): Maggi Hambling (born 1945)

Art in Dialogue: Duccio | Caro (13 June–8 November 2015): Anthony Caro (1924–2013)

Soundscapes (8 July–6 September 2015) (exh. cat.): Janet Cardiff (born 1957) and George Bures Miller (born 1960); Susan Philipsz (born 1965) (a few composers and musicians were also included)

Chris Ofili: Weaving Magic (26 April–28 August 2017)
(exh. cat.): Chris Ofili (born 1968)

Monochrome: Painting in Black and White
(30 October 2017–18 February 2018) (exh. cat.): Josef
Albers (1888–1976), Vija Celmins (born 1938), Chuck
Close (1940–2021), Marlene Dumas (born 1953), Olafur
Eliasson (born 1967), Alberto Giacometti (1901–1966),
Jasper Johns (born 1930), Ellsworth Kelly (1923–2015),
Kazimir Malevich (1879–1935), Gerhard Richter
(born 1932), Bridget Riley (born 1931), Frank Stella
(born 1936), Cy Twombly (1928–2011)

Tacita Dean: Still Life (15 March–28 May 2018)
(exh. cat.): Tacita Dean (born 1965)

Ed Ruscha: Course of Empire (11 June–7 October 2018)
(exh. cat.): Ed Ruscha (born 1937)

Rachel Maclean: The Lion and the Unicorn
(29 November 2018–3 February 2019): Rachel Maclean
(born 1987)

Sea Star: Sean Scully at the National Gallery
(13 April–11 August 2019) (exh. cat.): Sean Scully
(born 1945)

Young Bomberg, Old Masters (27 November 2019–
1 March 2020) (exh. cat.): David Bomberg (1890–1957)

Dance to the Music of Our Time: A Live Exhibition
(15 October–10 December 2021): Florence Peake (born
1973), Hetain Patel (born 1980), Zadie Xa (born 1983)
and Benito Mayor Vallejo (born 1981)

Kehinde Wiley at the National Gallery: The Prelude
(10 December 2021–18 April 2022) (exh. cat.): Kehinde
Wiley (born 1977)

Lucian Freud: New Perspectives (1 October 2022–
22 January 2023) (exh. cat.): Lucian Freud (1922–2011)

Paula Rego: Crivelli's Garden (20 July–29 October
2023) (exh. cat.): Paula Rego (1935–2022)

APPENDIX 7
ARTIST IN RESIDENCE AT THE NATIONAL
GALLERY, 1980–9 (List comprising date of the
residency, date of associated exhibition, and any works
created during the residency and gifted afterwards to

the National Gallery. The works dated 1991 relate to
a separate project, called the National Gallery Print
Portfolio (GROUP146), for which see p. 67.)

Maggi Hambling (born 1945): October 1980–
March 1981 (there was no exhibition)
Portrait of Archie MacDonald, 1980–1 (H11),
presented 1981
A Laugh with the Rokeby Venus, 1991 (H20)

Jock McFadyen (born 1950): October 1981–
March 1982; exhibition 2–30 June 1982
Disco Dancing at Home, 1981–2 (H10),
presented 1982
Canary, 1991 (H18)

Michael Porter (born 1948): October 1982–
April 1983; exhibition 1–30 June 1983
A Walled English Garden, 1982–3 (H9),
presented 1983
Sharp Frost, 1991 (H22)

Kevin O'Brien (born 1956): September 1983–
March 1984; exhibition 2 July–4 August 1984
The Man who gave away the Moon, 1983–4 (H32),
presented 1984
Sebastian, 1991 (H37)

Hughie O'Donoghue (born 1953): October 1984–
April 1985; exhibition 1–30 June 1985
View of Toledo, 1984–5 (H34), presented 1985
'Actaeon' after Titian, 1991 (H39)

June Redfern (born 1951): October 1985–April 1986;
exhibition 9 July–17 August 1986
On the Hill, 1985–6 (H17), presented 1986
After Bellini, 1991 (H19)

Vivien Blackett (born 1956): October 1986–
March 1987; exhibition 1–31 July 1987
The Three Hills, 1986–7 (H33), presented 1987
'Retreat' after Giovanni di Paolo, 1991 (H40)

Philip Mead (born 1948): October 1987–March 1988;
exhibition 1–31 May 1988
Untitled?, 1987–8 (H36), presented 1988
The Possibility of Loss, 1991 (H41)

Madeleine Strindberg (born 1955): October 1988–
March 1989; exhibition 1–30 June 1989
Soft Cut, 1988–9 (H35), presented 1989
Shadowlands, 1991 (H38)

APPENDIX 8
ASSOCIATE ARTISTS AT THE NATIONAL GALLERY,
1990–2016 (List comprising date of the residency, date
of associated exhibition and catalogue, and any works
created during the residency that now belong to the
National Gallery.)

Paula Rego (1935–2022): 1990–1; exhibition, *Paula Rego: Tales from the National Gallery*, 13 December 1991–1 March 1992 (before a touring exhibition in Plymouth, Middlesbrough, Manchester and Barnsley)
Crivelli's Garden (H12.1–5)
'Witches at their Incantations' after Rosa, 1991 (H21)

Ken Kiff (1935–2001): 1991–3; exhibition, *Ken Kiff at the National Gallery*, 20 October 1993–9 January 1994

Peter Blake (born 1932): 1994–6; exhibition, *Now We Are 64: Peter Blake at the National Gallery*, 25 September 1996–5 January 1997

Ana Maria Pacheco (born 1943): 1997–9; exhibition, *Ana Maria Pacheco: New Painting and Sculpture*, 29 September 1999–9 January 2000 (before a touring exhibition around England)

Ron Mueck (born 1958): 1999–2002; exhibition, *Ron Mueck: Making Sculpture at the National Gallery*, 19 March–22 June 2003

John Virtue (born 1947): 2003–5; exhibition, *John Virtue: The London Paintings*, 9 March–5 June 2005

Alison Watt (born 1965): 2006–8; exhibition, *Alison Watt: Phantom*, 12 March–22 June 2008

Michael Landy (born 1963): 2010–12; exhibition, *Michael Landy: Saints Alive*, 23 May–24 November 2013

George Shaw (born 1966): 2014–16; exhibition, *George Shaw: My Back to Nature*, 11 May–30 October 2016

APPENDIX 9
ARTIST IN RESIDENCE AT THE NATIONAL GALLERY, 2019–onwards
(List comprising date of the residency, date of associated exhibition and catalogue, and any works created as part of the residency and acquired by the partner UK gallery.)

Rosalind Nashashibi (born 1973): September 2019–December 2020; exhibition, *Rosalind Nashashibi: An Overflow of Passion and Sentiment*, Room 30, 3 December 2020–27 June 2021
Work acquired by the Pier Arts Centre, Stromness, Orkney: *Denim Sky* 2022, 16mm film transferred to HD video, 67 mins 24 seconds. Commissioned by the National Gallery, London, as part of the 2020 National Gallery Artist in Residence Programme. First edition presented to the Pier Arts Centre, Stromness, Orkney, by the Contemporary Art Society, 2022, with the support of Anna Yang and Joseph Schull.

Ali Cherri (born 1976): April 2021–March 2022; exhibition, *Ali Cherri: If you prick us, do we not bleed?*, Rooms 57, 58 and 59, 16 March–12 June 2022
Work acquired by the Herbert Art Gallery and Museum, Coventry: *The Madonna of the Cat, after Barocci*, 2022, taxidermy goldfinch, porcelain hand sculpture, wooden display cabinet, 147.7 × 81 × 40.6 cm. Commissioned by the National Gallery, London, as part of the 2021 National Gallery Artist in Residence Programme. Presented to the Herbert Art Gallery and Museum, Coventry, by the Contemporary Art Society, 2022, with the support of Anna Yang and Joseph Schull.

Céline Condorelli (born 1974): September 2022–September 2023; exhibition, *Pentimenti (The Corrections)*, Room 31, 13 September 2023–7 January 2024
Work acquired by the Royal Albert Memorial Museum and Art Gallery, Exeter: *Bulk, Everlasting Colour*, 2023, printed carpet, 640 × 340 cm and *Pentimenti (0751)*, 2023, giclée print on Hahnemühle Photo Rag, 54.5 × 39 cm. Commissioned by the National Gallery, London, as part of the 2023 National Gallery Artist in Residence Programme. Presented to the Royal Albert Memorial Museum, Exeter, by the Contemporary Art Society, 2024, with support of Anna Yang and Joseph Schull.

Katrina Palmer (born 1967): December 2023–December 2024

APPENDIX 10
NATIONAL GALLERY CONTEMPORARY FELLOWS WITH ART FUND, 2020–onwards
(List comprising date of the residency, date of associated exhibition and catalogue, and any works created during the residency, which now belong to UK galleries outside London.)

Nalini Malani (born 1946): 2020–2; exhibition, *Nalini Malani: My Reality is Different*, Sunley Room, 2 March–11 June 2023 (preceded by an exhibition at the Holburne Museum, Bath, 7 October 2022–8 January 2023).
Work acquired by the Holburne Museum, Bath: *My Reality is Different*, 2024, nine pencil, ink, acrylic, collage on digital pigment prints on Moab Entrada paper, 30 × 54 cm each. Presented by the Art Fund, 2024. Commissioned as part of the inaugural National Gallery Contemporary Fellowship with Art Fund in partnership with the Holburne Museum.

EXTRACTS FROM CORRESPONDENCE BETWEEN DAVID HOCKNEY AND THE NATIONAL GALLERY CONCERNING HIS *ARTIST'S EYE* EXHIBITION, *LOOKING AT PICTURES IN A ROOM*, 1981
(All the letters are in the exhibition file for David Hockney's *Artist's Eye* exhibition of 1981: NGA, NG32/135. Original styling, spelling and grammar in Hockney's letters have been retained.)

David Hockney to Michael Levey, 5 March 1979:
'I must tell you I enjoyed the exhibition Anthony Caro organised and the one Richard H. did. At the moment my only suggestion is this. In 1977 I made a picture called "looking at pictures on a screen". It was a portrait of Henry Geldzahler looking at reproductions pinned to a screen. All the reproductions were from the National Gallery. Vermeer, Van Gogh Piero and Degas. I know it would show up my work, – but I don't mind, – but that painting (at the moment its in Minniapolios but I'm sure we could borrow it) with a screen (thats in London) with the reproductions and then the real paintings on the wall.

If you would like a reproduction of my painting I'm sure Kasmin would let you have one. If you think the whole idea is crazy – I don't mind thinking again. I must tell you I <u>love</u> the collection of the National Gallery.'

Michael Levey to David Hockney, 22 January 1980:
'I am most attracted by your suggestion of displaying your painting *Looking at Pictures on a Screen* together with the screen as well as our pictures. Of course, this would be rather different from the <u>Artist's Eye</u> exhibitions as they have turned out so far, but all the better for that.'

David Hockney to Michael Levey, 5 February 1980:
'Ron tells me how much he is enjoying working on his exhibition and I'm sure I will.

Incidently, – here is a strange request, – or may be its not so strange. I have always wanted to do a copy of a Van Gogh painting, – yet stood in the N.G. every morning would be hard for me, – people would natter me, – I have drawn there before. Would it be possible to do it in the basement. I'm sure I could do it in 2 or three days. With Van Gogh you can actually see how he did the painting. (I have seen people copying your Rembrandts and working on white canvas. They hadn't taken the trouble to find out how Rembrandt began his painting). – Perhaps I could do the one in my picture, and then include it in the exhibition as well.

I have come to the conclusion that copying is a marvellous way to learn, it was good enough for Degas, Van Gogh and almost everybody before 1920. I recommend it to young students of painting now. I even think museums should encourage it in artists. They do have some responsibilities to artists working now, which sometimes they seem to forget. Every time I go in the Metropolitan Museum in N.Y. now I get very worked up when I see the notice they put up more and more 'No Photography or <u>Sketching</u>'. This seems to me to be insulting to students of painting and very unserious. They even had it up for their own Degas exhibition which of course included some of his own copies of other pictures, – done in the days before notices like that appeared. I mean to write to them about it yet when I try I seem to be like a preacher or moralist telling them their job. If libraries started being as unserious as that though where would we be?

Apologies for my digression. I look foreward to our meeting very much.'

Michael Levey to David Hockney, 14 February 1980:
'About your request to copy the Van Gogh, I'd like to be sympathetic and can well understand your wish to avoid being nagged and nattered at as would happen to you doing it on the Main Floor. I <u>think</u> we could arrange something for you, especially if it would only take you two or three days, and of course if we could justify breaking our own rules on the grounds that the copy would be included in your exhibition. In fact, it's a very exciting proposal and would be fascinating for visitors to the exhibition.

All you say about great painters of the past copying earlier painters' work is profoundly true. At least in this Gallery we – as you know – do take student copyists and permit sketching at any time. In [*sic*] can also sharpen the eyes of visitors, I think, to look at an artist making a copy – tiresome though it can be for the artist.'

Michael Levey to David Hockney, 28 July 1980:
'I was very glad to have the opportunity to meet recently and to talk about various things, not least of course your wish to take photographs in the Gallery. I was also delighted that you are so positively interested in doing "The Artist's Eye" exhibition next year, and I hope that you and Alistair Smith will be meeting to talk about this before you leave London.

I undertook to consider very seriously the points you raised about photography in the Gallery. While

obviously sympathetic to anything which sharpens
the eye of anyone going around, I don't believe it is
practical to allow anyone at any time to photograph. I
am convinced that in the long run this would only disturb
those who may well be looking just as intently and who
have a right to remain in front of paintings for as long as
they like.

However, I think it would be quite wrong on the
other hand if artists and other interested people were
not permitted at any time to take photographs of our
pictures. As you pointed out to me, the sort of detail
which may well interest the artist to record in this way is
something highly personal and is anyway unlikely to exist
among our own photographs. We have various publics
to satisfy, and the most reasonable solution seems to
me that private photography of the kind we are talking
about should be permitted for a period before the
Gallery opens at 10 a.m.

While this may not be ideal from every point of
view, it certainly meets any potential criticism that the
Gallery is not accommodating or indeed as flexible as
it can be. It shows that we are very far from forbidding
the activity. As for exact arrangements, we shall have
to see how things work out, but I envisage the Chief
Warder being given due notice that an artist like yourself
would like to come in on a given morning and take
some photographs. Not the least advantage of such a
system is that the Gallery will be free of crowds, making
photography very much easier.'

Alistair Smith to David Hockney, 20 August 1980:
'I enclose the Artist's Eye pamphlets so far published. I
remember your saying that you would like to have them.
As you can see, Anthony Caro's is slightly different,
this is because he could not decide what to have in the
exhibition until the very last minute. Therefore there is no
list of what he included. Also, he preferred to have a kind
of interview format for the pamphlet.

… I will collect as many reproductions of the four
pictures in question as I can. The whole thing is very
exciting. Incidentally, if you want us to arrange the
transport of the chair (I believe you said it was in New
York) please do not hesitate to say so, and let us have
the necessary addresses. I have had a word with our
designer and publications people here. They are happy
to do all the work that you require later this year. Perhaps
the most important deadline is for the catalogue …

It was a great pleasure meeting you – I do not think
I have ever enjoyed an opera quite so much.'

Alistair Smith to David Hockney, 16 March 1981:
'Following on our telephone conversation, I am
sending you this black and white photograph of the van
Gogh. The National Gallery does not publish a colour
reproduction of it, and I cannot, at the moment, put my
hand on a colour reproduction published by any other
company. If I find one, I will send it to you …

I am now writing … to organise the photography
necessary for the poster.

Good luck with the text.'

**Michael Levey to David Hockney, 10 September
1981:**
'Please forgive me for not writing before to convey our
warmest thanks for the Artist's Eye exhibition which you
so kindly organised for us and which closed at the end of
August having been a very great success. It was visited
by just over 163,000 people.

Quite apart from the number of visitors, I feel
sure that the exhibition had the stimulating effect you
wished and we welcomed. It will have made many
people look and think about paintings – and all the more
thanks to your shrewd comments in the accompanying
booklet.

It really was good of you to create this exhibition for
us and we all remain profoundly grateful.

With greetings and best wishes from everyone here
– and hopes of having the pleasure of seeing you again
sometime.'

Michael Levey to David Hockney, 12 October 1981:
'When the Trustees met on 1 October, which was their
first meeting since "The Artist's Eye" exhibition closed,
they expressed their greatest gratitude to you for having
organised this stimulating exhibition for us.

As a small token of their appreciation they wished
to issue you in future with a privilege Pass to the Gallery,
which of course means that when you are in London
you will have the opportunity of coming in out of Gallery
hours … We also ask holders visiting the Gallery in this
way to bring no more than a maximum of six guests on
any visit.

I am delighted to convey the Trustees' warm thanks,
in which we of course join, and to enclose herewith your
Pass.'

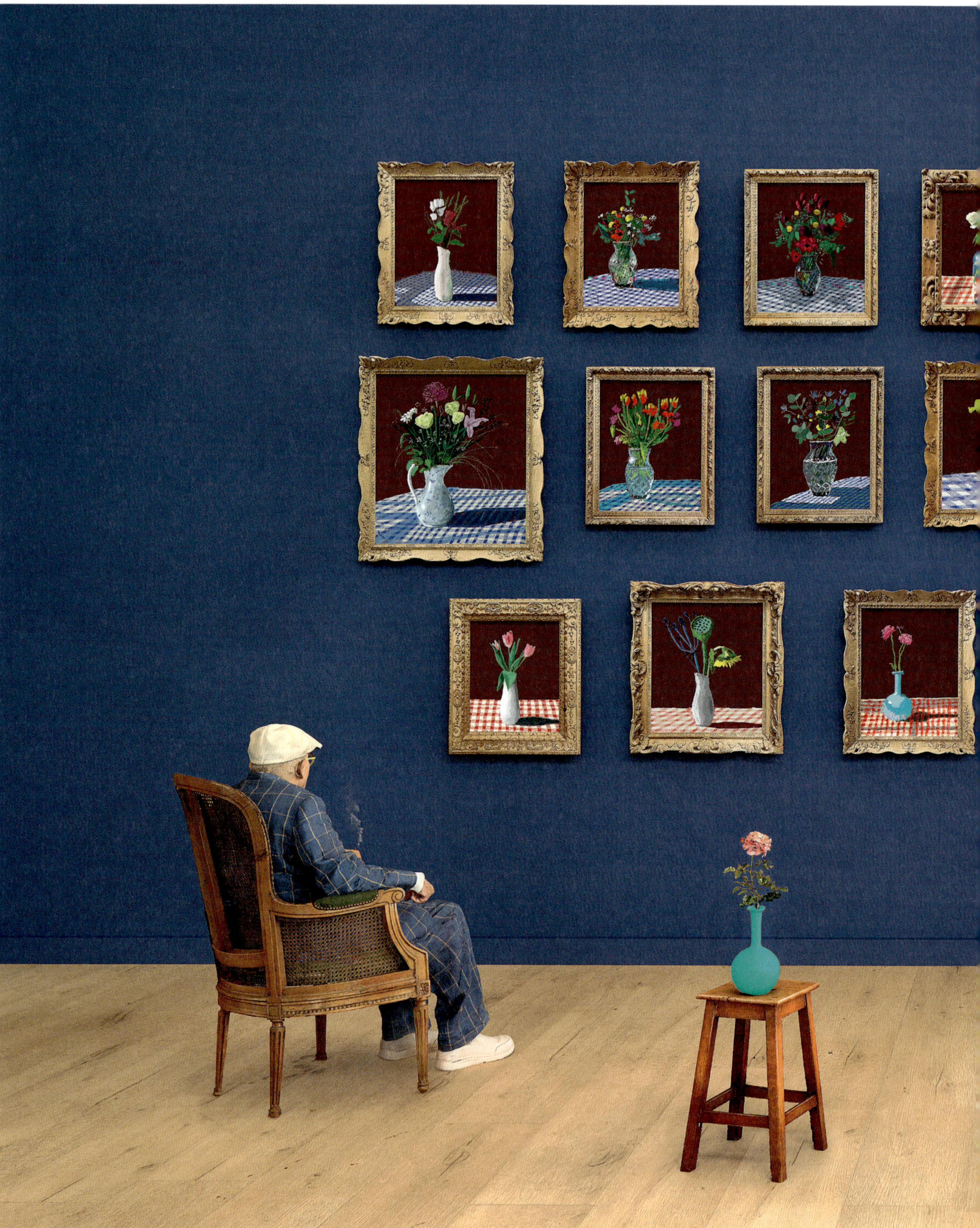

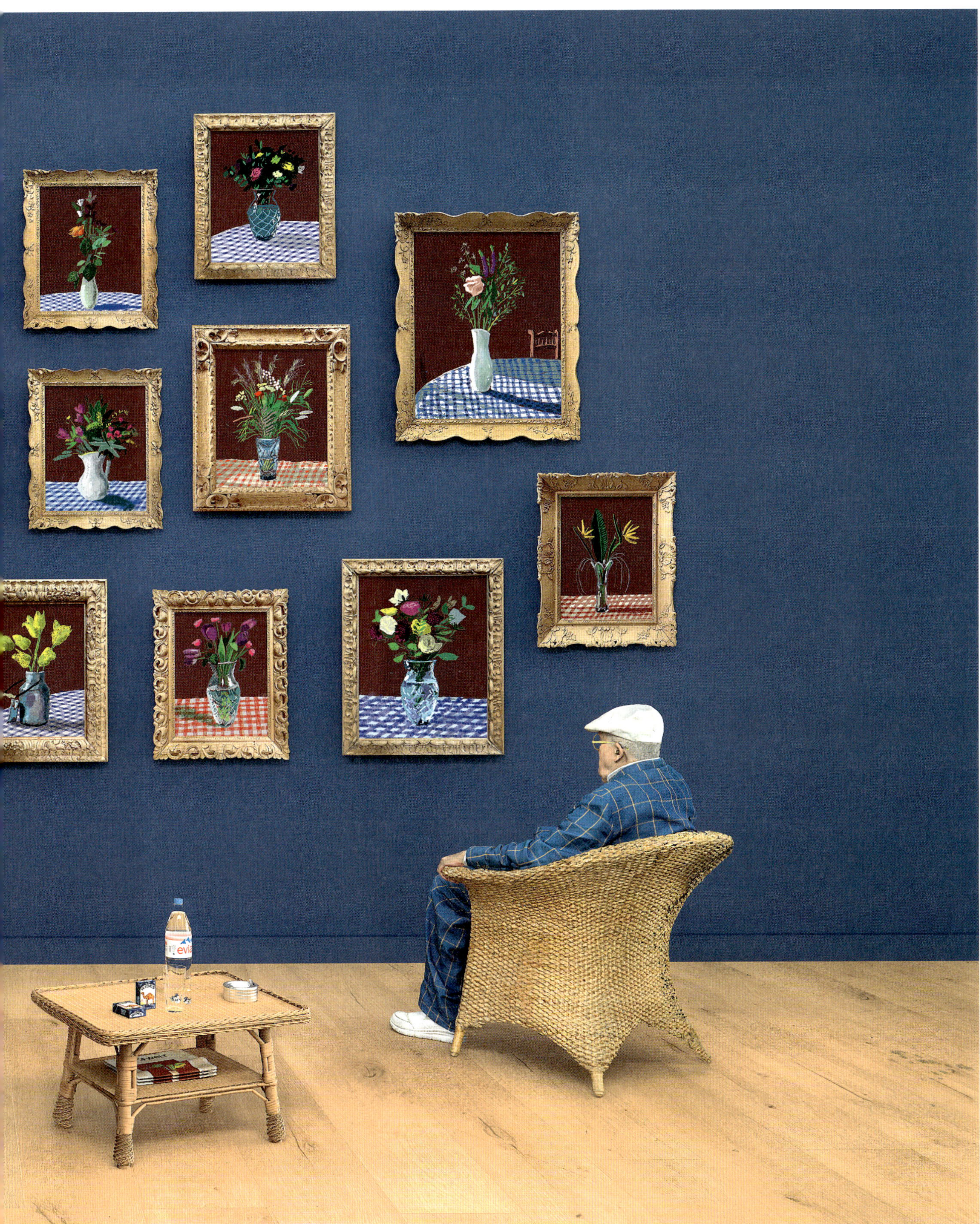

NOTES

NGA = National Gallery Archive

1 Looking at Pictures for a Long, Long Time

1　Quotation from Chapter 1, p. 26.

2 Transcending the Centuries: Artistic Conversations with Piero

1　Stangos (ed.) 1976, p. 61.

2　Rachel Spence, 'Tess Jaray's From Piero and Other Paintings – shadows of the masters', *Financial Times*, 10 February 2021, www.ft.com/content/406b6a9a-fa0d-4ff1-9c56-65375b966e4a (accessed 23 August 2023).

3　See Avery-Quash and Llewellyn 2022, pp. 3–16. Our research extends the scholarship of Luciano Cheles, Caroline Elam, Marilyn Aronberg Lavin, Nicholas Penny and Larry Witham, which has explored Piero's influence on twentieth-century art, and in particular on the British Modernist School centred around Roger Fry. See Cheles 2013, pp. 57–75; Elam 2004, and Elam 2016, pp. 315–23; Lavin 1981, and Lavin (ed.) 1995; Penny 2003, pp. 3–6; Witham, 2014.

4　NGA, NG17/2, *National Gallery Annual Report* for 1857–8, London 1858, p. 88.

5　Ralph Nicholson Wornum, revised by Charles Lock Eastlake, *Descriptive and Historical Catalogue of the Pictures in the National Gallery with Biographical Notices of the Painters: Foreign Schools Catalogue*, London 1858, pp. 85–6.

6　See Avery-Quash (ed.) 2011, vol. 1, p. 432.

7　NG585.

8　NG758.

9　Martin Davies, *National Gallery Catalogues: The Earlier Italian Schools*, London 1961, pp. 427–8. Due to the state of preservation of *The Baptism*, Eastlake initially considered acquiring it for himself; see Avery-Quash 2015, p. 20. Interestingly, Eastlake's wife, Elizabeth, appears to have been a great advocate of the purchase of Piero's *Baptism*. In a letter, dated 6 April 1861, to the Eastlakes' great friend, archaeologist, politician and diplomat Sir Austen Henry Layard, she wrote: 'Sir Chas is anxious that you sh[oul]d kindly inspect the Uzielli

P. della Francesca on view at Christies on Monday – with a view to giving him your opinion as to the policy of endeavouring to secure it for the N: G: He is irresolute – considering its injured condition – & the silence of Vasari, & the criticism of Passavant. He will also examine it afresh on Monday but has not empowered me to say whether fore or afternoon. I shall probably accompany him, & what influence I have will probably be executed in favour of trying to obtain it.' See Julie Sheldon (ed.), *The Letters of Elizabeth Rigby, Lady Eastlake*, Liverpool 2009, p. 208.

10　Avery-Quash 2011, 1, p. 570.

11　John Charles Robinson, 'To the Editor of the Times', *The Times*, 9 June 1874, p. 7, col. E. See also his subsequent letters published in *The Times*, 15 June 1874, p. 12, col. D, and 24 June 1874, p. 13, col. F.

12　See John Charles Robinson, *Catalogue of the various works of Art forming the Collection of Matthew Uzielli*, London 1860, no. 819.

13　NGA, NGA2/3/2/13, Ralph Nicholson Wornum's Diary: 10 and 11 May 1861.

14　Wilson 1991, p. 35; Amery 1991, p. 127.

15　NG667, NG668, NG669 and NG672, respectively.

16　'The National Gallery', *Illustrated London News*, 15 June 1861, pp. 546–7.

17　*Encyclopaedia Britannica*, London 1885, p. 82.

18　William George Waters, *Piero della Francesca*, London 1901, p. 55.

19　See Tim Hilton, 'Fresh-faced flush of venerable age: Five centuries have passed', *The Guardian*, 28 May 1992, p. 28.

20　E.V. Lucas, *A Wanderer in London*, London 1906, p. 96.

21　Charles Lewis Hind, *Landscape Painting from Giotto to the Present Day*, London 1923, p. 81; Charles Holmes, *An Introduction to Italian Painting*, London 1929, p. 62.

22　'The National Gallery Centenary: Pictures that please me most', *The Guardian*, 1–3 April 1924.

23　NG3266.

24　NG3860 and NG3908, respectively; both were purchased using the Courtauld Fund. The rediscovery of Piero in the late nineteenth century

in France was largely due to Charles Blanc, Director of the Ecole des Beaux-Arts in Paris, where Seurat was a student. This was pointed out by Victor Pasmore in the catalogue entries that he wrote for Piero's *Baptism* and Seurat's *Bathers at Asnières* in his *Artist's Eye* exhibition in 1990. For further details, see Chapter 4 and fig. 61. For more on the influence of Piero's *Baptism* on Degas, see Brown 2024, pp. 74–5.

25　Quoted in Virginia Woolf, *Roger Fry: A Biography*, New York 1940, p. 197.

26　Elam 2004, p. 36. See also Elam, *Roger Fry and Italian Art*, London 2019, pp. 213–38, where Fry's texts about Piero are reprinted.

27　Hendy 1968, p. 85, suggests that Piero was in certain ways a precursor not only of Cezanne but also of El Greco, Caravaggio and Van Gogh, and p. 125, where Piero's figures are compared with 'some great "Reclining Figure" by Henry Moore'.

28　André Lhote, *La Nouvelle Revue Française* (January 1930), quoted in Roberto Longhi (ed.), *Piero della Francesca*, trans. David Tabbat, New York 2002, p. 256.

29　Quoted in Lago 1996, p. 56.

30　The relationship between Vanessa Bell's and Piero's paintings was first pointed out by Frances Spalding in *Vanessa Bell*, London 1984, p. 124. See also Lisa Tickner, 'Vanessa Bell: *Studland Beach*, Domesticity, and "Significant Form",' in Tickner, *Modern Life & Modern Subjects: British Art in the Early Twentieth Century*, New Haven and London 2000, pp. 117–42.

31　Quoted in David Leighton, *Clare Leighton: The Growth and Shaping of an Artist-Writer*, The Estate of Clare Leighton 2009, pp. 8–9.

32　'Exhibitions of the Week', *The Athenæum* (9 January 1920), p. 138.

33　Michael Holroyd, *Augustus John: A Biography*, London 1976, p. 289.

34　'Grafton Galleries', *The Telegraph*, 6 May 1909.

35　Quoted in Gilbert Spencer, *Memoirs of a Painter*, London 1974, p. 99.

36　See Martineau 2023, pp. 952–67.

37　Postcard from Gwen Raverat to Gilbert Spencer, UCL Art Museum, London.

38　Quoted in Donald Hall, *Writers at Work: Second Series*, New York 1963, p. 44.

39　T.S. Eliot, *Poems*, New York 1920, pp. 10–14. Interestingly, David Hockney quoted the same passage in the catalogue that accompanied his 1981 *Artist's Eye* exhibition; see *Looking at Pictures in a Book*, London 1981, p. 14.

40　See gallery label, January 2019, on Tate's website, www.tate.org.uk/art/artworks/bomberg-the-mud-bath-t00656 (accessed 23 August 2023).

41　John D. Batten (ed.), *Papers of The Society of Mural Decorators & Painters in Tempera: Second Volume, 1907–1924*, Brighton 1925; www.eggtempera.com/about/ (accessed 23 August 2023).

42　The essay was published in Christiana J. Herringham (ed.), *Papers of the Society of Painters in Tempera, 1901–1907*, London c. 1907, pp. 23–7, here p. 25, where she further noted of *The Baptism* that it 'is as evidently painted over a particularly bright terra verte'. See Clarke 2019, doi: doi.org/10.16995/ntn.823 (accessed 20 May 2023).

43　Roger Fry, 'On a Profile Portrait by Baldovinetti', *The Burlington Magazine*, 18, no. 96 (1911), pp. 311–12.

44　*The Manchester Guardian*, 13 April 1927.

45　Quoted in Pamela Todd, *Bloomsbury at Home*, London 1999, p. 125.

46　Bertram 1951, pp. 120–3.

47　Quoted in Hassell 1999, p. 202.

48　In the case of visionary Swedish artist Hilma af Klint (1862–1944), whose colour palette is reminiscent of Piero and who likewise worked in the medium of egg tempera, her deliveries of so many eggs caused her to be accused of being a witch. See www.theguardian.com/artanddesign/2020/oct/06/hilma-af-klint-abstract-art-beyond-the-visible-film-documentary (accessed 15 November 2023).

49　Letter from Gordon House to Paul Liss, 1997, private collection. See also Smiles and Pratt in Exeter 1996, p. 26.

50　Quoted in William Feaver, *The Lives of Lucian Freud: Fame, 1968–2011*, London 2020, p. 198. See also

Wiggins 2024 (forthcoming), p. 77, who remarks: 'The whole of the early Renaissance was virtually written off and [Freud] took pride in dismissing Piero della Francesca, who has the status of near-sacred cow in art historical circles.' Wiggins also cites (p. 65) an interview with Nicholas Penny (National Gallery Director, 2008–15), in which Freud explained his relationship to the work of other artists: 'I've always had a natural or perhaps unnatural resistance against being influenced by things. I like looking and looking at them and taking them in. But if I thought that (my work) had emerged in some way that related to what I am looking at – I would not feel free about working like that.'
51 Hockney and Kitaj 1977, p. 76; cited in An 2021, p. 58.
52 See NGA, NG30/1981/24–26, 85–86, photographs in the Hockney *Artist's Eye* folder, and email from David Hockney to Sunnifa Hope, Head of Trafalgar Square Exhibitions, 16 March 2023: 'I really love your Piero. My mother had it in her bedroom for many years until she died (a reproduction of course).'
53 An 2021, p. 56.
54 Ibid., p. 61. More literally, it appears to be a reflection of the earlier version seen in fig. 25.
55 Hockney 1993, p. 154.
56 Quoted in Peter Clothier, *David Hockney*, New York 1995, p. 107. See also Chapter 1, p. 24.
57 London 1981, p. 10.
58 Scholar Gerard Hastings, writing on Vaughan, quoted in John Olsen, *Drawn from Life*, Sydney 1997, p. 11, cited in www.deutscherandhackett.com/auction/lot/baptism-1963 (accessed 15 November 2023).
59 Martin Gayford interview with Antony Gormley; information kindly supplied by the interviewer to Susanna Avery-Quash.
60 Lucy Davies, 'National treasures: Prince Charles, Mary McCartney and more on their favourite National Gallery artwork', *The Telegraph*, 3 July 2021, www.telegraph.co.uk/art/what-to-see/national-treasures-prince-charles-mary-mccartney-favourite-national/ (accessed 23 August 2023).

61 'Tess Jaray: Into Light', www.karstenschubert.com/publications/161-tess-jaray-into-light/ (accessed 15 September 2023).
62 'Tess Jaray: From Piero and other paintings', www.sculpture.uk.com/tess-jaray-from-piero-and-other-paintings (accessed 23 August 2023).
63 'Rachel Whiteread, *Ghost*, 1990', www.nga.gov/collection/art-object-page.131285.html (accessed 23 August 2023).
64 'Rachel Whiteread on Piero della Francesca', *Gagosian Quarterly*, 1 May 2020, gagosian.com/quarterly/2020/05/01/rachel-whiteread-piero-della-francesca/ (accessed 23 August 2023).
65 Bridget Riley, 'Painting Now', *The Burlington Magazine*, 139, no. 1134 (1997), pp. 616–22, here p. 617.
66 Ibid.
67 Riley's *Verve* brings to mind another work by Piero, his depiction of an arched vault in his *Annunciation* from the St Anthony Polyptych of Perugia; see useum.org/artwork/Polyptych-of-Perugia-Piero-della-Francesca-1469 (accessed 20 December 2023).

3 A 200-Year Dialogue between Living Artists and the National Gallery
1 Quotation from Chapter 1, p. 26.
2 There is very little secondary literature on this topic; see J. Putnam 2001; Crookham 2009, pp. 64–73; Chippindale 2010; and especially the invaluable text by Stearn 2016. For a recent discussion of the historic and ongoing centrality of the National Gallery's collection for living artists' engagement with works by their forebears, especially with reference to how its works by Degas have generated responses from Auerbach, Bourgeois, Hambling, Kitaj and Rego, see Brown 2024, esp. pp. 2, 13, 15, 17, 32–3, 51, 63–4, 180–1, 206–7.
3 See Robertson 1978, p. 290, also p. 292.
4 Stearn 2016, p. 52 notes incorrectly only Charlies Lock Eastlake as an artist director of the National Gallery. The situation in the UK contrasted with continental practice, where, from the mid-nineteenth century, scholarly art-

historical expertise, nurtured in the universities, was favoured over artistic ability, so that directors usually came with formal academic qualifications. See Avery-Quash and Carleton Paget 2013, pp. 33–47. The Gallery has acquired a handful of works by former artist keepers/directors, including oil sketches by Charles Lock Eastlake, the first Director (1855–65), and engravings after his work, a self portrait by William Boxall, second Director (1866–74), and some engravings by Charles Holroyd, fifth Director (1906–16); they are mostly preserved in the Gallery's Contextual Collection (see Appendix 1).
5 See Avery-Quash 2018, pp. 247–66.
6 When the Tate Gallery was given its own Board of Trustees in 1917 (previously, its Board was the same one that oversaw the operations of the National Gallery), it was established that three members of the National Gallery Board should sit on the Tate Board along with the National Gallery Director. When the two institutions separated fully in 1955, nothing about the shared trustees was mentioned in the National Gallery and Tate Gallery Act 1954. However, in the current legislation, as determined by the Museums and Galleries Act 1992, it is specified that, regarding the National Gallery, one Trustee 'shall be appointed by the Tate Gallery Board from among the members of that Board'; likewise, in relation to the Tate's Board, one of its members 'shall be appointed by the National Gallery Board' from among its members. These trustees do not need to be artists, although the Tate does have to include artists among its number. Twice during the last decade, the National Gallery has opted for one of the Tate artist trustees to act as its liaison trustee – Dexter Dalwood (served 2015–19) and Rosalind Nashashibi (served since 2023).
7 NG49 and NG726, respectively. See Esposito 2018, pp. 191–210.
8 NG666. See Avery-Quash 2015, pp. 11–37.
9 NG6620. See Robbins in London 2016, cat. 2, p. 25.
10 Transferred to Tate, N01205.

11 See Crookham in London 2012a, pp. 51–65.
12 See NGA, NG7/42/8, letter from Mr R.H. Nibbs re Turner's palette, 30 January 1883; NG7/96/6, letter from Miss Isabel Constable re her father's palette, 29 October 1887; NG7/173/5, letter from Mrs Hueffer re Ford Madox Brown's palette, 7 May 1894.
13 See NG6/1/271, letter to Mr James Hall re Wilkie's palette, 7 June 1842; NG7/261/11, letter from Mrs A. Lewis, re Phillip's palette, 9 January 1902.
14 See Crookham and Robbins 2016, pp. 99–116.
15 Both Sir David Wilkie's *The Village Holiday* of 1809–11 and William Hogarth's *The Painter and his Pug* of 1745 have been transferred to Tate, N00122 and N00112, respectively.
16 Quoted in Spalding 1999, pp. 9–10.
17 For a brief overview of this contentious bequest, see ibid., pp. 26–8.
18 NG621.
19 See Spalding 1999, especially Chapter 2, 'The Search for Identity', pp. 23–35; Crookham 2009, pp. 43–9.
20 For instance, the 1946 Massey Report stated that all international paintings at Tate would in time be transferred to the National Gallery, either when they were no longer regarded as 'modern' or at an earlier time if the National Gallery Director required them; see Spalding 1999, p. 91.
21 Pablo Picasso, *Fruit Dish, Bottle and Violin*, 1914 (NG6449); Gustav Klimt, *Portrait of Hermine Gallia*, 1904 (NG6434); Henri Matisse, *Portrait of Greta Moll*, 1908 (NG6450). Worth recalling, too, is the fact that it was the National Gallery and not the Tate Gallery that bought important French Impressionist paintings at the Edgar Degas Sale, Paris, in 1918. See Spalding 1999, pp. 185–6, who notes: 'No fixed and final policy emerged from all these discussions, but there was an acceptance of the National Gallery's wish to purchase into the twentieth century, combined with an awareness that the entire national holding of early twentieth-century art was still seriously thin.'
22 See Oliver 2004.

23   This commission was the subject of a focus exhibition at the Gallery, Room 46, 20 July–29 October 2023; see Mistry and Aridjis in London 2023. See also Wilson 1991, p. 23.

24   Both works are in the National Gallery's Contextual Collection, H26 and H47, respectively.

25   Ben Uri Gallery and Museum, 1987-159; see benuri.org/artists/69-lily-delissa-joseph/works/696-lily-delissa-joseph-the-art-gallery/ (accessed 21 December 2023); see also Tate, N00785.

26   'Denim Sky', lux.org.uk/work/denim-sky/. See also 'Vivian's Garden', another of Nashashibi's films in which interiors of the National Gallery appear: opencitylondon.com/events/denim-sky-vivians-garden/ (both accessed 20 December 2023). For Condorelli's exhibition, see www.youtube.com/watch?v=zFO3NI1gyEw (accessed 21 December 2023).

27   Wiggins in Münster 2014–15, p. 168.

28   Conlin 2006, pp. 28–45. Before the foundation of the National Gallery, artists working in the UK could copy works of the past in private collections, if they could gain privileged access. Otherwise, they were dependent on studying art in early public collections (Dulwich Picture Gallery, London, and the Fitzwilliam Museum, Cambridge, were both founded in the second decade of the nineteenth century) as well as in churches, cathedrals and other institutions, and also took advantage of preview days at auction houses, notably at Christie's in Pall Mall, London, and temporary exhibitions, including those arranged by the British Institution in Pall Mall. See Avery-Quash 2023, pp. 165–83.

29   In 1845 Charles Eastlake published a letter outlining problems arising from a lack of space at the National Gallery, including the 'insufficient room for the accommodation of artists and others copying in the Gallery' which meant that the number of 'students … allowed to copy in oil, on private days (Fridays and Saturdays) is limited to fifty'. See C.L. Eastlake, *The National Gallery. Observations on the unfitness of the present building for its purpose: in a letter to the Right Hon. Sir Robert Peel, Bart, By*

Charles Lock Eastlake, R.A., Keeper of the National Gallery, London 1845, pp. 16–17. The first official annual report of the Gallery, published by Eastlake as Director in 1856, stated that there was a limit of 70 places, of which 20 were reserved for Royal Academy students. Originally the student days were Fridays and Saturdays but they had moved to Thursdays and Fridays by 1859.

30   Cited in Potter (ed.) 2013, p. 10. See also Wiggins in Münster 2014–15, p. 168.

31   Quoted in Neil MacGregor's Foreword to *Encounters* in 2000, and by Wiggins in Münster 2014–15, p. 168, where he also cites Frank Auerbach's desire to surpass earlier artists' effort despite a feeling that 'one won't achieve it'.

32   See Hutchison 1968; Leslie 1914.

33   Frith 1887, vol. 1, p. 57.

34   On Eastlake's presidential 'Discourses', for instance, see Avery-Quash and Sheldon 2011, pp. 106–9. A similar relationship developed in Edinburgh between the Royal Scottish Academy and the National Gallery of Scotland; see Potter 2013, pp. 17–18.

35   Jan van Eyck, *Portrait of Giovanni(?) Arnolfini and his Wife*, 1434 (NG186); the Rossetti (N04872) and Millais (T07553) are both at Tate. See Smith et al. in London 2017–18, cat. 13, p. 34, and cat. 16, pp. 41–2, respectively.

36   Introduction by Hamilton to his 1978 *Artist's Eye* exhibition catalogue, n.p.

37   See, for instance, Emma Chambers, 'Prototype and Perception: Art History and Observation at the Slade in the 1950s', in Potter 2013, pp. 189–214.

38   See Langdale 1987, p. 11; see also p. 9.

39   NG838. See Langdale 1987, *The Duet*, cat. 3, pp. 133–4. The copy informed certain of Gwen John's own paintings, notably *Young Woman with a Violin*; see Langdale 1987, cat. 7, p. 134. See also Strickland 2013, pp. 131–3, who further notes (p. 136) that Gwen John's name appears in the National Gallery's Copyists Register, 1901–46.

40   From reminiscences of Opal Howard, cited in Hassell 1999, p. 202. Another Camberwell contemporary,

Donald Harris, mentioned being 'overwhelmed by the National Gallery' (p. 198), and Jennifer Kelly noted that her teacher William Coldstream 'pretended not to notice students if he saw them in the Gallery' (p. 210).

41   NG538. As noted by Cork 1981, p. 44.

42   NG130 and NG830, respectively. See letter from Vincent van Gogh to his brother, 4 August 1884, recommending what he should see on his upcoming trip to London; transcribed in Leo Jansen, Hans Luijten and Nienke Bakker (eds), *Vincent van Gogh: The Letters: The Complete Illustrated and Annotated Edition*, 6 vols, London 2009, vol. 3, p. 163. See also ibid., p. 238, where Vincent van Gogh mentions *Christ blessing the Children*, then attributed to Rembrandt (NG757; now catalogued as by Nicolaes Maes).

43   NG790. See Cork in London 2019–20, p. 36; the quotation is taken from Alice Mayes, 'The Young Bomberg 1914–1925', unpublished memoir, 1972, pp. 2–3, Tate Archive.

44   NGA, NG17/2, *Report of the Director of the National Gallery, 1856*, 'Admission of Artists and Others to Copy' and 'Private Days', pp. 18–19.

45   See Avery-Quash and Sheldon 2011, p. 214; NGA, *National Gallery, London: Rules for Admission of Students, 1894 … signed by Charles L. Eastlake, Keeper and Secretary*. The document was updated periodically, including by Allan Braham, Keeper, in November 1984. The rules remain in force today.

46   See Gerard 1893, pp. 119–23. See also Anon. 1885, pp. 534, 554. The rules for copyists, issued in September 1970, prohibited 'copying on commission or for sale', but this practice had originally taken place; Gerard explicitly stated that certain artists came 'to make copies either on commission or for sale on their own account' (p. 119).

47   For the student registers, see NGA, NG11/1 (1824–55), NG11/2 (1901–46), NG11/3 (1923–41), NG11/4 (1924–38). The register covering the years 1855 to 1901 is missing.

48   Gerard 1893, p. 123.

49   NG2057 was presented by the Art Fund in 1906; NG2475 was acquired

three years later by the same route but additionally 'with the aid of an anonymous donation'.

50   The wording is Fry's to William Rothenstein, quoted in Lago 1996, p. 56.

51   NGA, NG6/21, Letter book, 15 April 1897–11 May 1898, letter from the National Gallery's Chief Clerk, George Ambrose, to Christiana Herringham, 19 October 1897, about copying NG776. There is no reference in NGA, NG11/2, the copyists' register for 1909, about Herringham copying the Piero. See also NGA/NG7/286/5, letter dated 24 June 1904 from the Chapter of the Cathedral of San Sepolcro asking the Trustees to present them with a copy of Piero's *Baptism* formerly in that Cathedral, a request apparently supported by the then Director of the National Portrait Gallery, Lionel Cust, who was at San Sepolcro, taking photographs of what remained of the altarpiece ensemble. The Gallery's response was sympathetic up to a point. See the Board Minutes, 13 July 1904: 'The Secretary was instructed to reply that facilities would be gladly given for the making of the desired copy, but that there were no funds at the disposal of the Trustees to pay for it.' The author has not been able to establish if Herringham's copy, which, according to the label was made and donated in 1909, was related in any way to the earlier episode of 1904.

52   Alistair Smith, in an email to the author, 11 December 2023, noted of times spent with Hockney during the preparations for his 1981 *Artist's Eye* exhibition: 'Conversations were rambling, about what was on his shelves (and in his oeuvre) … Wallace Stevens, Proust, daily drawing (*nulla die sine linea*). And about fish-and-chips, and tripe, which I don't think appear in his work.'

53   For an account of Hockney's less straightforward relationship with Tate, see Spalding 1999, pp. 199–200.

54   NGA, NG32/135/1, letter from David Hockney to Michael Levey, 5 February 1980, and here, p. 55, fig. 39.

55   NGA, NG32/135/1, letter from Michael Levey to David Hockney, 14 February 1980.

56 London 1981, p. 22.

57 Ibid., p. 24.

58 Ibid., p. 22.

59 See Bosman 2008, pp. 91–9, and see list of 'Wartime Exhibitions at the National Gallery', p. 126.

60 NG270.

61 See Baeza 2017, pp. 179, 188–93.

62 NGA, NG17/26, *The National Gallery Report, January 1980– December 1981*, p. 20.

63 NGA, NG24/1981/19, Emmanuel Cooper, *Gay News* (July 1981). 'Desert Island Discs' is a popular weekly UK radio programme, broadcast since 1942, in which a guest discusses their life through a selection of favourite musical pieces, a book and a luxury item that they would take with them if they were cast away on a desert island.

64 Pasmore, uniquely, produced a new work for his *Artist's Eye* exhibition: *Living Water*, 1990, which was reproduced in the exhibition catalogue, pp. 6–7.

65 Michael Levey, 'Introduction', in London 1977, n.p.

66 Michael Levey, 'Preface', in London 1979, p. 2. See also Chippindale 2010, pp. 27–9.

67 See Crookham in London 2012a, p. 52.

68 Richard Hamilton, 'Introduction', in London 1978, n.p. See also Cork 1981, pp. 48–9.

69 NGA, NG24/1981/19, *Cosmopolitan* (London), July 1981.

70 NGA, NG24/1981/19, Waldemar Januszczak, *The Guardian*, 2 July 1981, p. 10.

71 London 1981, p. 8.

72 NGA, NG24/1981/19, Michael Shepherd, 'Art: Room with a View', *What's On in London*, 10 July 1981; Hockney's phrase 'which is one of the great delights of art' appears in a discussion of his friendship with Geldzahler. On Geldzahler's influence on Hockney's way of seeing, see An 2021, pp. 50–62.

73 NGA, NG24/1981/19, *Art & Antiques Weekly*, 31 July 1981.

74 NGA, NG24/1981/19, *The Sunday Times*, 5 July 1981.

75 See, for instance, Michael Levey's Preface in London 1979, p. 2: 'While it might be thought tempting to consider extending the invitation to organisers other than artists, that would miss the tacit reminder that pictures are the product of individual painters …' See also NGA, NG32/179/2, letter from Jacob Rothschild, Chair of Trustees, to Robert Reid, Chair of Shell UK Limited, 7 August 1989: 'Next year will of course mark the end of this particular series of five. We should, however, welcome the opportunity of talking to you about expanding the range of selectors to include writers, philosophers and public figures interested in painting. The idea of a personal choice clearly appeals strongly to a wide public and we believe that we could exploit it in new ways to reach new audiences …' Again, the idea was never developed.

76 NGA, NG24/1981/19, William Packer, 'Arts: Hockney's Choice', *The Financial Times*, 25 July 1981. Brown 2024, p. 51, points out that Rego and Bourgeois were the only female artists to participate in *Encounters*.

77 Christopher Riopelle, in an email to the author, 9 February 2024. For further analysis, see Stearn 2016, pp. 92–101.

78 'Director's Foreword', in London 2000, p. 7.

79 NG4077. Wiggins 2024 (forthcoming) notes: 'After the exhibition [Freud] made one further etching, a closely cropped detail of that ear.'

80 Christopher Riopelle, in an email to the author, 9 February 2024.

81 Ibid. *Encounters* inhabited more than the 'three sites', noted by Stearn 2016, p. 94.

82 Mary Hersov in an email to the author, 14 November 2023.

83 The catalogue's introduction was written by Robert Rosenblum, and there were contributions from external specialists Judith Bumpus, Keith Hartley, Andrew Lambirth and Marco Livingstone.

84 Christopher Riopelle in an email to the author, 29 October 2023.

85 The exhibition took place at the National Gallery, 17 January–25 April 1999; see Gary Tinterow and Philip Conisbee (eds), *Portraits by Ingres: Image of an Epoch*, New York 1999.

86 The portraits of the room stewards were most recently exhibited at Cambridge's Fitzwilliam Museum in 2022, in an exhibition titled *Hockney's Eye: The Art and Technology of Depiction*.

87 For a recent exploration of Hockney's views on the use of technology by painters in the past, see Munro in Cambridge 2022, pp. 113–31.

88 NG1314. Holbein's two single portraits in the National Gallery are *Christina of Denmark, Duchess of Milan* (NG2475) and *A Lady with a Squirrel and a Starling (Anne Lovell?)* (NG6540).

89 Susan Foister in an email to the author, 3 November 2023. Hockney published correspondence between himself and Foister in Hockney 2006, pp. 280–1.

90 Stearn 2016, p. 65.

91 See Wiggins in Münster 2014–15, p. 171; www.nationalgallery.org.uk/ stories/frank-auerbach (accessed 20 September 2023). Of the 141 Auerbach drawings donated in 2000 and preserved in the Gallery's Contextual Collection (H50–H190), 140 were lent to the exhibition – the exception being H50. There were nine further loans from other individuals or institutions.

92 Quoted in Wiggins in Münster 2014–15, p. 172.

93 'Director's Foreword', in Wiggins in London 1995, p. 4.

94 Ibid.

95 Wiggins in London 2023–4, p. 27.

96 Wiggins was also largely responsible for the film produced to accompany the exhibition, which he notes (ibid., note 88) included 'sensitive and perceptive contributions from long-term friends Peter Blake, David Hockney and Frank Auerbach, all of whom were more than pleased to give up their time to pay tribute to their old friend'.

97 Wiggins in Münster 2014–15, p. 171.

98 Stearn 2016, p. 31; for further analysis, see ibid., pp. 216–24.

99 For an in-depth discussion of *Scratch the Surface* and the wider phenomenon of artists and 'institutional critique', both outside and within the art museum, see Stearn 2016, pp. 123–4, 143–51, 165–82.

100 Since the 1960s, Artist Residencies in non-artistic institutions have become an important form of both socially engaged practice and institutional critique. In the British context, particularly the work of the Artist Placement Group (APG) pioneered this approach from an artist-led point of view with 'open-brief' placements in a variety of settings. See Simon Rycroft, *Cultural Geographies*, vol. 26, no. 3 (July 2019), pp. 289–304; Hudek and Sainsbury in London 2012b; and Slater 2001. The invitations of artists into an establishment institution such as the National Gallery absorbed the form of the artist's placement but substituted the subversive potential of the 'open brief' with a traditional arrangement that retained the gallery hierarchy.

101 Colin Wiggins in an email to the author, 10 November 2023.

102 Ibid.

103 Alistair Smith in an email to the author, 13 November 2023.

104 See 'Director's Foreword' in London 1991–2, p. 4.

105 Colin Wiggins in an email to the author, 10 November 2023.

106 See Stearn 2016, p. 65. For detailed discussion of Paula Rego and Ken Kiff as National Gallery Associate Artists, see ibid., pp. 71–86.

107 Quoted in Mistry and Aridjis in London 2023, p. 13.

108 For further discussion of this painting, see Greer and Wiggins in London 1991–2, p. 27; Stearn 2016, pp. 71, 73–9.

109 Nashashibi exhibited *Winter Solstice*, *Phosphorus Malvolio*, *A Drop of Scent* and *An Overflow* (all 2020).

110 Rosalind Nashashibi: *An Overflow of Passion and Sentiment*; see www.youtube.com/ watch?v=Ccckt1KQcy0 (accessed 20 September 2023).

111 Hambling produced other portraits of the sitter, including *Mac with Shadows*, which was purchased by Southampton City Art Gallery in 1982 (see fig. 47). See Susanna Avery-Quash and Jemma Craig, *Creating a National Collection: The Partnership between Southampton City Art Gallery and the National Gallery*, exh. cat., Southampton City Art Gallery, 2021, cats 52–3, pp. 150–1.

112 Miller 1991, pp. 444–7.

113 Ibid., p. 447.

4 Looking (Back) at Pictures in a Room: *The Artist's Eye* Exhibitions

1 Quoted in Kara Weisenstein, 'Nude Dudes and Swimming Pools: Inside the David Hockney Documentary', *Vice*, 19 May 2016, www.vice.com/en/article/pgq4y7/painter-david-hockney-documentary (accessed 11 November 2023).

2 Artists acting as curators in public collections sit, of course, in a longer tradition of artistic intervention and institutional critique. For an excellent introduction, including a discussion of the role of the National Gallery, see Musteata 2018, as well as Claire Bishop's critical assessment in 'History Depletes Itself', *Artforum*, 54, no. 1 (2015), pp. 324–9, 408, 410. Important context is provided by Ana Baeza in her PhD thesis (Baeza 2017), while Alison Green, *When Artists Curate: Contemporary Art and the Exhibition as Medium*, London 2018, provides a wider, international angle. Finally, *The Artist as Curator: An Anthology*, Milan 2017, draws together foundational research into the phenomenon of artists as curators. For an introduction to the National Gallery's display history under different directors from the perspective of one of their own, see Charles Saumarez Smith, 'Narratives of Display at the National Gallery, London', *Art History*, 30, no. 4 (2007), pp. 611–27. An important precedent for an artist making a selection from a permanent collection is Andy Warhol's *Raid the Icebox* (1979–80) at the Rhode Island School of Design; see Stearn 2016, p. 51.

3 NGA NG32/116, letter from Alistair Smith to American abstract artist Kenneth Noland, 18 February 1977.

4 There is very little published secondary literature on *The Artist's Eye* exhibition series; see Stearn 2016, who discusses in depth *The Artist's Eye* exhibitions of Caro (1977), Bacon (1985), Riley (1989) and Pasmore (1990), pp. 53–66; Wiggins in Münster 2014–15, pp. 168–72, and Wiggins 2024; see also Smith 2012, esp. Chapter 3, 'Artists as Curators/Curators as Artists'; and Robins 2013. For relevant primary sources held in the National Gallery Archive, which include exhibition planning files, press files, interpretation material, documentary photography and public correspondence, see: ANTHONY CARO, *Artist's Eye* (1 Jun–24 Jul 1977): NGA, NG32/116: Exhibition File; NG60/29: Poster; NG23/1977: Press Releases; NG24/1977/17: Press cuttings (May–Aug 1977); NG30/1977/24–28: Photographs; RICHARD HAMILTON, *Artist's Eye* (5 Jul–31 Aug 1978): NGA, NG32/120: Exhibition File; NG60/37: Poster; NG23/1978: Press Releases; NG24/1978/17: Press cuttings (May–Aug 1978); NG30/1978/42–59: Photographs; HOWARD HODGKIN, *Artist's Eye* (20 Jun–19 Aug 1979): NGA, NG32/124: Exhibition File; NG60/42: Poster; NG23/1979: Press Releases; NG24/1979/13: Press cuttings (Feb 1979–Feb 1980); NG30/1979/28: Photographs; R.B. KITAJ, *Artist's Eye* (21 May–20 Jul 1980): NGA, NG32/124: Exhibition File; NG60/49: Poster; NG23/1980: Press Releases; NG24/1980/10: Press cuttings (May–August 1980); DAVID HOCKNEY, *Artist's Eye* (1 Jul–31 Aug 1981): NGA, NG32/135: Exhibition File; NG60/57: Poster; NG23/1981: Press Releases; NG24/1981/19: Press cuttings (May–Aug 1981); NG30/1981/24–26; 85–86: Photographs; FRANCIS BACON, *Artist's Eye* (23 Oct–15 Dec 1985): NGA, NG32/161: Exhibition File; NG60/95: Poster; NG23/1985: Press Releases; NG24/1985/23: Press cuttings (May–Dec 1985); NG30/1985/75–76: Photographs; PATRICK CAULFIELD, *Artist's Eye* (4 Jun–10 Aug 1986): NGA, NG32/163: Exhibition File; NG60/100: Poster; NG23/1986: Press Releases; NG24/1986/23: Press cuttings (Feb–Oct 1986); NG30/1986/92–93: Photographs; LUCIAN FREUD, *Artist's Eye* (17 Jun–16 Aug 1987): NGA, NG32/169: Exhibition File; NG60/112: Poster; NG23/1987: Press Releases; NG24/1987/21: Press cuttings (May 1987–May 1988); BRIDGET RILEY, *Artist's Eye* (28 Jun–31 Aug 1989): NGA, NG32/179: Exhibition File; NG60/131: Poster; NG23/1989: Press Releases; NG24/1989/25: Press cuttings (Sept 1989–Jan 1990); VICTOR PASMORE, *Artist's Eye* (4 Jul–7 Oct 1990): NGA, NG32/184: Exhibition File; NG60/140: Poster; NG23/1990: Press Releases; NG24/1990/23: Press cuttings (Jul–Nov 1990); NG30/1990/27: Photographs.

5 Alistair Smith recalled the origins of *The Artist's Eye* in an email to the author, 6 February 2024: 'This is how I remember the sequence of events that culminated in the three series of small exhibitions, the first being shown in the old Board Room, with others in the Northern (Orange Street) Extension when space became available there. I did the first *Painting in Focus* in 1974 highlighting Holbein's *Ambassadors*. I coined the series title and established the format, as I did with *The Artist's Eye* and the third series that followed, namely *Second Sight*.'

6 Michael Levey, 'Introduction', in London 1977, n.p. As noted above, Smith had recently introduced the *Painting in Focus* exhibition series, starting with Hans Holbein the Younger's *The Ambassadors* (NG1314).

7 For instance, Levey launched new 'audio-visual presentations', one of the first being a film that Levey wrote and narrated about 'British Painting in the National Gallery'; see NGA, NG23/1976, Press Release, 28 June 1976.

8 Alistair Smith in an email to the author, 12 November 2023.

9 Ibid. Smith noted: 'John Hale, I was told, lived near the Caros, and had met them at dinner, or some other social gathering.'

10 NGA, NG32/116, letter from Michael Levey to Anthony Caro, 6 July 1976. This letter has led to a misunderstanding that the 'first *Artist's Eye* exhibition was initiated by the artist Anthony Caro, rather than the institution', an error made repeatedly by Stearn 2016, pp. 19, 53, 210.

11 NGA, NG32/116, letter from Anthony Caro to Michael Levey, 25 July 1976, and Levey's response to Caro, 30 July 1976.

12 See, for instance, NGA, NG32/179/1, letter from Chris Bullock to Neil MacGregor, 30 November 1989. Notably, a question was raised about Shell UK Limited's activities in South Africa, specifically its 'proven links of supporting and involvement with the South African apartheid regime'; see NGA, NG32/169/1, letter from Elizabeth Myers and Emma Bryant to Neil MacGregor from the 'Artists Support Peace' organisation, 24 August 1987, which included 'the petition forms [they] collected during [their] protest outside the National Gallery'. See also internal memo, 23 June 1989, which, in anticipation of potential protests over the partnership, notes that 'information packs with facts explaining Shell's involvement in South Africa … will be kept at the information desk' and 'the warders … primed in case anything does happen'. Nothing further is reported in the Exhibition File in this connection.

13 See NGA, NG32/184, letter from Gilbert Lloyd to Neil MacGregor, 23 February 1990, confirming Marlborough Fine Art's sponsorship; also subsequent letters of gratitude from MacGregor, 29 May 1990 and 12 October 1990.

14 Alistair Smith, in an email to the author, 12 November 2023, noted: 'I attended a lecture which [Hamilton] gave at the Institute of Contemporary Arts and I found myself in the queue of his admirers … I told him that I now worked at the National Gallery … that he was my "favourite" artist … [and] could I have his autograph? He seemed amused … I said maybe there was some way that he might want to be involved with the Gallery.'

15 Susan Foister in an email to the author, 8 November 2023.

16 Colin Wiggins in an email to the author, 10 November 2023.

17 NGA, NG23/1990, Press Releases (1990) Victor Pasmore.

18 See Kenneth Clark, *Another Part of the Wood: A Self-Portrait*, London 1974, p. 251.

19 See Neil MacGregor 'Foreword', in London 1987, n.p.

20 Susan Foister, in an email to the author, 8 November 2023, noted that there were 'attempts to give rooms more contemporary settings in these years, such as orange carpet for the Botticellis in old Room 3,

brown carpet and chrome for the Poussins, etc.'

21 MacGregor 'Foreword', in *Freud*, 1987, n.p.

22 Cork 1981, p. 44. Cork is speaking about NG599 and NG3951.

23 NGA, NG32/179, transcription of Critics' Forum Broadcast, BBC Radio 3, 1 July 1989. The speakers were: Alexander Walker (chair), William Feaver, Gillian Tindall and Jeremy Treglown.

24 NGA, NG32/184, transcription of Critics' Forum Broadcast, BBC Radio 3, 14 July 1990. The speakers were: Christopher Cook (chair), Michael Billington, John Carey and Marina Vaizey.

25 Cork 1981, p. 44.

26 Ibid.

27 NGA, NG32/116, letter from Michael Levey to Anthony Caro, 30 July 1976.

28 Quoted in John McEwen, 'An Introduction to Patrick Caulfield's Selection', in London 1986, p. 6.

29 NGA, NG32/184, note from Neil MacGregor to Colin Wiggins, 4 January 1990. See also letter from Victor Pasmore to Alistair Smith, 5 May 1989.

30 See NGA, NG32/128, letter from Alan Bowness to Michael Levey, 17 March 1980.

31 See NGA, NG32/120, letter from Alistair Smith to Richard Hamilton, 12 January 1978.

32 Cork 1981, p. 45. The picture in question is NG3294.

33 For more concerning Hockney's *Play within a Play*, which depicted his dealer John Kasmin, and its inspiration from a National Gallery painting, Domenichino's fresco of *Apollo killing the Cyclops*, itself painted as a trompe l'oeil tapestry (NG6290), see Stangos (ed.) 1976, p. 90.

34 NGA, NG32/184, see letter from Alistair Smith to Victor Pasmore, 5 May 1989, who noted that an artist's own work was 'not necessarily displayed "next to Leonardo", as you said, but in a vestibule leading into the exhibition'.

35 See Michael Levey, 'Director's Foreword', in London 1985, n.p.

36 NGA, NG32/161, document titled 'National Gallery Artist's Eye Exhibition: Francis Bacon: Summary and Conclusions'.

37 Cork 1981, p. 49.

38 NGA, NG32/120, letter from Alistair Smith to Richard Hamilton, 12 January 1978.

39 NGA, NG32/184, letter from Victor Pasmore to Alistair Smith, 12 October 1989. NB For the Room 46 exhibition in 2024, for which this book serves as exhibition catalogue, David Hockney happily responded to the Gallery's request to select the wall colour. Hockney chose a dark blue, the same one that he used for the walls of his London studio.

40 NGA, NG32/120, letter from Alistair Smith to Richard Hamilton, 12 January 1978.

41 'A limited number of posters, individually signed by the artist, is available [for] £50 (via post £51)', as advertised in *The New Standard* (July 1981), p. 18.

42 NGA, NG32/184, letter from Alistair Smith to Victor Pasmore, 11 August 1989.

43 NGA, NG32/184, letter from Alistair Smith to Victor Pasmore, 5 May 1989.

44 Ibid.

45 Alistair Smith in an email to the author, 11 December 2023.

46 NGA, NG32/179, letter from Alistair Smith to Bridget Riley, 24 June 1987.

47 NGA, NG32/179, memo, 'Meeting with Bridget Riley', 14 February 1989.

48 Ibid.

49 Colin Wiggins was responsible for collaborating with various living artists to produce the following films, listed in chronological order, about their work and their connections with the National Gallery's collection (until 2013, they were produced in-house): 'Frank Auerbach: Working after the masters' (1995), 'Peter Blake: Now I'm 64' (1996), 'Ana Maria Pacheco' (1999), 'Kitaj: In the aura of Cezanne and other masters' (2001), 'Travelling Companions: Chardin and Freud' (2001), 'Ron Mueck' (2002), 'Tom Hunter' (2005), 'Leon Kossoff' (2007), 'Alison Watt' (2008), 'Kienholz: The Hoerengracht' (2009), 'Bridget Riley' (2010, a short 4-minute film, shown in conjunction with the film she made for the National Gallery's *Artist's Eye* exhibition of 1989), 'Michael Landy' (2013, started by the Gallery's AV department and finished by freelance producer Jared Schiller), 'George Shaw' (2016, Jared Schiller).

50 NGA, NG32/184, transcription of Critics' Forum Broadcast, BBC Radio 3, 14 July 1990.

51 Francis Bacon, untitled text, in London 1985, n.p. (see also fig. 56).

52 NGA, NG23/1985, Press Release, 23 August 1985.

53 NGA, NG32/169, letter from Alistair Smith to Lucian Freud, 25 September 1986.

54 NGA, NG32/169, letter from Lucian Freud to Alistair Smith, 13 October 1986.

55 NGA, NG32/169, letter from Neil MacGregor to Lucian Freud, 4 March 1987.

56 NGA, NG32/169, letter from Alexander Walker to the Hon. Jacob Rothschild, Chair of Trustees, 20 July 1987.

57 NGA, NG32/169, letter from Neil MacGregor to Alexander Walker, 24 June 1987.

58 NGA, NG32/169, letter from Alistair Smith to Hazel Barbour, at Shell UK, 14 July 1987.

59 NGA, NG32/116, letter from Michael Levey to Anthony Caro, 30 July 1976.

60 For a detailed analysis of Freud's choice of paintings for his *Artist's Eye* exhibition, see Wiggins 2024 (forthcoming). Rembrandt was one of a number of painters of the past whom Freud noted he thought 'about all of the time', the others being Ingres, Rubens, Titian and Velázquez; see Wiggins in Münster 2014–15, p. 169.

61 See NGA, NG32/116, note from Sarah Spare, 9 May 1977: 'Piero della Francesca – either (preferably) The Baptism of Christ – NG 665 or The Nativity – NG 908 – if either of these Piero paintings can be used for the exhibition, Mr. Caro himself would like it out of its outer frame, but still in its inner frame.'

62 National Gallery paintings that appeared in three different *Artist's Eye* exhibitions: Manet, *The Execution of Maximilian*: Caro 1977, Hodgkin 1979, Bacon 1985; Velázquez, *Kitchen Scene with Christ in the House of Martha and Mary*: Hamilton 1978, Kitaj 1980, Caulfield 1986; Chardin, *The Young Schoolmistress*: Hamilton 1978, Caulfield 1986, Freud 1987; Goya, *Don Andrés del Peral*: Hamilton 1978, Kitaj 1980, Bacon 1985; Degas, *After the Bath, Woman drying herself*: Kitaj 1980, Hockney 1981, Bacon 1985; Rembrandt, *Portrait of Margaretha de Geer, Wife of Jacob Trip* (NG1675): Bacon 1985, Freud 1987, Pasmore 1990; Ingres, *Madame Moitessier*: Bacon 1985, Freud 1987, Pasmore 1990; Seurat, *Bathers at Asnières*: Bacon 1985, Freud 1987, Pasmore 1990. National Gallery paintings that appeared in two different *Artist's Eye* exhibitions: Pieter Saenredam, *The Interior of the Grote Kerk at Haarlem*: Hamilton 1978, Caulfield 1986; Degas, *Young Spartans Exercising*: Kitaj 1980, Freud 1987; Van Gogh, *Van Gogh's Chair*: Kitaj 1980, Bacon 1985; Piero della Francesca, *The Baptism of Christ*: Hockney 1981, Pasmore 1990; Van Gogh, *Sunflowers*: Hockney 1981, Pasmore 1990; Velázquez, '*The Rokeby Venus*': Bacon 1985, Freud 1987; Probably by Rembrandt, *Portrait of Margaretha de Geer, Wife of Jacob Trip* (NG5282): Bacon 1985, Freud 1987; Cezanne, *The Painter's Father, Louis-Auguste Cezanne*: Caulfield 1986, Freud 1987; Carel Fabritius, *A View of Delft, with a Musical Instrument Seller's Stall*: Caulfield 1986, Hodgkin 1979; Manet, *Corner of a Café-Concert*: Caulfield 1986, Pasmore 1990; Jan van de Velde, *Still Life: A Goblet of Wine, Oysters and Lemons*: Caulfield 1986, Pasmore 1990; Constable, *The Hay Wain*: Freud 1987, Pasmore 1990; Bouts, *Portrait of a Man (Jan van Winckele?)*: Hamilton 1978, Caulfield 1986; El Greco, *Christ driving the Traders from the Temple*: Riley 1989, Pasmore 1990. Analysing *The Artist's Eye* series as a whole, in terms of the artists who had the most numbers of repeated works (i.e., works that appeared in more than their own *Artist's Eye*), Bacon, Freud and Pasmore are at the top of the list, each with nine paintings. They are followed by Caulfield with eight; Hamilton and Kitaj with five; Hockney with three; and Hodgkin with two. Caro and Riley each had a single painting in

their exhibitions, which appeared in another *Artist's Eye*.

63 John McEwen, 'An Introduction to Patrick Caulfield's Selection', in Caulfield 1986, p. 6.

64 NGA, NG32/184, letter from Victor Pasmore to Alistair Smith, 5 May 1989.

65 NGA, NG32/184, John Carey's comment in the transcription of Critics' Forum Broadcast, BBC Radio 3, 14 July 1990.

66 Michael Levey, 'Preface', in London 1979, p. 2.

67 NGA, NG32/116, Caro's answers, first version, to Smith's interview questions for the 1977 *Artist's Eye* exhibition pamphlet; shorter answers were printed in the final version.

68 Neil MacGregor, 'Foreword', in London 1990, p. 3.

69 NGA, NG32/184, transcription of Critics' Forum Broadcast, BBC Radio 3, 14 July 1990.

70 'Bridget Riley interview with Robert Kudielka: The Colour Connection', in London 1989.

71 See Tindall's remarks in NGA, NG32/179, transcription of Critics' Forum Broadcast, 1 July 1989.

72 Richard Hamilton, 'Introduction', in London 1978, n.p.

73 NGA, NG32/120, letter from Alistair Smith to Richard Hamilton, 3 March 1978.

74 Cork 1981, p. 53.

75 For a thorough and insightful analysis of Hamilton's exhibition at the National Gallery, see Lotery 2017, pp. 55–85.

76 Alistair Smith in an email to the author, 14 November 2023.

77 Howard Hodgkin, 'Introduction', in London 1979, p. 3.

78 Michael Levey, 'Introduction', in London 1977, n.p.

79 Levey, 'Preface', in London 1978, n.p.

80 NGA, NG23/1977, Press Release, 'Artist's Eye: Victor Pasmore', 3 October 1989.

81 Colin Wiggins in an email to the author, 10 November 2023.

82 NGA, NG32/184, transcription of Critics' Forum Broadcast, BBC Radio 3, 14 July 1990.

83 Ibid.

84 NGA, NG32/169/1, letter from Neil MacGregor to Alexander Walker, 6 July 1987.

85 Alistair Smith in an email to the author, 11 December 2023.

86 London 1981, p. 5.

87 Ibid.

88 Ibid., p. 10.

89 Ibid., p. 12.

90 Ibid., p. 16. See also Chapter 1, p. 22, where Hockney notes that he himself would not mind contemplating Piero's *Baptism* for an hour a day.

91 NGA, NG32/135/1, letter from Michael Levey to David Hockney, 10 September 1981.

92 NGA, transcription of Critics' Forum Broadcast, BBC Radio 3, 14 July 1990.

93 London 1990, p. 8.

94 London 1981, p. 10.

95 Ibid., p. 6. Hockney included in his *Artist's Eye* exhibition, a framed version of a postcard he had bought from the Toulouse-Lautrec Museum at Albi of a portrait of Toulouse-Lautrec by fellow painter Edouard Vuillard, *Henri de Toulouse-Lautrec at Villeneuve sur Yonne*, 1898. In his exhibition catalogue (p. 6), Hockney noted that he 'thought the painting was delightful', so had sent copies to friends who found it just as 'thrilling', a reaction which proved to Hockney that 'you can get the magic to come, even off reproductions'. See also Hockney's recent comments about the postcard in Chapter 1, p. 14 and fig. 6.

96 NGA, NG32/179, transcription of Critics' Forum Broadcast, 1 July 1989.

97 NGA, NG32/184, letter from Victor Pasmore to Joanna Kent, 7 September 1990.

98 Cork 1981, p. 53.

99 NGA, NG32/116, letter from Anthony Caro to Michael Levey, 9 October 1976.

100 For instance, see NGA, NG32/116, letter from Caro to Levey, 2 June 1977. Rego likewise confessed to feeling daunted; for more on her reaction to working alongside the 'old masters' and for further discussion on the complex matter of 'the anxiety of influence' see Stearn 2016, pp. 67–71, 72.

101 NGA, NG32/116, letter from Caro to Levey, 28 July 1977.

102 In 2023, the National Gallery embarked on a series of digital reconstructions of *The Artist's Eye* series, the first being the 1987 Lucian Freud exhibition. The second of these 3D virtual-reality environments focuses on David Hockney's 1981 exhibition, reconstructing the exhibition space, selection of paintings and the artist's choice of exhibition furniture for the display, emphasising Hockney's consistent awareness of modes of viewing and the position of the beholder when enjoying works of art or their reproductions in all their forms. See nationalgallery.org.uk/exhibitions/hockney-and-piero-a-longer-look (accessed 19 May 2024).

103 NGA, NG32/116, letter from Levey to Caro, 27 July 1977.

104 Alistair Smith in an email to the author, 14 November 2023. Colin Wiggins, in an email to the author, 10 November 2023, also noted that a practical reason why the series came to an end was because the artists were 'tending to choose all the same pictures'; on this topic, see also note 62 above. For further discussion of other frustrations surrounding *The Artist's Eye* exhibition series, see Stearn 2016, p. 13.

105 Stearn 2016, p. 51. See also ibid., pp. 203–14, for a discussion of *The Tomb of the Unknown Craftsman*, an exhibition that Grayson Perry curated at the British Museum in 2011, which Stearn describes as 'a direct descendant' of the *The Artist's Eye* series, while acknowledging Perry's deliberate emphasis on imagination and emotional engagement.

106 NGA, NG25/326, Board Paper, May 2018, Item 9.

107 www.nationalgallery.org.uk/events/unexpected-views (accessed 11 November 2023).

SELECTED BIBLIOGRAPHY

AMERY 1991
C. Amery, *A Celebration of Art & Architecture: The National Gallery Sainsbury Wing*, London 1991

AN 2021
J. An, 'The Curator as the Artist's Friend: Henry Geldzahler Negotiating Artistic Autonomy in the 1960s', unpublished PhD dissertation, University of California, Los Angeles, 2021

ANON. 1885
Anon., 'Lady Students at the National Gallery', *Illustrated London News*, 21 and 28 November 1885

AVERY-QUASH 2015
S. Avery-Quash, '"A gallery of art": Fresh light on the art collection of Sir Charles Eastlake (1793–1865)', *The British Art Journal*, 15, no. 3 (2015), pp. 11–37

AVERY-QUASH 2018
S. Avery-Quash, 'John Julius Angerstein and the development of his art collection at No. 100, Pall Mall, London', in Avery-Quash and Retford, 2018, pp. 247–66

AVERY-QUASH 2023
S. Avery-Quash, 'Building(s) for Art: The Evolution of Public Art Galleries in England, 1780–1840', in M. McCue and S. Thomas (eds), *The Edinburgh Companion to Romanticism and the Arts*, Edinburgh 2023, pp. 165–83

AVERY-QUASH (ed.) 2011
S. Avery-Quash (ed.), 'The Travel Notebooks of Sir Charles Eastlake', *Walpole Society*, 73, 2 vols (2011)

AVERY-QUASH AND CARLETON PAGET 2013
S. Avery-Quash and J. Carleton Paget, 'The artist as director at the National Gallery, London: Intention or happenstance?', in M. Pye and L. Sandino (eds), *Artists Work in Museums: Histories, Interventions, Subjectivities*, Bath 2013, pp. 33–47

AVERY-QUASH AND LLEWELLYN 2022
S. Avery-Quash and S. Llewellyn, 'Piero della Francesca and British art: "That unfinished *Adoration* in the National Gallery has produced many descendants in our times!"', *The British Art Journal*, 23, no. 2 (2022), pp. 3–16

AVERY-QUASH AND RETFORD (eds) 2018
S. Avery-Quash and K. Retford (eds), *The Georgian London Town House: Building, Collecting and Display*, London 2018

AVERY-QUASH AND SHELDON 2011
S. Avery-Quash and J. Sheldon, *Art for the Nation: The Eastlakes and the Victorian Art World*, London 2011

BAEZA 2017
A. Baeza, 'The Road to Renewal: Refiguring the Art Museum in Twentieth-Century Britain', unpublished PhD dissertation, University of Leeds 2017

BERTRAM 1951
A. Bertram, 'Piero della Francesca and the Twentieth Century', *The Studio* (1951), pp. 120–3

BOSMAN 2008
S. Bosman, *The National Gallery in Wartime*, London 2008

BROWN 2024
K. Brown, *Dialogues with Degas: Influence and Antagonism in Contemporary Art*, London, New York, Oxford, New Delhi and Sydney 2024

CAMBRIDGE 2022
J. Munro, 'Ingres and Hockney: Art, Science and Uniformity', in M. Gayford, M. Kemp and J. Munro (eds), *Hockney's Eye: The Art and Technology of Depiction*, exh. cat., The Fitzwilliam Museum, Cambridge 2022, pp. 113–31

CHELES 2013
L. Cheles, 'Les recyclages de Piero della Francesca', in L. Cheles and G. Roque (eds), *L'image recyclée*, Pau 2013, pp. 57–75

CHIPPINDALE 2010
J. Chippindale, 'Something old, something new: Contemporary Artists at the National Gallery', unpublished MA dissertation, Courtauld Institute of Art, University of London, 2010

CLARKE 2019
M. Clarke, 'Women in the Galleries: New Angles on Old Masters in the Late Nineteenth Century', *19: Interdisciplinary Studies in the Long Nineteenth Century*, 28 (2019)

CONLIN 2006
J. Conlin, *The Nation's Mantelpiece: A History of the National Gallery*, London 2006

CORK 1981
R. Cork, 'Report from London: "The Artist's Eye"', *Art in America* (February 1981), pp. 43–55

CROOKHAM 2009
A. Crookham, *The National Gallery: An Illustrated History*, London 2009

CROOKHAM AND ROBBINS 2016
A. Crookham and A. Robbins, 'Im Angesicht der Moderne. Die Gründung der Britischen Nationalsammlung moderner ausländischer Gemälde, 1914–18', in C. Kott and B. Savoy (eds), *Mars und Museum: Europäische Museen im Ersten Weltkrieg*, Cologne 2016, pp. 99–116

ELAM 2004
C. Elam, *Roger Fry and the Re-Evaluation of Piero della Francesca*, New York 2004

ELAM 2016
C. Elam, 'Roger Fry e l'amore per Piero della Francesca in Inghilterra: Cambridge, Bloomsbury e la Slade School', in A. Paolucci (ed.), *Piero della Francesca: Indagine su un mito*, Milan 2016, pp. 315–23

ESPOSITO 2018
D. Esposito, 'Artist in Residence: Joshua Reynolds at No. 47, Leicester Fields', in Avery-Quash and Retford 2018, pp. 191–210

EXETER 1996
S. Smiles and S. Pratt, *Two-Way Traffic: British and Italian Art, 1880–1980*, exh. cat., Royal Albert Memorial Museum, Exeter, published Plymouth 1996

FRITH 1887
W.P. Frith, *My Autobiography*, 2 vols, London 1887

GERARD 1893
F.A. Gerard, 'Students' Day at the National Gallery', *Cassell's Family Magazine*, 1893, pp. 119–23

HASSELL 1999
G. Hassell, *Camberwell School of Arts and Crafts: Its Students & Teachers 1943–1960*, London 1999

HENDY 1968
P. Hendy, *Piero della Francesca and the Early Renaissance*, New York 1968

HERSOV 2017
M. Hersov, 'The Temporary Exhibition Galleries in the Sainsbury Wing, The National Gallery: Commission, Design and Outcome', unpublished PhD dissertation, University of Essex, 2017

HOCKNEY 1993
D. Hockney, *That's the Way I See It*, London 1993

HOCKNEY 2006
D. Hockney, *Secret Knowledge: Rediscovering the Lost Techniques of the Old Masters*, London 2006

HOCKNEY AND KITAJ 1977
D. Hockney and R.B. Kitaj, 'David Hockney and R.B. Kitaj in Conversation', *The New Review*, 3 (1977), pp. 75–7

HUTCHISON 1968
S.C. Hutchison, *The History of the Royal Academy, 1768–1968*, New York 1968

LAGO 1996
M. Lago, *Christiana Herringham and the Edwardian Art Scene*, London 1996

LANGDALE 1987
C. Langdale, *Gwen John: With a Catalogue Raisonné of the Paintings and a Selection of the Drawings*, London 1987

LAVIN 1981
M.A. Lavin, *Piero della Francesca's Baptism of Christ*, New Haven 1981

LAVIN (ed.) 1995
M.A. Lavin (ed.), *Piero della Francesca and his Legacy*, Washington DC and New Haven 1995

LESLIE 1914
G.D. Leslie, *The Inner Life of the Royal Academy, with an account of its schools and exhibitions principally in the reign of Queen Victoria*, London 1914

LONDON 1977
A. Caro, *The Artist's Eye: An exhibition selected by Anthony Caro at the National Gallery*, exh. cat., The National Gallery, London 1977

LONDON 1978
R. Hamilton, *The Artist's Eye: An exhibition selected by Richard Hamilton at the National Gallery*, exh. cat,. The National Gallery, London 1978

LONDON 1979
H. Hodgkin, *The Artist's Eye: An exhibition selected by Howard Hodgkin at the National Gallery*, exh. cat., The National Gallery, London 1979

LONDON 1980
R.B. Kitaj, *The Artist's Eye: An exhibition selected by R.B. Kitaj at the National Gallery*, exh. cat., The National Gallery, London 1980

LONDON 1981
D. Hockney, *The Artist's Eye: David Hockney: Looking at Pictures in a Book*, exh. cat., The National Gallery, London 1981

LONDON 1985
F. Bacon, *The Artist's Eye: Francis Bacon: An exhibition of National Gallery paintings selected by the artist*, exh. cat., The National Gallery, London 1985

LONDON 1986
P. Caulfield, *The Artist's Eye: Patrick Caulfield: An exhibition of National Gallery paintings selected by the artist*, exh. cat., The National Gallery, London 1986

LONDON 1987
L. Freud, *The Artist's Eye: Lucian Freud: An exhibition of National Gallery paintings selected by the artist*, exh. cat., The National Gallery, London 1987

LONDON 1989
B. Riley, *The Artist's Eye: Bridget Riley: An exhibition of National Gallery paintings selected by the artist*, exh. cat., The National Gallery, London 1989

LONDON 1990
V. Pasmore, *The Artist's Eye: Victor Pasmore: An exhibition of National Gallery paintings selected by the artist*, exh. cat., The National Gallery, London 1990

LONDON 1991–2
G. Greer and C. Wiggins, *Paula Rego: Tales from the National Gallery*, exh. cat., The National Gallery, London 1991–2

LONDON 1995
C. Wiggins, *Frank Auerbach and the National Gallery: Working after the Masters*, exh. cat., The National Gallery, London 1995

LONDON 2000
R. Morphet, *Encounters: New Art from Old*, exh. cat., The National Gallery, London 2000

LONDON 2012a
A. Crookham, 'The Turner Bequest at the National Gallery', in I. Warrell, *Turner Inspired: In the Light of Claude*, exh. cat., The National Gallery, London 2012, pp. 51–65

LONDON 2012b
A. Hudek and A. Sainsbury, *The Individual and the Organisation: Artist Placement Group, 1966–79*, exh. cat., Raven Row, London 2012

LONDON 2016
A. Robbins, *Painters' Paintings: From Freud to Van Dyck*, exh. cat., The National Gallery, London 2016

LONDON 2017–18
A. Smith with C. Bugler, S. Foister and A. Koopstra, *Reflections: Van Eyck and the Pre-Raphaelites*, exh. cat., The National Gallery, London 2017–18

LONDON 2019–20
R. Cork, *Young Bomberg and the Old Masters*, exh. cat., The National Gallery, London 2019–20

LONDON 2023
P. Mistry and C. Aridjis, *Paula Rego: Crivelli's Garden*, exh. cat., The National Gallery, London 2023

LONDON 2023–4
C. Wiggins, 'Kitaj in Los Angeles: "London died for me when Sandra died."', in A. Dempsey, M. Livingstone and C. Wiggins, *R.B. Kitaj: London to Los Angeles*, exh. cat., Piano Nobile, London 2023–4, pp. 27–31

LOTERY 2017
K. Lotery, 'Rooms: Richard Hamilton and Postmodernism', *October*, 159 (2017), pp. 55–85

MARTINEAU 2023
J. Martineau, 'Stanley Spencer, postcards, small books and old masters', *The Burlington Magazine*, 165, no. 1446 (2023), pp. 952–67

MILLER 1991
S. Miller, 'Ten "Artists in Residence"', *Print Quarterly*, 8, no. 4 (1991), pp. 444–7

MÜNSTER 2014–15
C. Wiggins, '"This is the family from which we spring": The National Gallery Collection and Post-war British Painting', in *Bare Life: Bacon, Freud, Hockney and Others: London artists working from life, 1950–80*, exh. cat., LWL-Museum für Kunst und Kultur, Münster 2014–15, pp. 168–72

MUSTEATA 2018
N. Musteata, 'The Origins of the Transhistorical Museum: The Artist as Curator', Conference Paper, Frans Hals Museum, Haarlem (2018)

OLIVER 2004
L. Oliver, *Boris Anrep: The National Gallery Mosaics*, London 2004

PENNY 2003
N. Penny, 'Journey to Arezzo', *London Review of Books*, 25, no. 8 (17 April 2003), pp. 3–6

POTTER (ed.) 2013
M.C. Potter (ed.), *The Concept of the 'Master' in Art Education in Britain and Ireland, 1770 to the Present*, Farnham 2013

PUTNAM 2001
J. Putnam, *Art and Artifact: The Museum as Medium*, London 2001

RILEY 1997
B. Riley, 'Painting Now', *The Burlington Magazine*, 139, no. 1134 (1997), pp. 616–22

ROBERTSON 1978
D. Robertson, *Sir Charles Eastlake and the Victorian Art World*, Princeton 1978

ROBINS 2013
C. Robins, *Curious Lessons in the Museum: The Pedagogic Potential of Artist Interventions*, Farnham 2013

SLATER 2001
H. Slater, 'The art of governance: The Artist Placement Group, 1966–1989', *Variant 11* (Summer 2001)

SMITH 2012
T. Smith, *Thinking Contemporary Curating*, New York 2012

SPALDING 1999
F. Spalding, *The Tate: A History*, London 1999

STANGOS (ed.) 1976
N. Stangos (ed.), *David Hockney by David Hockney*, London 1976

STEARN 2016
M.R.R. Stearn, 'Museum-commissioned Interventions by Contemporary Artists with Historic Art Collections, 1985 to the Present', unpublished PhD dissertation, Courtauld Institute of Art, University of London 2016

STRICKLAND 2013
A. Strickland, 'Opening Doors: The Entry of Women Artists into British Art Schools, 1871–1930', in Potter 2013, pp. 127–44

WIGGINS 2024 (forthcoming)
C. Wiggins, 'Lucian Freud and Painting of the Past', in T. Treves and C. Lampert, *Lucian Freud: A Catalogue Raisonné of the Paintings*, London 2024 (forthcoming)

WILSON 1991
M. Wilson, *A Guide to the Sainsbury Wing at the National Gallery*, London 1991

WITHAM 2014
L. Witham, *Piero's Light: In Search of Piero della Francesca: A Renaissance Painter and the Revolution in Art, Science, and Religion*, New York 2014

LIST OF EXHIBITED WORKS AND LENDERS

LIST OF EXHIBITED WORKS

Piero della Francesca
(about 1415/20–1492)
The Baptism of Christ, probably
about 1437–45
Egg tempera on wood, 167 × 116 cm
The National Gallery, London.
Bought, 1861
NG665
Fig. 2

David Hockney (b. 1937)
Looking at Pictures on a Screen, 1977
Oil on canvas, 188 × 188 cm
Private collection
Fig. 1

David Hockney (b. 1937)
My Parents, 1977
Oil paint on canvas, 182.9 × 182.9 cm
(frame 194 × 194.1 × 8.5 cm)
Tate: Purchased 1981
T03255
Fig. 3

Contact sheet of photographs showing
the installation of David Hockney's
Artist's Eye exhibition, 1981
National Gallery Archive: NG32/135/2
The National Gallery, London
Fig. 42

Letter from David Hockney to
Michael Levey, 5 February 1980
National Gallery Archive: NG32/135/1
The National Gallery, London
Fig. 39; see also p. 96

Letter from Michael Levey to
David Hockney, 14 February 1980
National Gallery Archive: NG32/135/1
The National Gallery, London
See p. 96

Letter from Michael Levey to
David Hockney, 28 July 1980
National Gallery Archive: NG32/135/1
The National Gallery, London
See pp. 96–7

Looking at Pictures in a Book by
David Hockney, 1981 (two copies of
the catalogue appear in the exhibition)
Exhibition catalogue, 15.3 × 12 cm
National Gallery Library: (P.) NC 30
LONDON N.G. =3 1981
The National Gallery, London
Private collection, London
Figs 6 and 7

Photograph of David Hockney in his
London studio, 1981
National Gallery Archive: NG32/135/2
The National Gallery, London
Fig. 7

Poster designed by David Hockney for
his *Artist's Eye* exhibition, 1981
Paper, 76 × 50.5 cm
National Gallery Archive: NG60/57
The National Gallery, London
Fig. 55

Two postcards included at the back
of *Looking at Pictures in a Book* by
David Hockney, 1981
National Gallery Library: (P.) NC 30
LONDON N.G. =3 1981
The National Gallery, London
Fig. 43

LIST OF LENDERS

London
Tate
Martin Perrin

And those lenders who wish to remain
anonymous

PHOTOGRAPHIC CREDITS

INDEX OF NAMES

ACKNOWLEDGEMENTS

The exhibition, catalogue and associated programme of public events for *Hockney and Piero: A Longer Look* have come about through the hard work and creative collaboration of inspiring and expert colleagues across the National Gallery and beyond. The publication and exhibition would not have been possible without the generous support of both Riverstone and the Capricorn Foundation for the H J Hyams Exhibition Programme – to them I remain deeply grateful.

I would like to thank David Hockney for his unwavering support for the exhibition and its accompanying catalogue. It was thrilling to be told by him at our first meeting that he loved the National Gallery and the work of Piero della Francesca; I am most grateful that he has been able to assist with choosing the colour of the walls for the exhibition as well as with an interview for the catalogue and with reading through and approving the catalogue text and exhibition interpretation. I have also benefited from the close collaboration with the Hockney Studio, especially Shannan Kelly and Jonathan Wilkinson, over all aspects of the project. Deep thanks are due too to Erica Bolton.

I wish to acknowledge that the concept for keeping the focus of the exhibition on Hockney's work in relation to Piero came from Christine Riding, who as Director of Collections and Research has been a constant source of encouragement. I am also indebted to Katherine Miller, whose expert guidance and patience have been crucial; working with her, Lydia Cooper, Alice Cox, Sunnifa Hope and Phoebe Newman from the Exhibition Department has been a very happy experience. I have particularly enjoyed lively meetings about the exhibition's design with the gifted designers Martin Perrin, Chris Oberon, Belinda Philpot and Sophie Ballinger, as well as Stephen Guest, Helen Loveday and Joshua Page from Framing. As ever, the Gallery's Art Handling team, under the able leadership of Patrick O'Sullivan and Mark Slattery, has come up trumps. I have been fortunate in receiving much assistance on the Digital front from Beks Leary and Lizzie Phillips, and in relation to Press matters from Tracy Jones and from Alexandra Moskalenko. It has been extremely stimulating to work with Gallery educators Anne Fay, Joseph Kendra, Bethany Lloyd-King and Josie Wood to devise appropriate public-facing activities to accompany the exhibition.

Thinking about the catalogue, my interactions with National Gallery Global, constantly happy and fruitful, have made the writing and designing of this book a joyous experience. My editor, Catherine Hooper, has been an utterly wonderful support and source of encouragement and inspiration from start to finish; indeed, countless conversations with her stimulated my thinking in creative directions. I am also indebted to Laura Lappin, who understood my vision and agreed to a longer book to accommodate more text, images and a rich appendix. My thanks are due also to Jenny Wilson for her meticulous copy-editing, to Phoebe Colley for her thorough proofreading, and to Bridget Harley and Diana Adell for their help with final corrections.

I am deeply grateful for the thought-provoking contributions to the catalogue by my fellow author Sacha Llewellyn and to Martin Gayford, with whom I enjoyed a delightful afternoon in his home discussing his interview with Hockney for Chapter 1. For help with content concerning *The Artist's Eye* series and other modern and contemporary elements of the Gallery's history, I am particularly grateful to Daniel Herrmann and Priyesh Mistry. There are numerous internal readers of draft chapters to whom I feel happily indebted – certainly the text has been enhanced by their suggestions: Annabel Bai Jackson, Alan Crookham, Karen Eslea, Susan Foister, Sarah Herring, Jon King, Christopher Riopelle, Emily Stone and Imogen Tedbury, as well as Ayla Lepine, a former Gallery colleague. I am especially grateful to Alistair Smith, as well as to both Colin Wiggins and Mary Hersov, former colleagues at the Gallery, for their generosity in sharing intriguing and insightful recollections of their interactions with living artists over National Gallery projects, which certainly helped to bring those episodes to life. For answering some specific queries, I am grateful to Suzanne Bosman and Zara Moran. For assistance with checking the Appendices, my thanks go to Hugo Brown, Sterre Overmars, Nicholas Smith and Hannah Stovin. For help with accessing relevant archival and bibliographical material for both the exhibition and catalogue, my thanks go to the Gallery's ever trusty team of librarians and archivists, especially Hannah Woodley. I would like to thank picture researcher Rebecca Thornton for her sterling work; and for her efficient and effective help with arranging new photography for the book, I would like to thank Rachael Fenton. For the handsome design of the book, I am most grateful to Adam Hooper of Hoop Design. Last but certainly not least, I would like to thank National Gallery Director Gabriele Finaldi for his support throughout, especially for drawing my attention to Christiana Herringham's copy of Piero's *Baptism*.

Susanna Avery-Quash

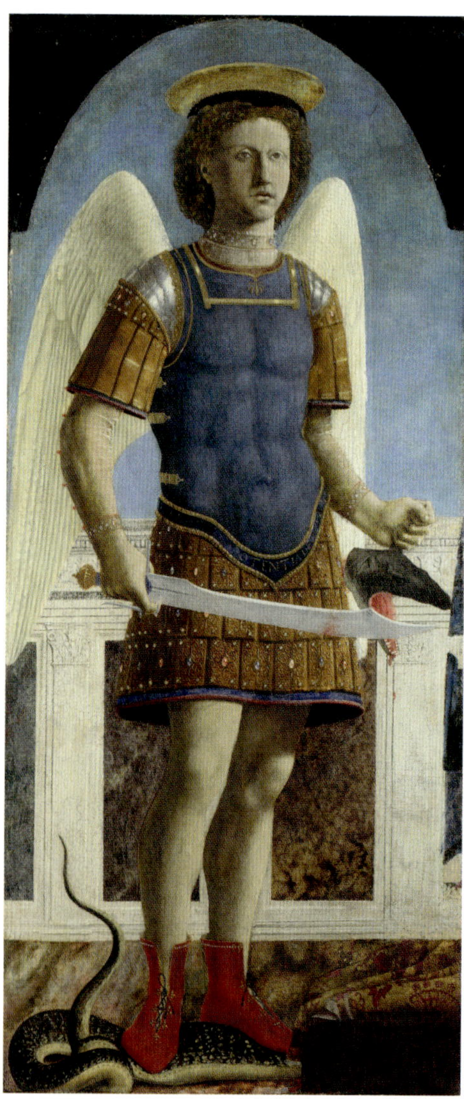

Fig. 64
Piero della Francesca
(about 1415/20–1492)
Saint Michael, completed 1469
Oil on wood, 133 × 59.5 cm
The National Gallery, London